Rewards and Intrinsic Motivation

REWARDS AND INTRINSIC MOTIVATION

Resolving the Controversy

Judy Cameron and W. David Pierce

Bergin & Garvey
Westport, Connecticut • London

Library of Congress Cataloging-in-Publication Data

Cameron, Judy, 1953–

    Rewards and intrinsic motivation : resolving the controversy / Judy Cameron and W. David Pierce.

    p. cm.

    Includes bibliographical references and index.

    ISBN 0–89789–677–7 (alk. paper)

    1. Employee motivation. 2. Achievement motivation. 3. Organizational behavior. 4. Psychology, Industrial. 5. Interpersonal relations. I. Pierce, W. David. II. Title.

    HF5549.5.M63C35   2002

    158.7—dc21   2001043794

British Library Cataloguing in Publication Data is available.

Library of Congress Catalog Card Number: 2001043794
ISBN: 0–89789–677–7

First published in 2002

Bergin & Garvey, 88 Post Road West, Westport, CT 06881
An imprint of Greenwood Publishing Group, Inc.
www.greenwood.com

Printed in the United States of America

The paper used in this book complies with the Permanent Paper Standard issued by the National Information Standards Organization (Z39.48–1984).

10 9 8 7 6 5 4 3 2 1

Acknowledgment

Our research was supported by the Social Science and Humanities Council (SSHRC) of Canada.

Contents

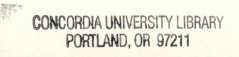

PART I
INTRODUCTION

Chapter 1

An Introduction to the Rewards and Intrinsic Motivation Controversy

Most parents and educators would agree that the ideal student is one who performs academic tasks at a high level, shows high interest and involvement in school activities, is willing to take on challenging assignments, and is an overall self-motivated learner. Most of us would agree that in an ideal workplace, people are productive, happy, and proud of their accomplishments. More generally, most of us want to live in a society where people contribute to the welfare of others, are free to choose among a variety of activities, have a sense of competence and achievement, and feel contentment in most aspects of their life. We agree with these values. However, how to attain these ideals has aroused far less consensus.

One way in which society attempts to achieve its goals is to punish undesirable behavior. Teachers give detentions for incomplete school assignments in the hope that students will develop a sense of responsibility for their work. Parents criticize their children's work habits to instill standards of high achievement. Employers threaten loss of jobs to motivate workers to be more productive. The legal system punishes those who break the laws in order to teach responsibility, maintain order, and protect the freedom of others.

Systems of punishment have been designed and maintained as ways to achieve the aims of high productivity, satisfaction with achievement, caring for others, and so on. The fact is, however, that punitive systems have never attained these goals. Instead, the use of punishment has resulted in resentment, discontent, feelings of low self-worth, and attempts to overthrow those who wield power. In other words, punishment backfires.[1]

PUNISHMENT SYSTEMS

MEANS	ENDS/GOALS	EFFECTS
• Detention • Criticism • Loss of Job • Legal penalties	• Sense of responsibility • High standards of achievement • Productivity • Responsibility, order, and freedom	• Resentment • Discontent • Low self-worth • Attack or subvert those in power

Punishment is a major source of external control over human behavior. The fact that punitive systems result in serious negative effects has led some social advocates to condemn the use of any form of external influence, including reward. For example, a prominent spokesperson in education and business, Alfie Kohn, rejects both punishment and reward as means of social influence.[2] Kohn's premise is that because punishment involves external control and has many negative detrimental consequences, positive external influence based on the use of rewards will also lead to pervasive negative effects. Kohn echoes the sentiments of many researchers and writers in social psychology, education, business, and the media.

THE CLAIM THAT REWARDS ARE HARMFUL IS BASED ON THE FOLLOWING LOGIC:

• Punishment produces negative effects.
• Punishment is an external influence.
• Reward is an external influence.

Therefore, rewards must produce negative effects.

In the early 1970s, Edward Deci, a social psychologist and researcher, claimed that external rewards should not be used because they take away people's interest and enjoyment of activities. Deci set out to show scientifically that rewards and positive reinforcement could harm people's intrinsic motivation.[3] From the time of Deci's initial study, literally hundreds of experiments have been carried out to investigate the negative effects of reward. The general conclusion from this literature is that reward systems and positive reinforcement have extensive negative effects. This conclusion has filtered into the popular media and is continually reiterated in introductory textbooks on psychology, education, and business management.

Although the claim that rewards (and positive reinforcement) have general negative effects is popular, it is also wrong. It is wrong because it is based on an idealistic and faulty view of human nature, because the evidence does not support the claim, because of serious overstatement and distortion of the research findings, and because of conceptual confusion, faulty reasoning, and misunderstandings. Finally, it is wrong because there is no acknowledgment of the vast literature showing that rewards can be used effectively without negative by-products.[4]

The claim that rewards have general negative effects is not only wrong; it is harmful. It is harmful because teachers and educators who accept this view resist using rewards when there is no need to do so. Students enjoy school and work hard when a positive reinforcement system is properly arranged. Employees strive to attain high standards in the workplace when they are rewarded for their accomplishments. These positive means of influence are being denied to individuals based on the claim that reward systems are detrimental. The view that rewards are harmful is preventing us from designing better work and learning environments. The result is that many people no longer have the means to achieve the personal and social goals that we all strive for in our society.

There is an even more insidious aspect to the claim that rewards are negative: the claim is elitist. We all admire children who enjoy learning and who do so without any obvious rewards. The child who is apparently self-motivated to learn is valued in our society—but who is this child? Usually, he or she comes from a well-educated family, which teaches the child the skills and values of learning. Children from such families go on educational excursions, travel with their parents to other parts of the world, and have the means and resources to inquire about the world in which they live. These children receive praise, recognition, and privileges for their accomplishments. In a school system based on self-motivation, these children excel.

THE CLAIM THAT "REWARDS ARE NEGATIVE" IS WRONG AND HARMFUL	
Why is it wrong?	*Why is it harmful?*
• Based on an idealistic and faulty view of human nature • Evidence does not support the claim • Based on serious overstatement and generalization of research findings • Based on conceptual confusion, faulty reasoning, and misunderstandings • Research shows that rewards can be used effectively	• Prevents us from designing better work and learning environments • Denies people the means to achieve personal and social goals • Denies less privileged individuals opportunities and access to resources

But what is the fate of less privileged children? In a school system that has rejected the use of positive reinforcement and reward programs, less privileged children are still expected to inquire and discover on their own. The problem is, however, that they may not have the desire, the skills, or the resources to succeed without help. Such children come from families who have been unable to provide them with educational opportunities and positive consequences prior to entering school. Without positive reinforcement for progress in learning, less privileged children fall to the wayside in the school setting. They become classroom management problems and eventually encounter the punitive aspects of the educational system and society in general. In other words, our reluctance to use positive incentives results in a major injustice to a large segment of children in our society.

We agree with those who seek to reduce the use of social punishment. The negative side effects of punishment are well established.[5] It is also true that rewards can be used in a way to benefit those in power and control those subjected to the reward system. Such a reward system would be negative. But let us be clear. There is no need to equate punishment with reward. Rewards and positive reinforcement can be used effectively to enhance people's performance, interest, and enjoyment. The view that rewards are inherently detrimental is a wrong-headed notion, which must be rectified if we are to see improvements in education, work, and other applied settings.

Basic principles of positive reinforcement are now well established.[6] In addition, there is a large body of research on how to implement these principles in education and business.[7] Designing social environments through the use of rewards and positive reinforcement is not an easy task, but it can be done. Those who participate in the design of such environments must have an experimental attitude and be willing to adjust and fine-tune the system based on measures of its effectiveness. As part of an ongoing assessment, people within the system must be consulted and their evaluations must be used to improve it. Most important, people will express satisfaction and like what they are doing if positive reinforcement and rewards are properly arranged.

AN EFFECTIVE REWARD SYSTEM REQUIRES:

- an experimental attitude
- continual fine-tuning of the system
- input from people within the system
- ongoing evaluation of the effectiveness
  of the system

AN EFFECTIVE REWARD SYSTEM LEADS TO:

- increased satisfaction for students and employees
- recognition of accomplishments
- a desire to attain high standards
- a means to achieve personal and social goals
- high productivity
- feelings of competence and freedom

The claim that rewards and reinforcement are destructive has a long history that involves many cherished beliefs about human nature as well as numerous misunderstandings about a science of human behavior. This book is our attempt to clarify major historical and contemporary issues surrounding this topic, present current findings, address misconceptions about the use of reward within a science of behavior, and describe how rewards can be used effectively within applied settings.

In the next section (Part II), we describe and assess the initial research on rewards and intrinsic motivation that was conducted in the early 1970s. Although the findings from the initial studies were weak and inconclusive, they are frequently cited as evidence that rewards have generalized negative effects on human behavior. This view has been touted for the past three decades in newspaper articles, major psychology textbooks, education and business journals, and many other outlets. Our evaluation of the early studies, however, shows that producing a negative effect of reward requires an unusual combination of conditions that is not characteristic of the actual use of rewards in everyday life. Nonetheless, the idea that rewards disrupt an individual's intrinsic motivation has captured a great deal of attention. Numerous theories have been put forward to predict and account for the effects of rewards, and a large body of experimental research has accumulated on the topic.

Different theoretical perspectives are presented in Part III of the book. Chapter 4 deals specifically with theories that view rewards as harmful; Chapter 5 covers theories that focus on positive effects of reward and reinforcement. In Part IV, we review and evaluate more than 30 years of research (over 100 experiments) on rewards and intrinsic motivation. A major feature of this section is our meta-analysis of the literature. The meta-analysis presented in Chapter 8 is designed to address shortcomings of previous reviews on the topic, while drawing on strengths. Based on our findings, we show that negative effects of reward are a limited phenomenon. At the same time, we identify conditions under which rewards can be used effectively to enhance and maintain performance and motivation. In Chapter 9, these findings are discussed in terms of theoretical and practical implications.

In Part V of this book, the rewards and intrinsic motivation literature is examined in a sociohistorical context, specifically, in light of the debate between behaviorism and other psychologies. Our contention is that the hypothesis that rewards undermine intrinsic motivation was propagated because it provided an apparent empirical attack on behavioral conceptions of human nature. The notion that rewards sap people's intrinsic motivation can be understood as an offshoot of other sentiments and concerns that were popular in the 1960s and 1970s. External rewards, structured workplaces and classrooms, competition, performance evaluations, and so on were all viewed as forms of control that constrain individual freedom and expression. Thus, although the research findings do not support the view that rewards are inherently harmful, given the views that dominated the period when this research was instigated, it is not surprising that the literature was interpreted in this way.

Part VI of the book deals with practical applications of rewards. In Chapter 11, we discuss how to enhance performance and motivation in educational and business settings through the effective arrangement of rewards and reinforcement. The final section of the book, Part VII, provides an overall summary of the controversy over rewards and intrinsic motivation.

Our premise in this book is that there is no inherent negative property of rewards. They are not harmful to human nature. If anything, rewards are a natural part of human nature. What is important is to ensure that reward systems promote, rather than restrict, human freedom. This is exactly what we mean by the phrase, *the effective use of rewards*. As we enter the new millennium, the time is ripe to debunk old myths and to bring rewards back into the picture. An uncritical reliance on weak experimental data and on a philosophy asserting that rewards are harmful to human nature has been maintained at the expense of building a better world in which to live.

NOTES

1. Sidman, 1989. Sidman provides an analysis of punishment and other forms of aversive control and shows that these forms of control of human behavior produce numerous problems for society.

2. Kohn, 1993a.

3. Deci, 1971.

4. The reader is referred to the *Journal of the Experimental Analysis of Behavior*, the *Journal of Applied Behavior Analysis*, and textbooks on modern behavior theory (e.g., Pierce and Epling, 1999; Mazur, 1998).

5. Azrin and Holtz, 1966.

6. Skinner, 1953.

7. Kazdin, 1994; Martin and Pear, 1999.

PART II

REWARDS AND INTRINSIC MOTIVATION: A LOOK AT THE EARLY RESEARCH

Chapter 2

How Rewards Got a Bad Reputation

The contemporary view that rewards and reinforcement are harmful is grounded in a literature from social psychology concerning intrinsic motivation. A prominent view states that rewards and reinforcement decrease a person's intrinsic motivation to engage in an activity. Essentially, the concern is that although money, high grades, prizes, and even praise may get people to perform an activity, the motivation to continue the activity will be lost once the rewards stop coming. For example, if a child who enjoys reading is rewarded with money for reading, the claim is that he or she will read less and enjoy reading less once the money is discontinued. In other words, rewards are said to have a negative effect on people's intrinsic motivation.

Although this sounds straightforward, the relationship between rewards and intrinsic motivation is riddled with problems. There are problems with the concept of intrinsic motivation, the basic experimental situations used to show that rewards are harmful, and the conclusions drawn from these experiments. We begin this chapter with a definition of intrinsic motivation; we show that the concept involves complexities and confusions. Next, we describe the research hypothesis that rewards are harmful to intrinsic motivation. This hypothesis has guided most of the research in this area. We provide an overview of two highly cited experiments on the effects of rewards and intrinsic motivation. Although the results of these studies are not definitive, they set the stage for the view that rewards are harmful. A consideration of the details of these studies helps to reveal problems with procedures, measures, and overgeneralized conclusions.

WHAT IS INTRINSIC MOTIVATION?

Intrinsic motivation is a term used mostly in social psychology.[1] In everyday language, the term is simply another way of saying that people are interested in, and enjoy, what they are doing. According to the social psychological literature, people are said to be intrinsically motivated when they do an activity for its own sake, rather than for any extrinsic reward.[2] The term *intrinsic motivation* is often used in contrast to *extrinsic motivation*. Extrinsically motivated behaviors are those in which an external controlling factor can be readily identified. For example, if people solve puzzles, play games, or paint pictures for no obvious external reason, they are said to be intrinsically motivated. On the other hand, students who study hard to obtain high grades, employees who work extra hours for pay, and children who do their homework to please their parents are said to be extrinsically motivated.

INTRINSIC Motivation	EXTRINSIC Motivation
• used to refer to behaviors for which there is no apparent reward except the activity itself • performance in the absence of reward	• used to refer to behaviors in which an external controlling variable can be readily identified

Now, you can probably see a difficulty with these definitions. The term *intrinsic motivation* is defined by the absence of obvious external factors such as extrinsic rewards. If the reasons for doing and enjoying an activity are a result of past consequences, due to anticipated future benefits, not obvious, or unknown, the behavior is characterized as intrinsically motivated.[3] In other words, when we do not know why a person engages in a particular activity, we infer intrinsic motivation. Thus, the motives for engaging in many activities get lumped into the category of intrinsic motivation. As a result, behavior due to distant, hidden, or obscure external causes gets mistakenly labeled as intrinsically motivated.[4]

A further complication is that the terms *interest* and *motivation* are frequently used interchangeably; both are inferred from behavior. Technically speaking, intrinsic motivation is supposed to be the inner cause of an individual's interest in an activity. Substituting the term *interest* for *motivation* results in considerable confusion. Nonetheless, several social psychologists use the terms, and a research hypothesis concerning rewards and intrinsic motivation has been formulated. The conjecture is that external rewards destroy intrinsic motivation.

THE DETRIMENTAL EFFECTS OF REWARD HYPOTHESIS

In the 1950s and 1960s, the view was that intrinsic and extrinsic motivation were independent. Some theorists assumed that intrinsic and extrinsic rewards were additive and combined to increase overall performance and motivation.[5] In terms of work, the view was that the highest motivation to perform would occur in a system in which jobs were interesting and challenging and in which the employee was extrinsically rewarded for performance (e.g., with pay, recognition, etc.). That is, productivity and satisfaction would be highest when intrinsic motivation was supplemented with extrinsic incentives.

The notion that extrinsic rewards could be harmful to overall motivation was raised in the late 1960s by the psychologist R. DeCharms.[6] DeCharms speculated that intrinsic and extrinsic motivation may not be additive and that external rewards might actually interfere with intrinsic motivation. He further suggested that external rewards would change people's perceptions about the causes of their behavior.[7] If people were rewarded for engaging in activities, they would begin to see themselves as doing the activity for the reward rather than for interest and enjoyment. In this way, DeCharms suggested, external rewards undermine intrinsic motivation.

The idea that extrinsic rewards could disrupt an individual's intrinsic motivation led to the detrimental effects of reward hypothesis, which states that external rewards undermine intrinsic motivation, either by subverting perceptions of competence and self-determination or by deflecting the source of motivation from internal to external causes.

> ## THE DETRIMENTAL EFFECTS OF REWARD HYPOTHESIS
>
> ◆ ─────────────────────────── ◆
>
> Extrinsic rewards undermine people's intrinsic motivation.

The detrimental effects of reward hypothesis has been highly influential in social psychology and education, leading many researchers to investigate the relationship between external rewards and intrinsic motivation. Since the early 1970s, over 100 studies have been conducted on this topic. Part IV of this book deals with this enormous literature. In this chapter, we examine two early studies on rewards and intrinsic motivation. These studies are the most cited examples of the negative effects of reward. Based on these early experiments, the hypothesis gained wide public acceptance. Given this wide acceptance, it is informative to closely examine the procedures and details of the early experiments.

DECI'S ORIGINAL EXPERIMENTS

The first laboratory investigations to test the effects of rewards on intrinsic motivation were conducted by Edward Deci in the early 1970s.[8] In the first experiment, 24 college students, fulfilling a course requirement, were presented with a puzzle-solving task (using Soma™, a commercial puzzle composed of seven different shapes that can be fitted together to form an infinite variety of configurations). The Soma™ puzzle was chosen because the college students indicated high interest in it.[9] The study was made up of three one-hour sessions over a three-day period. Twelve students were assigned to an experimental group and the remainder, to a control group. During each session, the participants were individually taken to a room and asked to work on the Soma™ puzzles in order to reproduce various configurations that were drawn on a piece of paper. Four puzzles were presented in a session, and the students were given 13 minutes to solve each one. In the second session only, experimental participants were told that they would receive $1 for each puzzle solved. They were paid prior to the third session. The control group was not offered any money.

In the middle of each session, the experimenter made an excuse to leave the room for eight minutes. The participants were told that they could do as they pleased. The puzzles, three magazines, and an ashtray were available in the room. During the eight-minute period, the experimenter observed the participants through one-way glass and recorded the time that each individual spent engaged on the Soma™ task. The amount of time spent on the task during the free-choice period was taken as one measure of intrinsic motivation. A second measure of intrinsic motivation was the participants' self-reported interest (attitude toward solving puzzles).[10]

In accord with the detrimental effects hypothesis, Deci proposed that reward (money) would decrease subsequent intrinsic motivation and that participants in the experimental group would spend less time on the Soma™ puzzles in the third session than they had in the first. He predicted that there would be a statistically significant difference between the experimental and control groups on this free-time measure. Deci's findings indicated that the rewarded group did spend less time on the task in the free-choice period than the nonrewarded group, but the difference did not meet conventional levels of statistical significance.[11] On the second measure of intrinsic motivation—the self-reports of task interest—no significant differences were found between the two groups. That is, those who had received a reward reported as much interest in the Soma™ task as did those in the control group.

Thus, Deci's first study on the topic of rewards and intrinsic motivation showed no differences between the reward group and the control group on the task interest measure. And although there was a small difference between the two groups on the free-time measure, this difference was not statistically significant. In other words, the findings were not in accord with the detrimental effects hypothesis. Nonetheless, Deci claimed, "If a person is engaged in some activity for reasons of intrinsic motivation, and if he begins to receive the external reward, money, for performing the activity, the degree to which he is intrinsically motivated to perform the activity decreases."[12]

In another study, Deci used a somewhat different experimental design and further investigated the effects of external reward (money) on college students'

**DECI'S (1971) INITIAL STUDY ON THE
EFFECTS OF REWARDS ON INTRINSIC MOTIVATION**

Experimental Group:
12 college students offered money to solve puzzles

Control Group:
12 college students asked to solve puzzles
(no offer of money)

Task:
Solving Soma™ puzzles

Reward:
$1 for each of four puzzles solved

Measures of Intrinsic Motivation:
Difference between experimental and control groups on:
(1) Free time on task—time spent during free-
choice period without reward
(2) Self-reported task interest

Results:
(1) Free time—rewarded group spent less free time on task than
control group, but difference was not statistically significant
(2) Self-reported task interest—no difference between groups

---

intrinsic motivation.[13] The study involved two, rather than three, sessions. In the first session, experimental participants were offered money to solve Soma™ puzzles; the control group was not offered money but was asked to solve puzzles. The second session involved a free-choice period without reward; participants were free to do more Soma™ puzzles or to engage in alternate activities. As in Deci's first study, intrinsic motivation was indexed by the difference between rewarded and control participants on time spent on the Soma puzzles during the free-choice period (free-time intrinsic motivation). Interestingly, those who were promised and given the reward prior to the free-choice period spent *more* free time on Soma™ puzzles than the control group.[14] This difference was statistically significant. Although Deci continued to claim that external rewards reduce intrinsic motivation, what this study actually showed was that students who were rewarded showed an increase in the main measure of intrinsic motivation (free time). Thus, in terms of money as an extrinsic reward, Deci's early findings did not show significant decreases in measures of intrinsic motivation.[15]

Deci also investigated the effects of verbal rewards (praise) on students' intrinsic motivation in two early studies.[16] Participants were asked to solve Soma™ puzzles. Experimental participants were told after each puzzle that their performance was very good or much better than average. In both studies using verbal praise as the reward, Deci found that the praised group spent more free time on the task than those who received no praise. These findings were statistically significant in Deci's first study but not significant in the second experiment.

Overall, the results from Deci's early studies showed that verbal rewards appeared to increase motivation to perform an activity; tangible rewards (money) produced either an increase in intrinsic motivation measures or no reliable effects. In spite of the fact that the findings from Deci's initial experiments did not provide support for the detrimental effects of reward hypothesis, Deci's early experiments are frequently cited in textbooks as evidence for negative effects of reward.

THE STANFORD EXPERIMENT

One of the best known and most cited studies on the detrimental effects of reward on behavior comes from an experimental study conducted by Lepper, Greene, and Nisbett in the 1970s at Stanford University.[17] In this study, nursery school children were observed in a free-play period in order to determine their initial interest on a drawing activity. Two observers sat behind a one-way mirror and recorded the amount of time each child was engaged in drawing. The children who spent the most time on the task were selected as participants for the experiment. Three conditions were then set up. In the "expected-reward" condition, children were offered a "good player" award, which they received for drawing with magic markers. Children in the "unexpected-reward" group received the award but were not promised it beforehand, and "no-reward" participants did not expect or receive an award.

In a subsequent free-play session, those children who were promised an award (expected-reward group) spent significantly less time drawing than the other two groups. Furthermore, the expected-reward group spent less time drawing in the postexperimental session than they had in the initial session (pre-experimental free-play session). The unexpected-reward and no-reward groups did not differ significantly from one another; both groups showed slight increases in time on task from the pre-experimental to postexperimental sessions.

LEPPER, GREENE, AND NISBETT'S (1973) STUDY ON THE EFFECTS OF REWARDS ON INTRINSIC MOTIVATION

Experimental Group 1
(expected [promised] reward):
18 nursery school children offered an award to draw

Experimental Group 2
(unexpected reward):
18 nursery school children asked to draw
(no offer of reward—but reward was given after children had drawn)

Control Group:
15 nursery school children asked to draw
(no offer of reward, no reward given)

Task:
Drawing with magic markers

Reward:
Good player award

Measures of Intrinsic Motivation:
Difference between groups on free time on task—
time spent during free-choice period without reward

Results:
Free time
(1) expected reward group spent significantly less free time on task than unexpected reward group and control ($p < .05$).
(2) no significant differences between unexpected reward and control groups

---

Based on the findings, Lepper and his colleagues concluded that their results provided "empirical evidence of an undesirable consequence of the unnecessary use of extrinsic rewards."[18] Although they made this conclusion, it is interesting to note that those who had received an unexpected reward spent more time on the task during the postexperimental free-play period than either the expected-reward or the control groups. Because the unexpected and expected reward groups are both reward conditions, the conclusion that these results demonstrate

Table 2.1

A Summary of the Early Findings on the Effects of Rewards on Intrinsic Motivation

		INTRINSIC MOTIVATION MEASURE	
Study	**Type of reward**	**Free time**	**Task interest**
Deci (1971)	Expected tangible (money)	n.s.	n.s.
	Verbal praise	Increase*	n.s.
Deci (1972b)	Expected tangible (money)	Increase*	—
	Verbal praise	n.s.	—
Lepper, Greene, and Nisbett (1973)	Expected tangible (good player award)	Decrease*	—
	Unexpected tangible (good player award)	n.s.	—

Note: * = statistically significant at p < .05; n.s. = not significant.

the negative effects of reward is not correct. This is because reward was held constant in the unexpected-reward and expected-reward groups; what differed was the condition of promise or no promise. That is, the promises made must have produced the results.[19] As this is the case, the experiment actually showed that promises of reward (telling children that they would receive a reward for doing the activity), and not reward per se, reduced the time spent on the task.

A SUMMARY OF THE EARLY RESEARCH FINDINGS

The detrimental effect of reward hypothesis became prominent in the early 1970s. The claim was that rewards undermine people's intrinsic motivation. At the point when the detrimental effects hypothesis became popular, however, and rewards got a bad reputation, the experimental data did not, in fact, provide conclusive evidence for negative effects of reward. Findings from the early studies are summarized in Table 2.1.

Deci's (1971) first study showed that the effects of tangible rewards (money) were not statistically reliable and that verbal rewards had positive effects. Table 2.1 also shows that in a subsequent study by Deci (1972b), tangible rewards were found to increase free-time intrinsic motivation, whereas verbal rewards showed no significant effect. The study by Lepper and his associates (Lepper, Greene, and Nisbett, 1973) showed that when tangible rewards were delivered unexpectedly, free-time intrinsic motivation was unaffected. However, Lepper and colleagues did show a significant decrease in free-time intrinsic motivation when the reward was tangible and offered beforehand (expected). In Deci's first study, intrinsic motivation was also indexed by self-reports of task interest. No significant findings were detected for either tangible or verbal rewards.

Table 2.1 shows that the results from the early studies produced mixed effects. Clearly, the results did not indicate that rewards are generally harmful. In fact, the early research showed that rewards could be used to increase measures of intrinsic motivation. Nevertheless, the findings from the early research are often cited in newspapers, journal articles, and introductory psychology textbooks as evidence that extrinsic rewards undermine intrinsic motivation. Some writers equate reward with reinforcement and claim that the early studies are demonstrations of detrimental effects of positive reinforcement.[20]

POPULAR ACCEPTANCE OF THE VIEW THAT REWARDS ARE HARMFUL

Following the publication of the initial studies on rewards and intrinsic motivation, numerous statements began to appear in the psychological and educational literature warning practitioners of the dangers of implementing incentive programs based on rewards and reinforcement. In the 1970s, the message was that positive reinforcement techniques and token economy programs (programs in which, for appropriate behavior, individuals are given tokens that are exchangeable for goods, services, and activities) may be worse than ineffective. Drawing on the results of the early studies on rewards and intrinsic motivation, the authors of an *American Psychologist* article argued that "since tokens tend to decrease the intrinsic value of an activity, they may actually do more harm than good."[21]

Such comments and cautions have been echoed throughout psychology and education ever since. For example, in the 1990s, the authors of one prominent textbook cited Lepper's work and stated that

when an extrinsic reward is given, the motivation becomes extrinsic and the task itself is enjoyed less. When the extrinsic rewards are withdrawn, the activity loses its material value. The moral is: *A reward a day makes work out of play.*[22]

A trade book entitled *Punished by Rewards*, by Alfie Kohn, has received considerable attention for its general thesis that in business and education, the use of rewards has a detrimental impact.[23] The experiments from social psychology on rewards and intrinsic motivation are used to substantiate this claim. Kohn extended his critique of external rewards to include verbal rewards, particularly the use of praise.[24]

In a recent article in a top educational journal, Deci and his colleagues cautioned teachers and suggested that "there is indeed reason for teachers to exercise great care when using reward-based incentive systems."[25] As we have seen, the initial research findings were not conclusive. Nonetheless, the original experiments continue to be cited as evidence that rewards are detrimental. In a current edited volume titled, *Intrinsic and Extrinsic Motivation*,[26] several of the writers point to the early research and claim that the findings indicate that extrinsic incentives undermine intrinsic motivation.[27]

The popularization of the negative view of extrinsic rewards has fostered public attitudes against the use of rewards and incentives. In the United States, there has been public pressure to improve children's reading abilities. Business and philanthropic organizations have funded programs in which everything from money to pizza has been offered to increase the number of books children read. Articles appearing in the *New York Times* and *U.S. News and World Report* have complained that "read for reward" programs are making children into non-readers by destroying their enjoyment of reading.[28] Recent articles in Canadian newspapers have also focused on the topic. A concern is that rewarding children is akin to bribery and such bribery will prevent children from ever being motivated to learn for the sake of learning.[29]

There is no doubt that the early research on rewards and intrinsic motivation has had a powerful impact. Many drew conclusions from Deci's and Lepper and his colleagues' early studies that went well beyond the scope of the research. Statements that the results confirmed the negative effects of reward were soon picked up by the media and public. The rumor that rewards are harmful has filtered into psychology texts, educational journals, and business magazines.

Do rewards deserve such a bad reputation? Should rewards be removed from educational, business, and other applied settings? Our answer is a firm no. Rewards can be used as effective means for cultivating interest and increasing motivation and performance. In the following chapter, we describe why rewards do not deserve a bad image.

NOTES

1. A nativistic approach to motivation can be found in the first social psychology textbook by McDougall (1908) and may be one reason why concepts such as intrinsic motivation have some support in this discipline. That is, intrinsic motivation is thought by some to be an innate property of human nature in the same way that instincts were formerly thought to account for variation in human behavior. In dispute of a nativistic approach to motivation, Kuo (1931) raised cats with rats and showed that there was no basic instinct for the cats to kill the rats. He argued that much behavior was learned (acquired during the individual's lifetime). One basis of learning that we emphasize in this book is learning by consequences. Rewards are a source of consequences for human behavior that are arranged by other people. It is these socially arranged consequences that are said to disrupt intrinsic motivation.

2. Deci, 1975.

3. There may be many reasons why people do things in cases where external control is not obvious. See Kohn, 1993a, pp. 270–276.

4. The consequences of action are often difficult to observe because they are remote or intermittent.

5. Porter and Lawler, 1968; Vroom, 1964.

6. DeCharms, 1968.

7. Why do people want to see themselves as causes of their own actions? DeCharms (1968) tells us that this is another basic, innate need. Skinner (1971) suggests that the reasons are social. The less obvious are the external causes of behavior, the more credit for their actions people will receive from others. Actions that are due to clear external reasons receive little respect from others. On the other hand, if we cannot see the sources of influence that affect a person's behavior, we attribute it to that person. Thus, the need to see oneself as a causal agent is not innate. Rather, the social consequences of appearing to be self-motivated maintain this behavior.

8. Deci, 1971, 1972a, 1972b.

9. The issue of task interest is problematic. Only tasks of high initial interest are said to be undermined by external rewards. Students are often faced with tasks that they do not initially find interesting, and rewards can be used effectively to build interest and skillful performance in such cases (Bandura, 1986, pp. 241–242). The point at which rewards change from beneficial to harmful is not addressed by theories of intrinsic motivation.

10. Deci and Ryan (1985) initally claimed that the self-report interest measure is more closely related to intrinsic motivation than is the free-time measure. In a recent publication, Deci, Koestner, and Ryan (1999) suggested that a composite measure called "free choice" (free time and performance on a task during the free-choice session) is the best measure.

11. Social scientists work under the alpha .05 level of statistical significance. Results that do not meet this criterion are failures to reject the null hypothesis. This means that the researcher is unable to reject the hypothesis that there is no difference between experimental and control groups and therefore, should not favor the alternate, research hypothesis. Deci's results were not significant at the .05 level (the findings were reported as significant at $p < .10$, one tailed).

12. Deci, 1971, p. 108.

13. Deci, 1972b.

14. There were two reward groups in Deci's (1972b) study. Both groups were offered money to solve Soma™ puzzles. One group was paid prior to the free-choice period; the second group was paid after the free-choice period. Participants who were rewarded prior to the free-choice session spent significantly more free time on the task than control participants; there was no significant difference between controls and participants who were rewarded following the free-time session.

15. Deci (1972a) conducted another study using monetary rewards, in which participants were offered money simply for participating in the experiment. No significant differences were detected on the free-time measure for reward versus control participants.

16. Deci, 1971, 1972b.

17. Lepper, Greene, and Nisbett, 1973.

18. Ibid., p. 136.

19. Promises of reward fall under the category of verbal stimuli called instructions. Instructions regulate behavior because of a past history of consequences in their presence. For example, an instruction from a friend such as, "Eat at Joe's, you'll really like the food," will affect you if, in the past, the advice of this friend has been credible. That is, if past recommendations made by your friend have turned out well, you are likely to take future advice. In terms of promises of reward, a person will react to the promise on

the basis of past experiences of promises. Some types of promised rewards are usually described as bribes. Often, when a bribe is presented, people will react to it by doing the opposite. Thus, if the promise of reward is taken as a bribe, a person may do less of that activity in reaction to the social control implied by the bribe. Rather than a loss of intrinsic motivation, this reactance to implied control may account for the results of the early experiments on expected and unexpected reward.

20. Behavioral psychologists make an important distinction between the terms *reinforcement* and *reward*. Reinforcement is defined by its effects on behavior. A reinforcer is an event that has been shown to increase the frequency of the behavior that it follows. A reward, however, is defined socially. Rewards are stimuli that are assumed to be positive events but have not been shown to strengthen behavior. Incentive systems (e.g., classroom token economies) may be based on either reward or reinforcement and are designed to increase motivation.

21. Levine and Fasnacht, 1974, p. 819.

22. Zimbardo, 1992, p. 454.

23. Kohn, 1993a.

24. Although Kohn (1993a) recognized that the literature on intrinsic motivation does not support the conclusion that praise has detrimental effects, he still condemned the use of praise and other verbal reinforcement. His concern was that people use praise to get other people to do what they want. This is what we would call insincere praise. Sincere praise is praise given when a person accomplishes some level of performance that evokes a positive reaction. Sincere praise has positive effects on interest and performance. The point is not to condemn praise per se, but to effectively use it to reward accomplishments.

25. Deci, Koestner, and Ryan, 2001, p. 2.

26. Sansone and Harackiewicz, 2000.

27. For example, see Lepper and Henderlong, 2000.

28. Egan, 1995; Hawkins, 1995.

29. Smyth, 2001; Vanderberg, 2001.

Chapter 3

Why Rewards Do Not Deserve a Bad Reputation

The early experiments on rewards and intrinsic motivation have led many psychologists, parents, educators, and other practitioners to reject the use of rewards and be suspicious of programs based on the use of positive reinforcement. Numerous confusions and misunderstandings underlie the continued popularity of the view that rewards and reinforcement are harmful. In this chapter, we carefully analyze aspects of the early experiments in order to clarify many of the misunderstandings and misconceptions that permeate this literature. Based on this analysis, we conclude that there is no need to reject the use of rewards in everyday life.

PROBLEMS WITH THE EARLY EXPERIMENTS

Reinforcement versus Reward

The early research on reward and intrinsic motivation is often used to argue that rewards and reinforcement are destructive to human nature. In this context, it is useful to distinguish between reward and reinforcement. Technically, the term *reinforcement* means "to increase or strengthen"; reinforcement involves a procedure for strengthening behavior. A behavior is likely to be repeated (or increase in frequency) if certain kinds of consequences follow. The consequences that increase behavior are called reinforcers and are usually things that people (or other organisms) find rewarding or satisfying. For example, a teacher may say, "Correct, good job!" when a student successfully solves math problems. Most students like to succeed at their schoolwork, so the teacher's social reward is expected to reinforce the behavior of solving math problems.

Although one might suspect that rewards such as "correct," "right," or "yes" will strengthen behavior, the actual effects of these words on behavior is an open question. A test for reinforcement involves showing that the teacher's verbal rewards actually increase a student's math performance. If this is the case, verbal rewards are defined as reinforcement for the behavior of a particular student. On the other hand, verbal rewards may not reinforce academic peformance by another student. The point is that reinforcement must be tailored to the individual. This means that social and material rewards will not serve as reinforcement for all people. This is an important point. Teachers cannot count on their rewards serving as reinforcement for all students. What may work as a reinforcer for one person may not work for another. Depending on the person, rewards could have no effect, have a reinforcement effect, or even function as punishment (decreasing behavior). When rewards are perceived as bribes, they often have this latter effect.

Reinforcement procedures also usually involve repeated presentation of the reinforcer following the occurrence of the desired behavior. This means that the teacher arranges corrective comments for appropriate answers to math problems over an extended period (not on a onetime basis) so as to strengthen this behavior.

Events that are called rewards are socially defined and usually involve such things as gold stars, awards of excellence, pats on the back, recognition, money, opportunities to do preferred activities, and so on. These events are presumed to be positive and may be given for a variety of reasons. Rewards may be given for honorable service, to establish a positive attitude toward the reward giver, or to set up an obligation to reciprocate. Only when rewards are shown to strengthen behavior can they be equated with reinforcement.

In the original experiments by Deci (1971, 1972b) and by Lepper and his colleagues (Lepper, Greene, and Nisbett, 1973), there was no test to ascertain whether the rewards that were used functioned as reinforcement for the tasks of puzzle solving and drawing. In addition, the rewards were not delivered repeatedly. Instead, repeated delivery of reinforcement was replaced by instructions, promises of reward, and descriptions of reward contingencies. In other words, neither of these early studies involved positive reinforcement and intrinsic motivation. In fact, on close inspection, the studies did not really involve rewards either but rather promises and instructions about reward.

Promise of Reward versus Reward

The early studies on reward and intrinsic motivation involved promises of reward and descriptions of reward contingencies. That is, people were told what they had to do to get a reward. This is what the researchers called "expected reward." It is this expected-reward condition that was found to decrease time spent on the task in the free-choice phase of the experiment by Lepper and his colleagues.[1]

Alyce Dickinson provides a useful analysis of the distinction between reinforcement contingency and the description of contingencies.[2] She makes the point that describing what people are to do and offering them a reward for doing it may result in the occurrence of the desired behavior. But verbal descriptions of contingencies usually do not show all the features of behavior maintained by reinforcement. Similarly, what happens following the promises and actual exposure to contingencies may be quite different. Skinner made a similar distinction when he stated:

The manipulation of independent variables appears to be circumvented when, instead of exposing an organism to a set of contingencies, the contingencies are simply described in "instructions." Instead of shaping a response, the subject is told to respond in a given way. A history of reinforcement or punishment is replaced by a promise or threat. . . .

Descriptions of contingencies are, of course, often effective. . . . Verbal communication is not, however, a substitute for the arrangement and manipulation of variables.

There is no reason why a description of contingencies of reinforcement should have the same effect as exposure to the contingencies. A subject can seldom accurately describe the way in which he has been actually reinforced. Even when he has been trained to identify a few simple contingencies, he cannot then describe a new contingency, particularly when it is complex. We can scarcely expect him, therefore, to react appropriately to descriptions by the experimenter. Moreover, the verbal contingencies between the subject and experimenter must be taken into account. Instructions must in some way promise or threaten consequences not germane to the experiment if the subject is to follow them.[3]

Dickinson elaborates on Skinner's points, stating that promises of reward can be influenced by many factors, including

the sophistication of the subject's verbal repertoire, the subject's history with respect to whether the promised rewards were actually received, the nature of the subject's prior exposure to the object being offered as reward, whether the particular wording of the request to perform the task has been correlated with punishment for noncompliance and events that occur during the delay between the promise and reward delivery, such as the way the experimenter interacts with the subject.[4]

Most important, people may react to descriptions and promises of reward in a different way than the way in which they react to actual rewards or actual contingencies of reinforcement. In fact, the early research showed that the delivery of reward without a promise (unexpected reward) did not lead participants to spend less time on the task. In spite of this, the detrimental effect hypothesis is cast in terms of actual rewards rather than in terms of promises of reward or descriptions of reward contingencies. Based on findings of the early research, a more correct statement of the negative effect would be that time on task declines when people are promised a reward for doing some activity.[5]

Withdrawal of Promised Reward

The early experiments on rewards and intrinsic motivation are often cast as evidence for the negative effects of delivering rewards or reinforcement. However, it should be pointed out that the major effect came when the previously promised reward was withdrawn. The participants in the studies were offered and delivered a reward for doing some task. Following this, the reward was removed and time on task was measured. The findings indicated that those who had been promised a reward spent less time on the task once the reward was removed than those participants who had not been rewarded. This finding was interpreted as evidence that rewards reduced people's intrinsic motivation. A more logical interpretation, however, is that the change from a stated reward contingency to a no reward situation produced a temporary decline in time on task rather than a loss of intrinsic motivation.

To illustrate, suppose a local fast food restaurant offers to give free meals for each book a student reads during a month-long campaign. Suppose that one child decides to enroll in the campaign while a second child does not. Prior to the campaign, both children have been reading approximately the same number of books at the same level. During the campaign, the child who is enrolled increases the number of books read (due to the promised reward). That is, the promised reward enhances motivation to read. The other child continues to read at his or her own pace. Thus, while the offer of reward is in effect, the child who is enrolled in the program reads more than the child who is not enrolled. The offered reward increases the desired behavior, which is the objective of the campaign.

Once the campaign ends, the concern is that the child enrolled in the program will read less because of a loss of intrinsic motivation during the reward period. Will this happen in the restaurant example? One possibility is that the child enrolled in the program will read about as much as he or she did before the campaign. This seems highly likely as a long-range outcome. That is, in the long run, the restaurant's campaign may have no lasting effects on the child's reading. There could be a short-term decline in reading. This temporary reduction would not be due to a loss of intrinsic motivation but to the fact that child may have read so much during the month long campaign that he or she is momentarily tired of reading.

In addition, the signal that rewards have stopped for an activity often produces its immediate cessation. For example, an out-of-order sign on a vending machine will prevent a person from inserting money to get a drink. But this is a momentary effect, and the person will continue to use vending machines. In the same sense, the child who is told that the reading campaign has ended may stop reading temporarily but will return to reading later on. These types of transient effects could be what the early researchers observed in the laboratory studies during the brief free-time play period. The point is that the side effects of withdrawal of reward are fleeting. Statements that rewards have pervasive, long-lasting negative effects on people's intrinsic motivation are not supported by the early studies.

Effects of Choice and the Free-Time Measure

In order to measure intrinsic motivation, in the early studies, a free-time phase was arranged following the period of reward. During this phase, participants had the opportunity to engage in the experimental task or in a variety of other activities (e.g., reading a magazine, smoking a cigarette). A problem with this procedure is that these activities introduce an aspect of choice that was not present in the other phases.

The introduction of choice means that the rewarded participants went from a period of promised reward for a specific activity to a period of choice among activities. The decline in time spent on the rewarded activity could be due to this change. Consider the fact that individuals who were promised a reward for solving puzzles or drawing pictures did more of this activity in the reward phase than the control group, which was not promised a reward. When placed in the free-time setting, the rewarded participants could now distribute their time to the experimental task or to the other activities. Because they had spent more time doing the experimental task in the reward phase, the alternative activities in the choice phase would tend to become more attractive. That is, the experimental participants would choose the alternate activities rather than spend more time on puzzle solving or drawing. This would lead to a decline in absolute time spent on the experimental activity and account for a major part of the findings. In other words, the findings may have been due to the introduction of choice rather than to a loss of intrinsic motivation. If this is so, the results reflect an artifact of the procedures rather than a fundamental relationship between reward and intrinsic motivation.

Verbal versus Tangible Rewards

The detrimental effects of reward hypothesis concerns the use of external rewards. External rewards are those that come from outside the person and are usually arranged by other people. In Deci's first study (1971) and in Lepper, Greene, and Nisbett's (1973) experiment, time on task was found to decrease following the removal of a promised tangible reward (e.g., money, good player award) given for puzzle solving or drawing pictures. The first study by Deci, however, also indicated that not all external rewards produced a decline in intrinsic motivation.[6] Specifically, Deci found that when verbal praise was given for solving puzzles and then removed, the experimental participants spent more time on the task than the unrewarded control group. At the very least, this finding limits the generality of the detrimental effects of reward hypothesis. That is, only some external rewards produced a decline in time on task, whereas others enhanced performance.

Another point is that there is no inherent difference between verbal and tangible rewards. It is likely that verbal praise can be used in ways that make people less enthusiastic about an activity. For example, people who use praise to ingratiate themselves to others may find that other people do less for them. Using praise to confer status does not necessarily mean that it will enhance performance. That is, the finding that praise enhances intrinsic motivation does not mean that it does so in all situations and contexts. Clearly, it is the manner in which rewards are arranged and implemented that determines their effects on behavior.

Tangible Rewards Offered for Drawing versus Solving Puzzles

In Deci's early studies (1971, 1972b), participants were offered rewards to solve puzzles. As noted in Chapter 2, Deci found a negative effect of this type of reward in his initial study (although the result was not statistically significant),[7] but the same type of reward was found to increase free time on task in Deci's subsequent study.[8] Lepper and his colleagues (Lepper, Greene, and Nisbett, 1973), on the other hand, offered a reward to participants simply for doing the task (drawing). There was no requirement to achieve a certain level of performance. Lepper and his associates found a strong negative effect with this type of reward arrangement.

These differing findings suggest that it is not tangible reward or the offer of reward that produced the negative effect. Instead, the early findings indicate that reward effects depend on what is required for participants to receive the reward (the stated reward contingency). The Lepper and colleagues study (Lepper, Greene, and Nisbett, 1973) showed that when tangible rewards were offered but no performance requirement was specified, a negative effect occurred. However, in Deci's (1971, 1972b) studies, in which participants were offered a tangible reward to meet a performance standard (solve puzzles), there was no evidence of negative effects.

These findings show that tangible rewards are not inherently harmful. The implication is that tangible rewards can be used to enhance interest and performance when they are allocated correctly. For example, if a tangible reward is given for achieving some level of performance, there is no reason to expect a decline in performance and interest. Clearly, it is not helpful, at the practical level, to condemn the use of all external rewards. A better strategy is to understand how to use rewards effectively in applied settings.

Attitude Measure of Intrinsic Motivation

According to the early researchers, intrinsic motivation has a direct link with task interest. That is, the greater is the intrinsic motivation, the greater the interest. Rewards are expected to decrease intrinsic motivation, and therefore, expressed interest in the task is also expected to decline. Reported interest in puzzle solving was measured in Deci's (1971) original experiment; the results showed that interest in the task was not eroded by the promised rewards. Of course, this finding is rather devastating to the detrimental effects hypothesis, as it indicates that rewards can be used without reducing people's interest in a task.

The relationship between task interest and the free-time measure is also problematic. In Part IV of this book, we show that there is little agreement between these measures. That is, time on task may decrease, yet task interest tends to remain unchanged or even to increase. We only mention here that this is a serious problem for theoretical interpretations of intrinsic motivation; both measures should correlate if they reflect the common energy source of intrinsic motivation.

PROBLEMS WITH THE EARLY EXPERIMENTS ON REWARDS AND INTRINSIC MOTIVATION

- Rewards were not shown to be positive reinforcers.
- Rewards were offered or promised (by instructions)—people did not experience the contingency between doing the task and the reward.
- Change from reward to no-reward phase may produce a temporary decline in time on task—not a loss of intrinsic motivation.
- Change from no choice in the reward phase to choice in the free-time phase may lower time on task as an experimental artifact.
- No detrimental effect was found with verbal rewards.
- Rewards for merely doing an activity show detrimental effects of free time, but rewards for each unit completed do not.
- Time and attitude measures do not covary with reward manipulations.

SINGLE-SUBJECT DESIGNS ASSESSING THE EFFECTS OF REWARD

Following the work of Deci (1971, 1972b) and Lepper and his colleagues (Lepper, Greene, and Nisbett, 1973), some researchers designed studies in an attempt to address some of the concerns raised in this discussion. One of the problems in the original experiments was that the promised rewards were not shown to act as reinforcement. That is, there was no demonstration that the promised rewards increased the frequency of puzzle solving or drawing pictures (i.e., the target activities). Also, the procedures did not involve a repeated presentation of the rewards over time. Critics of Deci's and Lepper and colleagues' studies have noted that in everyday life, rewards are arranged and delivered over a considerable length of time. In the experiments by Deci and by Lepper and associates, the reward and intrinsic motivation procedures involved a single delivery of an offered reward.

In order to address these issues, in 1975, Feingold and Mahoney conducted an experiment using a single-subject, repeated-measures design.[9] Five second-grade children were studied individually. The children were given access to two activities (Dot-to-Dot or Etch-a-Sketch games). The experimenter observed the children's performance of these activities for eight 15-minute sessions. Following these baseline sessions, each child was individually informed that his or her Dot-to-Dot performance would subsequently be rewarded with points exchangeable for prizes. The researchers described the reward procedures as follows:

[Participants] earned one point for exceeding their highest baseline performance and an additional point for every 50 subsequent dots connected. Thus, a child who had completed 130 dot connections during his highest baseline session was required to complete 131 for one point, 181 for two points, and so on. These contingencies were specified by marking the 1–5 point criteria in each [participant's] booklet prior to each session. Points were redeemed on a daily basis and were not accumulated across days. Token reinforcement procedures were continued for four sessions.[10]

This reward phase was followed by a period during which the reward contingency was withdrawn and the children's rate of performing the Dot-to-Dot activity was observed for eight sessions. Two weeks after the experiment, the children returned and were again observed for ten sessions.

Results indicated that the rate of Dot-to-Dot connections more than doubled during the reward phase as compared to baseline. Thus, a reinforcement effect was demonstrated. Removal of the rewards for the activity resulted in a drop in performance to a level equal to the initial baseline. Thus, there was no difference between the pre- and postreward phases, indicating no evidence of a loss of intrinsic motivation. For the two weeks following the experiment, children continued to engage in the Dot-to-Dot activity at baseline level. Again, there was no evidence of a detrimental effect of reward or reinforcement. These results suggest that there is no detrimental effect of reward when the rewards are shown to be reinforcers and delivered repeatedly and repeated assessments of intrinsic motivation are made.

**FEINGOLD AND MAHONEY'S (1975) STUDY ON THE
EFFECTS OF REINFORCEMENT ON INTRINSIC
MOTIVATION**

Participants
Five second grade children

Task:
Making dot-to-dot connections

Reward:
Points exchangeable for prizes

Procedure:
Baseline phase—eight sessions on task without reward
Reinforcement phase—eight sessions on task with reward
Postreinforcement phase—eight sessions on task without reward
Follow-up phase (two weeks later)—ten sessions on task without
reward

Measures of Intrinsic Motivation:
Differences between postreinforcement phase, follow-up phase, and
baseline phase on rate of performance

Results:
(1) no differences
(2) no negative effects of reinforcement

Although Feingold and Mahoney's study showed that rewards were not harmful, the findings have not been readily accepted or acknowledged by those who argue against rewards and reinforcement. Critics have suggested that the results of single-subject designs are limited because too few participants are investigated and no-reward control groups are omitted.[11] Instead, those who advocate the detrimental effects hypothesis rely on evidence from between-group design studies like those conducted by Deci (1971, 1972b) and by Lepper, Greene, and Nisbett (1973).

SUMMARY

The view that external rewards negatively affect people's intrinsic motivation has its basis in early laboratory investigations into this phenomenon. The early experiments by Deci (1971, 1972b) and by Lepper, Greene and Nisbett (1973) have been heralded in psychology, education, business, and the media as evidence that rewards and reinforcement are damaging to basic human nature. Based on this assumption, many researchers and writers have argued against using rewards and positive reinforcement in classrooms, the workplace, and other applied settings.

A close examination of the early experiments on external rewards and intrinsic motivation is revealing. All in all, it turns out that the evidence does not support the claim that rewards are generally harmful. In addition, there is no evidence that the rewards used in the initial studies operated as reinforcement for the activities. Feingold and Mahoney (1975) showed that when rewards were shown to function as reinforcement, intrinsic motivation was not affected. In the initial studies by Deci and by Lepper, Greene, and Nisbett, intrinsic motivation was measured as time spent on a task following the removal of a promised reward; Deci also used a self-report measure of task liking to index intrinsic motivation. The early studies demonstrated that external rewards have different effects on these measures as a function of the type of reward (verbal or tangible), whether the rewards were promised beforehand (expected or unexpected), and what participants were required to do to obtain the reward (reward contingency).

Based on the early experiments, the detrimental effects of reward appear to be highly restricted. The reward procedures of these studies had no effects on the participants' attitude or interest in the activities. The participants were as interested in the activities after the rewards were promised and delivered as they were before.

In terms of time spent on the activity in the free-choice period, a statistically reliable decrease was found in the Lepper and colleagues study, but an unusual combination of conditions was necessary to produce the effect. Specifically, a negative effect was found when the delivery of rewards was stated beforehand. That is, the rewards were promised to participants before they did the task (expected); unexpected rewards did not produce a negative effect. In addition, the rewards were material or tangible; verbal praise did not produce a negative effect. In addition, the rewards were offered simply for doing the task with no performance requirement; rewards offered to meet a performance standard (solve puzzles) did not produce a negative effect.

Another condition necessary to produce a detrimental effect was that time on task had to be measured after the rewards were removed; measuring time on task during the rewarded period did not produce a negative effect. Finally, a negative effect was produced only when the reward was delivered in a single session followed by a onetime assessment of time on task after the reward was removed; repeated presentation of the reward followed by repeated assessments of intrinsic motivation did not produce a negative effect.

IMPLICATIONS OF THE EARLY RESEARCH

Conditions necessary to produce a negative effect of reward:

- Reward is tangible or material
- Reward is offered beforehand
- Reward is offered regardless of level of performance
- Reward is delivered once over a single session
- Intrinsic motivation is measured as time on task following the withdrawal of reward
- Intrinsic motivation is indexed by a single assessment of time on task following the removal of reward

---

Since the publication of the initial studies, an enormous amount of research on rewards and intrinsic motivation has been conducted. Part IV of the book provides an in-depth analysis of these experiments and shows that the results from the early studies have stood the test of time. That is, negative effects of reward remain highly circumscribed and occur only under the unusual conditions already described. Other reward procedures either have no effect on measures of intrinsic motivation or result in an increase.

Reward and reinforcement are critical elements in the design of effective learning and work systems. The literature on intrinsic motivation and reward has been used to convince educators and business managers that rewards are harmful to human nature, and consequently, the trend has been to shy away from the use of rewards. However, there is no need to avoid the use of reward; when properly arranged, it can enhance performance without a loss of interest or enjoyment. What we are saying, then, is that rewards do not deserve a bad reputation.

NOTES

1. Lepper, Greene, and Nisbett, 1973.
2. Dickinson, 1989.
3. Skinner, 1969, pp. 114–115.
4. Dickinson, 1989, p. 11.
5. The problem is, therefore, to account for the negative effects of promises, instruc-

tions, and descriptions of contingencies. One possibility is that vague instructions about what is required to get a reward are taken as attempts at social control. Participants in an experiment may subvert attempts of conspicuous control by undermining the experimenter's authority—spending less time doing the required activity. Reactance against social control rather than a loss of intrinsic motivation may explain the decrease in time spent on an activity. Rewards that are tied to specific performance accomplishments may serve to acknowledge a person's attainments and not evoke reactance.

6. Deci, 1971.

7. Ibid.

8. Deci, 1972b.

9. Feingold and Mahoney, 1975.

10. Ibid., p. 370

11. See Deci, Koestner, and Ryan, 1999.

PART III

THEORETICAL DISPUTES OVER REWARDS AND INTRINSIC MOTIVATION

Chapter 4

Theoretical Perspectives on Rewards as Harmful

The initial studies in the early 1970's on the effects of rewards and re-inforcement on intrinsic motivation instigated a great deal of research on the topic. Numerous experiments have been designed to test and generate a variety of hypotheses about how rewards alter people's intrinsic interest in activities. In this section of the book, we examine various theoretical perspectives on the effects of rewards. This chapter focuses on theories and perspectives that emphasize harmful effects of rewards and reinforcement.

Assertions that rewards and reinforcement are harmful to people's intrinsic motivation come mainly from an area of social psychology that embraces philosophical notions of human nature that stress individualism[1] and innate needs for freedom and competence, which are said to be suppressed or undermined by external (social) constraints imposed by society.[2] Some writers who adopt this position claim that all rewards, whether tangible or verbal, induce compliance but undermine the motivation to continue an activity once the rewards are withdrawn.[3]

An example of how rewards destroy intrinsic motivation is presented in Alfie Kohn's book *Punished by Rewards*.[4] Kohn presents a story about an old man who is taunted by a group of ten-year olds who pass his house on the way home from school each day. Kohn describes the scene:

One afternoon, after listening to another round of jeers about how stupid and ugly and bald he was, the man came up with a plan. He met the children on his lawn the following Monday and announced that anyone who came back the next day and yelled rude comments about him would receive a dollar. Amazed and excited, they showed up even earlier on Tuesday, hollering epithets for all they were worth. True to his word, the old man ambled out and paid everyone. "Do the same tomorrow," he told them, "and you'll get twenty-five cents for your trouble." The kids thought that was still pretty good and turned out on Wednesday to taunt him. At the first catcall, he walked over with a roll of quarters and again paid off his hecklers. "From now on," he announced, "I can give you only a penny for doing this." The kids looked at each other in disbelief. "A penny?" they repeated scornfully. "Forget it!" And they never came back again.[5]

Although this example is meant to be a joke, it is frequently cited as an illustration of how rewards kill intrinsic interest. The story is meant to show that the children were initially "intrinsically motivated" to scorn the old man. Once they began to receive money to insult him, however, their interest in taunting him became motivated by the pay rather than by the fun of it. When the reward was no longer there, the children had no reason to continue their gibes. The point to be made is that the rewards destroyed the children's intrinsic motivation.

Those who espouse the view that rewards are harmful suggest that this type of situation happens all the time in homes, educational settings, businesses, and other environments. The contention is that teachers, parents, and managers are destroying intrinsic interest by giving rewards to their students, their children, and their employees for engaging in particular activities.

A historical illustration of the supposed damage of rewards concerns craftspersons and the change from feudal relationships to a pay-for-service economy.[6] Proponents of the negative effects of reward argue that in feudal times, craftspersons made cabinets and other artifacts for sheer enjoyment (intrinsic motives). With the rise of capitalism, the view is that the reason for making cabinets changed from intrinsic to extrinsic sources (pay for services). From this perspective, contemporary craftspersons make items for money. They no longer engage in their craft because they enjoy it; instead, today, they make cabinets for the money. That is, their intrinsic motivation to make cabinets has been undermined by the pay-for-service capitalist system (a system presumably based on principles of reinforcement).

Of course, one can see problems with this argument. All of us know professional carpenters, artists, and musicians who build, paint pictures, or play music when they are not being paid to do so. Many of us know professional athletes who continue to play and enjoy their sport after they have retired.[7] And many parents have watched their children become avid readers following participation in a reward-for-reading program.

Yet it is precisely these contexts that are of great concern to those who argue against rewards. The view is that if we reward people for engaging in enjoyable activities, we will sap their intrinsic motivation. From this position, once there is no longer a reward for doing so, the child will not read, the artist will not paint, the athlete will not play, and the carpenter will not build. Our everyday observations of behavior do not support this view, nor do the research findings. Nonetheless, several psychologists and educators vehemently argue that pay and other rewards have lasting negative effects on people's motivation in these contexts. In fact, a variety of theories and hypotheses have been formulated to explain how and why rewards have negative effects. Currently, the most popular accounts of the presumed negative effect of rewards on intrinsic motivation come from cognitive evaluation theory and from an attribution approach to rewards and other external influences.

In this chapter, we describe a cognitive evaluation approach to intrinsic motivation, outline its claims in terms of the undermining effects of reward contingencies, and critically evaluate its merits. We end this chapter with a brief consideration of attribution approaches to rewards and intrinsic motivation.

COGNITIVE EVALUATION THEORY

One explanation for the existence of decremental effects of reward on intrinsic motivation comes from Deci and Ryan's cognitive evaluation theory.[8] In order to understand the theory, it is informative to first examine how the concept of intrinsic motivation is understood from this perspective. The claim is that people derive innate satisfaction from certain activities. This innate fulfillment is said to motivate people to engage, and sustain interest, in these activities. In cognitive evaluation theory, this innate energizing force is called intrinsic motivation. Deci and his colleagues discussed the concept in a recent article:

Intrinsic motivation energizes and sustains activities through the spontaneous satisfaction inherent in effective volitional action. It is manifest in behaviors such as play, exploration, and challenge seeking that people do for no external rewards. It is thus a prototypic instance of human freedom or autonomy in that people engage in such activity with a full sense of willingness and volition.[9]

According to cognitive evaluation theory, intrinsically motivated actions are ones that evoke a high degree of liking and interest but for which there is no reward beyond the activity itself.

Cognitive evaluation theory proposes that intrinsic motivation springs from two innate sources (the need for competence and the need for self-determination).[10] On the basis of their humanness, people strive to feel competent and free from external control. Thus, intrinsic motivation arises from activities that lead people to fulfill their needs for competence and self-determination. When people engage in activities such as puzzle solving, they are said to feel free and highly competent; these perceptions, in turn, activate the innate energy of intrinsic motivation. The energy of intrinsic motivation, according to cognitive evaluation theory, heightens interest and sustains involvement in an activity. Extrinsically motivated behaviors, on the other hand, refer to actions that are directly linked to an external cause such as an explicit reward, incentive, or threat. Extrinsically motivated actions are said to be characterized by pressure and tension and to result in a loss of perceived competence and personal freedom.

Although intrinsic and extrinsic motivation are alluring notions and basic to cognitive evaluation theory, numerous researchers and theorists have pointed out difficulties with the concepts. One issue is that many behaviors that appear to be intrinsically motivated are in fact motivated by anticipated future benefits, previous environment-behavior interactions, and the physical and social contexts (e.g., cultural patterns and practices).[11]

Another issue concerns the claim that intrinsic motivation involves an innate energy source. People are said to be intrinsically motivated when they draw pictures, write or play music, solve crossword puzzles, or play games or sports. But are children born with an interest in these activities? Clearly, the answer is no. Learning experiences are necessary to build interest and enjoyment of activities. Almost any activity can become interesting and enjoyable when instruction and rewards are initially used to promote engagement in it. The types of activities that children find enjoyable vary with culture and social learning. For example, in the United States, children play baseball, whereas Canadian children play hockey and European children play soccer. The point is that children are not born with an innate motivational force that drives them to engage in these games. The source of their interest and enjoyment lies in their culture and social learning history, not in an innate energy source.[12]

A further difficulty is that explanations in terms of intrinsic motivation involve circular reasoning. To illustrate, consider the following situation. You have a friend, Joe, who goes out to his lakeside cabin each weekend and spends his time drawing pictures. When asked why Joe draws pictures on the weekends, a psychologist states that Joe is intrinsically motivated to draw. But how does one know that Joe is intrinsically motivated? The answer from the psychologist is that Joe spends much of his time drawing and, because there are no obvious external reasons for him to do this, he must be intrinsically motivated. In other words, Joe's intrinsic motivation is inferred from his behavior (time spent drawing at the lake); it is then used to explain the same behavior (Joe draws because he is intrinsically motivated). Because intrinsic motivation is inferred from the very behavior it is said to cause, the concept involves circular reasoning and lacks explanatory power.[13]

DIFFICULTIES WITH THE CONCEPT OF INTRINSIC MOTIVATION

- Behavior said to be intrinsically motivation is often due to:
  - (a) anticipated benefits
  - (b) previous behavior-environment interactions
  - (c) cultural context
- Learning experiences are necessary to build interest and enjoyment of activities.
- The concept of intrinsic motivation involves circular reasoning.
- Circular reasoning means that the concept lacks explanatory power.

Clearly, intrinsic motivation is not a clear-cut concept. In spite of conceptual difficulties with the concept, cognitive evaluation theorists continue to contrast intrinsic motivation with extrinsic motivation. Of major concern is how extrinsic rewards act to harm one's intrinsic interests.

Cognitive Evaluation, Rewards, and Intrinsic Motivation

Building on the early work of social psychologists F. Heider and R. De-Charms, Deci and Ryan argued that the effects of extrinsic rewards on intrinsic motivation depend on an individual's interpretation (i.e., cognitive evaluation).[14] People who receive a reward are said to interpret the reward in relation to their feelings of self-determination and competence. When rewards are interpreted as controllers of behavior, they interfere with innate needs for freedom and undermine competence by shifting perceptions of causality from internal to external sources, with a resulting loss of intrinsic motivation. On the other hand, when rewards are interpreted as indicators of competence, these events can have positive effects on intrinsic motivation. That is, when rewards provide positive information about performance accomplishments, they are expected to satisfy the need for competence and thereby increase a person's intrinsic motivation.

Cognitive evaluation theory presumes that rewards have two conflicting effects: controlling and informational. The degree of loss (or enhancement) of intrinsic motivation depends on a person's interpretation of the reward in terms of control versus information. If the reward is interpreted as more controlling (undermining autonomy) than positively informational (indicating competence), the net effect is a loss of intrinsic motivation. Rewards that convey strong positive information about competence but with some degree of perceived control can have positive net effects on intrinsic motivation.

Thus, from a cognitive evaluation perspective, rewards can lead to a reduction or enhancement in intrinsic motivation, depending on their controlling and informational values. Given that cognitive evaluation theory predicts both positive and negative effects of reward, it is noteworthy that Deci and his associates continue to predict and find mainly negative effects of various reward contingencies.[15] As we shall see in Part IV of the book, the bulk of the research coming from the cognitive evaluation theorists has emphasized the negative effects of reward. That is, over the past 30 years, most of the research on rewards and intrinsic motivation has been explicitly designed to find negative effects. Positive informational effects of rewards are downplayed, and cognitive evaluation theorists highlight the controlling aspects of rewards. By doing so, they often leave readers of the vast experimental literature on rewards and intrinsic motivation with the impression that all rewards are harmful.

Predictions about the Effects of Reward on Intrinsic Motivation

Since 1971, when Deci first proposed cognitive evaluation theory to account for negative effects of reward, the theory has been reformulated and revised many times. A recent statement of cognitive evaluation theory appeared in a 1999 article in *Psychological Bulletin*, in which, Deci and his colleagues outlined their current position regarding cognitive evaluation theory and made predictions about the effects of rewards on intrinsic motivation.[16]

Cognitive evaluation theory proposes that intrinsic motivation is altered by feelings of competence and self-determination. Events that increase people's beliefs that they are skilled in performing a task or that their performance is based on personal preference are assumed to enhance intrinsic motivation. Events that decrease a person's perceptions of competence or self-determination will diminish intrinsic motivation. From this perspective, it is argued that tangible rewards (prizes, money, awards, medals, gold stars, and so on) elicit the strongest perceptions of external control.

Tangible Rewards and Intrinsic Motivation

According to cognitive evaluation theory, tangible rewards are most harmful when they are expected, that is, offered to individuals prior to their engagement in activities. If the rewards are unexpected, they are not predicted to affect intrinsic motivation. The explanation for this is that when the rewards are not offered beforehand, people do not experience a connection between the task and the reward. Therefore, the reward cannot be interpreted as controlling and cannot undermine perceptions of autonomy and intrinsic motivation. Unexpected rewards are also said to have no impact on intrinsic motivation because the cognitive evaluation process only takes place when the rewarded activity is in progress. When rewards are presented unexpectedly (without announcement), cognitive evaluation of the rewarded activity is not activated and no loss of intrinsic motivation is expected to occur.

With expected tangible rewards, however, individuals are able to make a connection between the offer of reward and the activity for which they are being rewarded. The rewards are said to be experienced as controlling, perceptions of autonomy and self-determination are reduced, and the result is a decline in intrinsic motivation.

As the research on rewards and intrinsic motivation was amassed over the years, not all studies found negative effects from expected tangible rewards. Thus, cognitive evaluation theory was altered a number of times to make it consistent with the evidence. In the most recent statement of cognitive evaluation theory, the precise predictions with regard to expected tangible reward are said to depend on the manner in which specific reward contingencies affect perceptions of both competence and self-determination.

Cognitive evaluation theory stipulates four types of expected tangible reward: task-noncontingent rewards, engagement-contingent rewards, completion-contingent rewards, and performance-contingent rewards. Task-noncontingent rewards are rewards offered regardless of any involvement in an activity. Engagement-contingent rewards are offered simply for doing a task without a requirement to complete it. Completion-contingent rewards are offered for doing and completing the assigned task, and performance-contingent rewards are those offered for performing well, meeting or surpassing a specified criterion, or achieving a standard of performance (for example, better than 80 percent of the other participants).

Cognitive evaluation theory is said to consider the controlling versus informational aspects of different reward contingencies in order to predict whether the contingency will undermine intrinsic motivation. With task-noncontingent rewards, there is no contingency between the reward and the task; thus, cognitive evaluation theory does not predict negative effects on intrinsic motivation. Deci and his associates argue that engagement-contingent rewards (those offered for working on a task with no requirement to complete it) are likely to be experienced as controlling; engagement-contingent rewards should act primarily to reduce perceptions of self-determination and thereby reduce intrinsic motivation. Engagement-contingent rewards are said to carry little or none of the competence information that can override the perceived control by rewards. Thus, rewards offered merely for doing (but not completing) a task are said to have a net negative effect on intrinsic motivation. The majority of research studies on rewards and intrinsic motivation have been conducted using this contingency.

Completion-contingent rewards require people to complete a task in order to obtain the reward. The contingency between completing the task and receiving rewards is said to be experienced as more controlling than for rewards given simply for doing the task (engagement contingent), although the exact details of the evaluation process are not given. On the other hand, completion-contingent rewards are said to convey some level of competence, especially for skilled tasks. The positive information for competence is claimed to offset some of the controlling aspects of completion-contingent rewards, so these rewards should have less of an undermining effect on intrinsic motivation than engagement-contingent rewards.

A final type of reward contingency addressed by cognitive evaluation theory is called performance contingent (rewards for doing well at a task, meeting a standard, or performing to a set criterion). Performance contingent rewards are said to lessen self-determination because the recipient interprets the use of the reward as an attempt at behavioral control. At the same time, performance-contingent rewards can increase one's perceptions of competence by providing information concerning ability. Deci, Koestner, and Ryan (1999) concluded that the decrement in perceived self-determination will have a stronger effect than the increment in perceived competence and that the net effect will be an undermining of intrinsic motivation. They further predicted that the negative effect of performance-contingent rewards should be less than those of engagement- or completion-contingent rewards. They went on to state that the effects of performance-contingent rewards will be more variable and will depend on additional factors (e.g., interpersonal context for administering the rewards).[17]

Verbal Rewards and Intrinsic Motivation

In Deci's initial research on rewards and intrinsic motivation, verbal rewards (e.g., praise and positive feedback) were found to result in positive effects on measures of intrinsic motivation.[18] That is, people who received verbal rewards spent more free time on the activity and showed increased interest.[19] According to cognitive evaluation theory, verbal rewards are generally said to convey positive information about competence that overrides the controlling component of rewards. In this case, cognitive evaluation theorists propose a net positive effect of verbal rewards on intrinsic motivation.[20]

Although cognitive evaluation theorists acknowledge the beneficial effects of verbal rewards, they tend to dismiss the positive impact and instead emphasize possible negative effects of these rewards. In their recent statement of cognitive evaluation theory, Deci and his associates conceded the positive effects of verbal rewards but then provide a warning:

> According to CET [cognitive evaluation theory], the informational aspect of verbal rewards is generally expected to be salient and thus verbal rewards are generally predicted to enhance intrinsic motivation. However, verbal rewards can also have a significant controlling component—that is, people sometimes engage in behaviors to gain acknowledgment or approval—so verbal rewards can also have the potential to undermine intrinsic motivation. CET suggests that, just as with tangible rewards, the interpersonal context within which positive feedback is administered influences how it is interpreted and thus what effect it has.[21]

This reasoning is difficult to follow. The authors are telling us is that verbal rewards usually convey high competence to people but can also have a significant controlling component. What is meant by this is that there are ways to administer verbal rewards that are coercive and that result in a loss of intrinsic motivation.

One way to reduce intrinsic motivation by verbal rewards is to have an authority figure (the experimenter) say something like, "Excellent, you should keep up the good work," as opposed to saying the same statement without the word "should" or the pressure to behave. Under conditions of social pressure, people show a loss of intrinsic motivation. This loss of intrinsic motivation, however, cannot be attributed to the use of verbal reward; rather, it is the coercive implications (implied threat) of the social pressure that lowers motivation. Equating verbal rewards with implied threats is confusing and leads to misconceptions about this form of reward. Teachers, parents, and administrators may draw the conclusion that verbal rewards are often harmful when, in fact, it is the use of threats or other coercive strategies that is at issue.[22]

Rewards and Interpersonal Context

Cognitive evaluation theorists state that the effects of rewards (both verbal and tangible) depend on the interpersonal context. The interpersonal context, according to cognitive evaluation theory, "refers to the social ambiance of settings such as homes, classrooms, or work groups as they influence people's experience of autonomy, competence, or relatedness."[23]

The most important aspect of interpersonal context is whether the ambiance (mood, feel, or atmosphere) is perceived as controlling. When the interpersonal context is set up to reflect control or pressure, cognitive evaluation theory states that performance-contingent rewards (and verbal rewards) will be viewed as controlling and will undermine intrinsic motivation. Rewards that are administered in a noncontrolling style are said to be experienced as more informational and lead to less of a loss of intrinsic motivation.

In a study published in 1982, Ryan compared performance-contingent rewards administered in a controlling manner with the same rewards administered without pressure. A strong undermining effect was reported only when people were pressured to perform and offered a reward for their performance.[24] This finding suggests that performance-contingent rewards have no direct undermining effect on intrinsic motivation. That is, performance-contingent rewards, per se, are not harmful. It is the interpersonal context that produces positive or negative effects.

The implication of this finding is that performance-contingent rewards (and verbal rewards) take their meaning from the interpersonal context. When people are pressured, giving them rewards for performance leads to a loss of interest in the target activity (recall that social pressure can even alter the positive effects of verbal rewards). This is not the case when rewards are given without pressure. Thus, the effects of a reward procedure depend on the style of administration. In other words, cognitive evaluation theory predicts a loss of intrinsic motivation only when rewards are presented in an authoritarian supervisory style (using pressure to get people to perform). The implication of this prediction is that even from a cognitive evaluation perspective, reward systems have no inherent negative effects; it is the aversive control tactics of supervisors and administrators that are at issue.

Rewards and Initial Task Interest

Deci and associates have indicated that the field of research on rewards and intrinsic motivation is concerned with activities that people find intrinsically motivating (e.g., solving puzzles).[25] Of course, not all activities are initially interesting (i.e., intrinsically motivating). Many academic skills and performances hold no initial interest, and other routines may be dull and boring (e.g., completing pages of addition and subtraction problems). However, according to Deci and his colleagues, the cognitive evaluation process is only operative for activities that are high on initial interest. The authors stated:

CET was explicitly formulated to explain the effects of external events such as rewards on intrinsic motivation for interesting tasks. If an activity stimulates little or no initial intrinsic motivation, one would not expect to find external events undermining intrinsic motivation, and the principles of CET would not apply. Instead, with boring tasks, the critical theoretical issue is how to facilitate internalization of the regulation of such tasks if they are deemed important within the social environment. . . . The theoretical principles relevant to motivation for dull, boring tasks are different from those relevant to motivation for interesting tasks.[26]

Thus, cognitive evaluation theory applies only to initially interesting tasks that are intrinsically motivating. The theory has nothing to say about activities that lack initial interest.

Although this view sounds straightforward, an analysis of initial interest reveals several problems for cognitive evaluation theory. Consider first the fact that not all activities are absolutely dull or absolutely interesting. It is more useful to think of activities as varying in degree of initial interest. If tasks vary on a continuum of interest (from dull to extremely interesting), this creates a problem of scope (i.e., boundary conditions) for cognitive evaluation theory. At what point does increasing interest become indicative of intrinsic motivation, so that cognitive evaluation theory applies? In other words, how are we to know when rewarding people for doing a task of some initial interest will activate the cognitive evaluation process (reducing intrinsic motivation) and when it will not? The problem is that there is no answer to this question from cognitive evaluation researchers. All that we can fall back on is that cognitive evaluation theory works best for tasks of high initial interest.

This fallback, however, leads to more problems and questions. For instance, what constitutes high initial interest and intrinsic motivation? Does an activity possess an absolute amount of interest or is interest a relative concept? Consider an activity such as solving crossword puzzles and the usual measure of intrinsic motivation (or interest) based on time spent on the activity. If this activity is presented by itself, people may spend much of their time on it; in absolute terms, according to cognitive evaluation theory, this would be a task of high initial interest and intrinsic motivation.

But now consider a situation involving several optional tasks as well as cross-word puzzles. When faced with a choice among crossword puzzles, computer games, and books or magazines, people may spend more time on computers and books than on crossword puzzles. In a relative sense, crossword puzzles are low in initial interest. If this is so, is the activity of solving puzzles no longer in-trinsically motivating? By changing the number of optional tasks, we can make the relative time spent on crossword puzzles rise and fall. In one context a task is interesting, whereas in another it is not (or less so). These conceptual problems about initial interest mean that it is impossible to know when a task is "high in initial interest" and when to apply cognitive evaluation theory.

Deci and colleagues concede that performance of dull tasks may require the internalization of behavior regulation based on requirements set by the social environment (i.e., sources of external control). Presumably, rewards and incen-tives would be an essential aspect of the external influences that generate inter-nalized regulation of behavior; however, this is not addressed by Deci and his colleagues. We suggest that during the process of internalization, dull or neutral tasks become more interesting. Based on this process, when people express interest in certain activities, their interest may reflect past experience with re-wards rather than the fulfillment of innate needs for competence and self-determination. In other words, individuals may be interested in a variety of activities for which they were not initially intrinsically motivated.

According to cognitive evaluation theory, only those initially interesting tasks that possess intrinsic motivation (by satisfying the innate needs for competence and autonomy) are said to be susceptible to the undermining effects of reward. Other tasks in which initial interest reflects a past history of reward would not be expected to show an undermining effect of reward because in such tasks, there is no intrinsic motivation to undermine. Because the only way we can know if someone is interested in a task is by observing the time spent on the task or by asking the person about his or her attitude toward the activity, cog-nitive evaluation theory is faced with a problem.

In order to make use of cognitive evaluation theory and its predictions about rewards, it is necessary to know if an initially interesting task reflects intrinsic motivation or a past history of rewards. Unfortunately, cognitive evaluation the-orists do not provide a method to distinguish these alternative sources of interest, and therefore cannot predict which interesting tasks will show the undermining effects of rewards. Instead, cognitive evaluation theorists rely on self-reports of task interest and time on task as indications that people are intrinsically moti-vated. If individuals report high task interest and spend time on the activity, the assumption is that they are intrinsically motivated and that under these condi-tions, rewards will affect the cognitive evaluation process.

Table 4.1

Predictions According to Cognitive Evaluation Theory about the Effects of Reward on Intrinsic Motivation

HIGH INTEREST TASKS

Reward condition	Predicted change in perceptions of competence	Predicted change in perceptions of self-determination	Predicted change in intrinsic motivation
Verbal	Increase	Increase	**INCREASE**
Tangible Unexpected	No change	No change	**NO CHANGE**
Expected Task noncontingent	No change	No change	**NO CHANGE**
Engagement contingent	Decrease	Decrease	**DECREASE**
Completion contingent	Small increase	Large decrease	**DECREASE**
Performance contingent	Small increase	Large decrease	**DECREASE**

Summary of Predictions Made by Cognitive Evaluation Theory

Since 1971, numerous experiments have been conducted to test and generate the predictions of cognitive evaluation theory. The specific predictions of the theory are summarized in this section.

First, cognitive evaluation theory concerns the effects of rewards on activities of high initial intrinsic interest. Cognitive evaluation theory makes no predictions about the effects of reward on low-interest tasks as, from this perspective, there is no intrinsic motivation to alter. In terms of high-interest tasks, general predictions of the theory are presented in Table 4.1. Rewards are said to be experienced as controlling or informational, and changes in intrinsic motivation come about from changes in perceptions of competence and self-determination. Table 4.1 presents cognitive evaluation theory's predictions about how rewards will affect feelings of competence and self-determination as well as predicted changes in intrinsic motivation.

An inspection of Table 4.1 shows that negative effects of reward are predicted when the rewards are tangible, expected (offered beforehand), and engagement contingent (offered for doing a task), completion contingent (offered for completing a task), and performance contingent (offered for doing well or for surpassing a performance standard). In each of these situations, the prediction is that participants who receive a reward will feel controlled by the reward and their feelings of self-determination and autonomy will decline. In the case of completion-contingent and performance-contingent rewards, however, the receipt of reward may signal a degree of competence. Nonetheless, the controlling aspect of these rewards is expected to be stronger than the competence information and intrinsic motivation is predicted to decrease.

Table 4.1 indicates that verbal rewards are predicted to lead to an increase in intrinsic motivation. However, verbal rewards can reduce intrinsic interest when they are administered in a coercive context. Under conditions of threat and social pressure, according to cognitive evaluation theory, verbal rewards will decrease feelings of competence and self-determination will be reduced.

A further qualification of the theory regards the effects of expected, tangible, performance-contingent rewards. Again, as with verbal rewards, performance-contingent rewards can have opposite effects to those predicted in Table 4.1. Performance-contingent rewards are only predicted to be harmful when they are presented in an authoritarian supervisory context. When such rewards are given without pressure, however, negative effects are not predicted.

Although the effect of rewards on different age groups has not been a critical component of cognitive evaluation theory, Deci and his colleagues recently made some new propositions with regard to children versus adults. Specifically, they suggest that all types of rewards may be more undermining for children. According to Deci and associates, this is because children frequently experience adults as controlling their behavior; in addition, children are less able to separate the controlling and informational aspects of rewards.

In sum, cognitive evaluation theory predicts both positive and negative effects of rewards. However, the major focus of the theory is on harmful effects of reward and, as we shall see in Part IV of the book, the majority of experiments conducted by cognitive evaluation theorists have been designed to detect negative effects.

A CRITICAL ASSESSMENT OF COGNITIVE EVALUATION THEORY

Cognitive evaluation theory has provided a conceptual framework that has guided a considerable amount of research on the effects of rewards on people's intrinsic motivation. However, major ambiguities exist in this framework. Our overall assessment of cognitive evaluation theory is that it lacks sufficient details on a number of theoretical issues. This lack of specification often means that there is low predictive utility to the theory. With low predictive power, the theory is difficult to disconfirm by scientific evidence and is often applied to experimental findings in an after-the-fact manner.

One problem is that it is difficult to know how controlling or informational a reward contingency is before its effects are known. That is, if a reward procedure results in less time on the task in the free-choice period, the contingency is said to be more controlling than informational. Thus, cognitive evaluation theory is of limited predictive power because the process of cognitive weighting of a reward contingency is not well specified. How much control or informational perceptions does a given reward contingency activate? There is nothing in the theory to provide the answer. Further, how do perceptions of control combine with perceptions of competence to yield the net effects of a reward contingency on intrinsic motivation? Are perceptions of control and competence combined additively, averaged, or brought together in some other way? These issues are not resolved, even in recent statements of cognitive evaluation theory. Instead, the informational and controlling aspects of reward are inferred from their effects.

A second issue is that it is difficult to know how Deci and his associates arrived at the net effects of different reward contingencies. For example, completion-contingent and performance-contingent rewards are said to have some controlling aspects and some positive informational aspects. But how much controlling versus informational value do these reward procedures activate? Could these types of rewards activate high perceptions of competence that override the presumed controlling effect of these contingencies? If so, completion-contingent and performance-contingent rewards should have net positive effects on intrinsic motivation. Overall, it is not clear how cognitive evaluation theory claims a net negative effect of completion-contingent and performance-contingent rewards.

A further concern involving both completion-contingent and performance-contingent rewards is that some people in these situations receive less than maximal reward.[27] For example, a person who is required to complete puzzles for money may solve only half the problems and thus receive half the available money. In this case, less than maximum reward indicates a failure to solve some of the problems and low competence at the task. Thus, the undermining effects of completion-contingent and performance-contingent rewards (predicted by cognitive evaluation theory) may be due to failure feedback and derogation of competence, and not to the controlling nature of these rewards. This issue is not addressed in cognitive evaluation theory.

Our point here is that failure feedback should not be equated with a reward system. In businesses, schools, and homes, rewards can be arranged to encourage behavior and generate interest without indicating failure. When rewards are arranged for successive approximations to skillful performance or are based on graduated steps from one skillful performance to another, they are programmed for success and not for failure. Rewards tied to success, gradual challenge, and mastery can enhance measures of intrinsic motivation.[28] Unfortunately, these positive reward procedures have not been investigated by social psychologists who instead promote the view that rewards are inherently damaging.

Cognitive evaluation theory claims that people evaluate rewards, weighing the controlling aspects of rewards against the competency information that they contain. In this weighing of information, cognitive evaluation researchers typically predict that rewards will have pervasive negative effects. However, it is clear from the theory that rewards can have positive effects when the reward procedures convey high competence with low perceived control. To date, cognitive evaluation researchers continue to denounce the use of rewards, even though this is not a requirement of their theory.

A problematic aspect of cognitive evaluation theory is the notion of intrinsic motivation. Cognitive evaluation theorists imply that people must be intrinsically motivated to engage in certain activities. However, task interest is not absolute;

instead, it varies on a continuum. In addition, there are many tasks that take a great deal of skill and instruction (e.g., learning to play the piano, learning to read, etc.) and are of little initial interest to individuals. Cognitive evaluation theory does not address the issue of how people become interested in such tasks. Most activities people engage in were not initially interesting to them. Because cognitive evaluation theory restricts its claims to the concept of innate intrinsic motivation, it has very little to say about what actually goes on in everyday settings.

A final concern is that cognitive evaluation theory does not consider differences in social learning and acculturation that may eliminate or reduce the decremental effects of rewards on self-determination. Cognitive evaluation theory incorporates the view of philosophical romanticism that self-determination is an inherent human motive.[29] Currently, however, there is no evidence that self-determination is innate. What we do know, however, is that such motivation is greatly influenced by culture. Whereas Western culture highly promotes individualism, many Eastern cultures promote collectivist values—working together as a family, a work group, an ethnic group, and so on.[30] The regulation of behavior by rewards and by other people may be much less troubling for people acculturated to collectivist values than to those who have been socialized to seek individualism. Additionally, many people value both individualism and collectivism; the strength of these orientations differs from one individual and one context to another.[31] Because individualism and collectivism are competing values, we must look to people's learning histories, personality characteristics, and cultural background to understand why some individuals may react more negatively than others to constraints on their feelings of freedom and self-determination.[32]

ATTRIBUTION, OVERJUSTIFICATION, AND DISCOUNTING

Whereas some social psychologists advocate cognitive evaluation theory, other social psychologists have used an attribution approach to understand when and why rewards undermine intrinsic motivation.[33] Attribution theory concerns our reasoning about the causes of behavior. From an attribution perspective, the causes of behavior may be either internal or external. People attribute their behavior to internal or external sources. For example, a person who runs away from a dog may say that he or she ran away because of fear (internal causes) or because there was a vicious dog (external causes).

From the perspective of self-perception theory, Daryl Bem argued that people infer their feelings and attitudes (internal causes) from an analysis of their behavior and the situation.[34] When people reason that their behavior is caused by an external source, they do not attribute the behavior to their feelings and attitudes. During the summer, if you reason that you are spraying fertilizer on lawns because you are paid well to do so, you will not assume that you do it because you enjoy it. That is, after looking at your behavior and the situation, you will make an external attribution (I spray lawns for the money) and not an internal attribution (I enjoy spraying lawns and serving people). Of course, a person could enjoy the job and also do it for money. The internal and external factors could add together, giving greater overall motivation to becoming a lawn service representative.

According to attribution theory, when the external causes of behavior are conspicuous or salient, people discount the extent to which internal causes play a role. More generally, the discounting principle (or subtraction rule) states that people reduce (discount) a potential cause of behavior to the extent that other potential causes also exist. The process of discounting has been applied to an analysis of motivation to engage in activities and our subsequent interest in, and enjoyment of, those activities.

As discussed in Chapters 2 and 3, Mark Lepper and his associates published one of the most cited articles on rewards and loss of interest in young children.[35] The discounting principle was used to predict an "overjustification effect" when rewards were used to motivate children to engage in interesting activities (i.e., drawing pictures). According to the overjustification hypothesis, intrinsic interest in an activity is assumed to be influenced by attributions concerning whether performance of the activity resulted from influences internal or external to the person. When individuals are offered a reward to do an activity they already enjoy, the reasoning is that they will have a new potential explanation for their behavior (doing the activity for the reward). Based on the discounting principle, this should increase the likelihood that they will attribute their behavior to the reward (external cause) rather than to task enjoyment (internal cause). Thus, because there is more than adequate justification (overjustification) for performing the task, intrinsic motivation is predicted to decline.

A few researchers have suggested that use of the discounting principle does not occur until a child reaches a developmental stage commonly found at about eight years of age.[36] In a typical discounting experiment, participants are given a scenario in which one person engages in a task for intrinsic reasons and another person engages in the task because of external pressure. When participants are asked which person in the scenario prefers the task, young children do not reason in accord with the discounting principle; they tend to infer that extrinsic reasons indicate greater task liking. Because Lepper and his associates found decremental effects of reward on intrinsic motivation in very young children, some researchers have argued that overjustification cannot account for the changes in intrinsic motivation.[37]

On the other hand, other researchers have suggested that, if tested appropriately, the discounting principle can be used by young children and applied to overjustification-type situations. In two experiments, Newman and Ruble demonstrated that children were able to use and understand the discounting principle when the comparison they were asked to make was between objects and events (e.g., preference for a toy over an activity) and not between people.[38]

Newman and Ruble pointed out that this type of choice situation is similar to the situation in overjustification experiments in which participants may attribute their behavior to a reward or an activity. Given these findings, it has been argued that the discounting effect is a plausible explanation for decremental effects of reward.

According to Lepper and his associates, young children develop simple rules about the use of rewards in everyday life.[39] By this developmental account, young children learn the rule, "If adults give me rewards to do something, the activity must be boring." This rule is extracted from specific experiences, as when a parent says, "When you clean your room you can go out and play," or "If you wash the car, you can have $10 for your date tonight." Given a number of these experiences, the child learns that the offer of reward is tantamount to telling the child, "The rewarded activity is something you do not want to do."

In this expanded version of attribution theory, the more salient is the means-end relationship (instrumentality) between an activity and reward, the more likely it is that the reward will undermine intrinsic motivation. In children, salient rewards activate the simple rule that the activity is probably not enjoyable; adults use the more abstract discounting principle to arrive at the same conclusion. On the other hand, when rewards convey information about competence, this information is said to offset the instrumentality of the reward and lessen the detrimental effect on intrinsic motivation.

Predictions about the Effects of Rewards on Intrinsic Motivation

The attribution approach to rewards and intrinsic motivation makes predictions similar to those of cognitive evaluation theory, even though the underlying processes are different. Attribution theory emphasizes the instrumentality of the rewards whereas cognitive evaluation theory points to perceptions of control. Attribution theorists predict decrements in intrinsic motivation when there is a high degree of interest in an activity and extrinsic rewards are offered beforehand (expected). Because an individual would have to know about the reward in advance to attribute performance to its influence, unexpected reward is not predicted to alter intrinsic interest. In addition, Lepper and his colleagues accept the assumption of cognitive evaluation theory that intrinsic interest will not be undermined by rewards that increase perceived competence without lessening perceived self-determination, such as verbal approval delivered in an uncontrolling manner.[40]

According to Lepper and his associates, "rewards that enhance an individual's sense of competence and accomplishment will increase his or her intrinsic motivation; conversely, contingencies that reduce a person's sense of competence or accomplishment will decrease his or her intrinsic motivation."[41] Thus, as with cognitive evaluation theory, Lepper and his associates predict that expected tangible rewards contingent on engaging in an interesting activity (engagement-contingent rewards) will reduce intrinsic motivation because they do not convey competence information.

Lepper and his associates do not make specific predictions about how completion-contingent and performance-contingent rewards will affect intrinsic motivation. They do suggest, however, that

enhanced perceptions of competence may also play a role in determining motivation . . . but only after successful performance at the activity. If one lacks confidence in one's ability to perform well enough to earn a reward, that reward is not likely to prove an effective incentive.[42]

The implication of this statement is that the effects of completion-contingent and performance-contingent reward depend on whether an individual is successful at an activity. It follows from this that if individuals are successful and able to obtain the full reward, their sense of competence should be enhanced and intrinsic motivation should increase. On the other hand, when people do not perform well enough to obtain the full reward, their intrinsic motivation should decrease.

Thus, although Lepper and his colleagues do not predict positive effects of completion- or performance-contingent rewards, their theoretical approach would suggest that these reward contingencies should produce positive effects on motivation if people succeed at a task and obtain the maximum reward. In contrast, completion-contingent and performance-contingent rewards should produce negative effects when individuals are not entirely successful and receive less than the maximum reward, which would indicate failure feedback. These predictions were not made by cognitive evaluation theorists who do not address the issue of rewards given for successful performance. Instead, cognitive evaluation theory predicts overall negative effects for both completion- and performance-contingent rewards, regardless of whether rewarded participants are successful at the task.

Like cognitive evaluation theory, an attribution approach does not require that all rewards decrease people's intrinsic motivation. But also like cognitive evaluation theorists, those who advocate the overjustification hypothesis focus their research and discussion on the negative effects of reward. The bulk of research coming from this perspective is designed to detect negative effects. This focus on negative effects has led to the misleading conclusion that all rewards are harmful.

EVALUATION OF ATTRIBUTION THEORY AND THE OVERJUSTIFICATION HYPOTHESIS

The attribution approach to rewards and intrinsic motivation is based on an analysis of causal reasoning, the discounting principle, and the generalization that rewarded activities are boring to children. At the present time, there is a lack of evidence that this kind of causal reasoning mediates the effects of reward contingencies on measures of intrinsic motivation. That is, rewards given for doing an activity may result in less free time spent on the task, but there is a lack of evidence to show that (1) people's causal judgments are altered by reward contingencies, and (2) that these causal judgments produce a reduction in measures of intrinsic motivation.

In order to solve these difficulties, attribution researchers should repeatedly measure participants' causal judgments during the experiment. Measurement of causal judgments during the reward and free-choice phases is necessary to show the mediating effects of attributions. Once measured, statistical techniques can be used to establish the mediating role of causal judgments for any decline in intrinsic motivation. As a cautionary note, the measurement of causal judgments after the experiment (during debriefing) is not adequate. This is because postexperimental attributions may be a result of the exposure to the reward and free-choice phases rather than a mediator of the loss of interest and time spent.

A final issue concerns the discounting principle and its application to rewards and intrinsic motivation. Attribution theory, like cognitive evaluation theory, generally predicts that external rewards undermine intrinsic motivation. The internal factors of interest and enjoyment are said to be discounted by attributing the activity to the salient external rewards. The undermining effects of rewards are not, however, an inevitable outcome of an attribution process. That is, the discounting principle does not require that the external rewards always subtract from internal causes.

When external rewards are provided for an activity, interventions that highlight the internal factors could result in the discounting of the external rewards. For example, prior to implementing a reward contingency, an attribution procedure could be used to focus participants' attention on the interest and enjoyment of the activity (e.g., "You must really enjoy the task because you spend much more time on it than most people.") Under these conditions, the external reward contingency might be discounted and the activity attributed to the internal causes of enjoyment and interest. If this were so, reward contingencies, combined with attribution procedures to enhance the salience of internal factors, could be used to increase performance without a loss of interest in the activity.

NOTES

1. Sampson, 1988.
2. Rousseau, 1762/1974.
3. See Kohn, 1993a. Most social psychologists accept the findings that verbal rewards are not destructive to intrinsic motivation. Kohn, however, questions these findings and argues that most praise and feedback are harmful.
4. Kohn, 1993a.
5. Ibid., pp. 71–72.

6. Schwartz, Schuldenfrei, and Lacey (1978) argued that reinforcement captures behavior but is ultimately destructive of human value (see also Schwartz, 1990).

7. The famous hockey player Wayne Gretzky recently retired from the game, however, he continues to coach it. Even though the rewards for playing hockey are no longer forthcoming, Gretsky continues to be involved in the sport. This anecdote is contrary to the view that rewards destroy one's motivation for an activity.

8. Deci and Ryan, 1985.

9. Deci, Koestner, and Ryan, 1999, p. 658.

10. Ibid., p. 658.

11. Bandura (1986) suggests that behavior can show persistence and have nothing to do with intrinsic motivation (p. 243). Bandura points out that a person may appear to be intrinsically motivated in a specific activity when there is nothing better to do. On the other hand, the person will appear to be unmotivated to do the same activity when more attractive options are available. Hence, from Bandura's perspective, any theory of motivation must take into account the wide variety of interactions that take place between personal and situational variables.

12. Another issue concerns the relatively low frequencies of human behavior said to be due to an underlying force of intrinsic motivation. For example, according to cognitive evaluation theory, music and artistic painting are activities that should be sustained by intrinsic motivation. Based on innate energy or drive, all we have to do is expose our children to these activities and they should become captivated, pursuing lifelong careers in the arts. But is this what we see? Most children who take piano (or another instrument) do not become accomplished musicians. Also, few children who take up drawing and painting become acclaimed artists. If each child has a reservoir of innate drive released by these activities, how is it that so few continue to the highest levels? The point is that there is more variability in proficiency, interest, and enjoyment of artistic activities than would be expected if all of us had the innate energy of intrinsic motivation. A more parsimonious explanation is that variation in proficiency and interest is due to culture and social learning.

13. In the more complex case of theories relating intrinsic motivation to innate needs for competence and self-determination, circular reasoning occurs when the hypothetical motivator (intrinsic motivation) and the innate needs (competence and self-determination) are all inferred from the same behavior they are said to explain. That is, the needs for self-determination and competency are inferred from the fact that Joe spends much of his time drawing at the lake, which is the same fact that indicated to us that Joe was intrinsically motivated to draw. Both the innate needs and the resulting intrinsic motivation have no referent other than Joe's behavior. Our point is that innate needs and motivators fail to explain human behavior unless these concepts are anchored to measures or procedures independent of the behavior itself.

14. Heider, 1958; DeCharms, 1968; Deci and Ryan, 1985.

15. Deci, Koestner, and Ryan, 1999.

16. Ibid.

17. Ibid.

18. Deci, 1971, Experiment 3.

19. The difference between verbal and tangible rewards and their effects on intrinsic motivation may have less to do with the type of reward than with its allocation. Studies

that use tangible rewards usually involve a single presentation of the incentive, and the rewards cannot function as positive reinforcement. The effects of tangible rewards are more likely due to the offer of a reward than to a reinforcement process. In contrast, studies that use verbal rewards usually involve repeated presentations of praise or positive feedback. Such rewards are likely to function as positive reinforcement for the activity, and in doing so, enhance interest in it. See Carton, 1996.

20. Deci and his colleagues predicted that expected tangible reward contingencies (based on the cognitive evaluation of positive information and controlling aspects of rewards) always result in a net loss of motivation. However, it is not obvious why the positive information about competence outweighs the controlling component with verbal rewards but not with expected, tangible, performance-contingent rewards. Rather than explain this inconsistency, cognitive evaluation theory is made to fit the evidence, providing little understanding or prediction about the cognitive process that leads verbal rewards (as opposed to tangible rewards based on performance) to enhance intrinsic motivation.

21. Deci, Koestner, and Ryan, 1999, p. 629.

22. The coercive use of rewards may underlie much of the negative effects on intrinsic motivation. Kohn (1993a) talked about punishment by reward, and Sidman (1989) talked about the coercive use of rewards. When rewards are given and people then threaten to remove them, the procedures are aversive. The coercive use of rewards generates escape and avoidance and should not be confused with positive reinforcement.

23. Deci, Koestner, and Ryan, 1999, p. 629.

24. Ryan, 1982.

25. Researchers in the area of rewards and intrinsic motivation often use puzzle solving as the intrinsically motivated activity. It should be apparent, however, that not all (or perhaps even most) people like solving puzzles. If interest in puzzle solving stems from an innate source of energy, how is it that there is so much variation in people's interest?

26. Deci, Koestner, and Ryan, 1999, p. 635.

27. Deci, Koestner, and Ryan (1999) brought up the issue of maximum and less than maximum rewards. In their meta-analysis on the topic, they showed that for performance-contingent rewards, less than maximum rewards led to a large decrease in intrinsic motivation. They attributed this effect to the reward contingency rather than to failure-feedback.

28. Bandura, 1986.

29. Geller, 1982; Hogan, 1975.

30. Triandis, 1995.

31. Kuhlman, Camac, and Cunha, 1986; Kuhlman and Marshello, 1975; Kuhlman and Wiberley, 1976.

32. This criticism of cognitive evaluation theory was first noted by Bob Eisenberger (personal communication), 1996.

33. Lepper, Greene, and Nisbett, 1973.

34. Bem, 1972.

35. Lepper, Greene, and Nisbett, 1973.

36. Karniol and Ross, 1977; Morgan, 1981.

37. Deci and Ryan, 1985.

38. Newman and Ruble, 1982.
39. Lepper, Sagotsky, Dafoe, and Greene, 1982.
40. Lepper and Gilovich, 1981.
41. Lepper, Keavney and Drake, 1996, p. 24.
42. Ibid., p. 24.

Chapter 5

Theoretical Perspectives on Rewards as Helpful

Many of the activities that people enjoy doing for their own sake held little or no interest for them initially. From a learning viewpoint, young children are not born with an innate interest in artistic activities such as drawing and painting. An interest in playing piano, singing operas, solving mathematical equations, writing novels, or playing baseball needs to be cultivated. Psychologists in the area of learning and motivation reject the claim that rewards are basically harmful to human motivation. Instead, they point to the beneficial effects of rewards in establishing performance and interest.

The cultivation of interest in activities, from a learning viewpoint, depends on environmental experiences that originally involved the use of extrinsic rewards. For example, a child may initially practice scales on a piano for an opportunity to play with friends. The relationship between practicing scales and the reward of playing with friends is arbitrary and socially arranged. As proficiency in music increases, external rewards are gradually withdrawn in favor of the usual consequences of musical performance (i.e., the sounds of music).[1] In this example, external rewards are a necessary part of teaching complex performances that eventually result in their own, automatic rewarding consequences.

Today, the view that rewards are a necessary part of teaching and learning comes from two branches of psychology: social learning and behavioral psychology. Both these approaches to learning state that rewards and reinforcement play an important role in the regulation of human behavior. Rewards are viewed as powerful influences on human performance and interest, and at the same time, reward procedures that are used incorrectly may result in negative effects or by-products. These by-products of reinforcement have been observed in the laboratory, and some of the negative effects have been well documented and analyzed.[2] What is clear, however, is that rewards and other reinforcements do not have inherent negative effects on human motivation. From an applied learning perspective, the objective is to specify how to use the principles of reinforcement in everyday settings without generating as by-products negative effects on performance and interest.

In this chapter, we present Albert Bandura's social learning theory of rewards and intrinsic interest and point to the role that rewards play in human learning and motivation from this perspective. Social learning theory emphasizes the informational aspects of rewards and how rewards influence thoughts about future outcomes of action. In this regard, social learning researchers share much with cognitive social psychologists. The difference is that social learning theorists suggest that rewards play a positive and important role in learning and motivation.

In contrast to the social learning approach, behavior theory emphasizes the role of rewards in the learning of contingent relations between behavior and its consequences.[3] From the behavioral perspective, people do things that result in rewarding consequences and thus learn the contingent effects of their actions (i.e., If I do X, then Y happens.). Based on contingency learning, individuals are more likely to do similar actions in the future. Thinking about the contingencies as well as the actions that are taken both result from the interaction of the person's behavior with its consequences. That is, both thought and action by a person are viewed as behavior that has been selected by its success in meeting the requirements for reward or reinforcement.

In this chapter, we will describe how social learning theorists stress the antecedent effects of rewards as incentives for thought and action whereas behavioral psychologists (behavior analysts) point to the learning of contingencies through the consequences of action. Throughout the chapter we provide critical commentary on the social learning and behavioral perspectives on rewards and intrinsic motivation.

SOCIAL LEARNING, REWARDS, AND MOTIVATION

As part of his comprehensive theory of human behavior, Bandura presents a social learning analysis (also called social cognitive theory) of rewards and human motivation.[4] Bandura's analysis of incentive motivators is particularly relevant to the reward and intrinsic motivation debate and the hypothesis that external rewards reduce intrinsic motivation.

In contrast to social psychologists who see rewards and incentives as intrusions on human motivation, Bandura contends that human behavior is extensively regulated by its consequences. Bandura states:

If people acted with foresight on the basis of informative cues but remained unaffected by the results of their actions, they would be too insensible to survive very long. Behavior is, in fact, extensively regulated by its effects. Actions that bring rewards are generally repeated, whereas those that bring unrewarding or punishing outcomes tend to be discarded. Human behavior, therefore, cannot be fully understood without considering the regulatory influence of response consequences.[5]

In social learning theory, rewards and other response consequences are said to influence human behavior through their incentive function. People use the pattern of feedback from rewards over time as information about how to produce or increase these outcomes. That is, rewards for certain actions create expectations of these outcomes in the future. In social learning theory, behavior in a situation is increased by expected rewards and reduced by anticipated punishment.

Bandura further proposes that people show little change in behavior unless they are aware of what actions are being rewarded or punished. Awareness of the contingency between behavior and its consequences builds expectations of reward. Once expectations of reward have been established, behavior can be maintained by intermittent rewards that occasionally confirm outcome expectations. Generally, rewards and punishment are said to help people anticipate the outcomes of future actions, and in so doing, these events aid in the regulation of adaptive behavior.[6]

Extrinsic and Intrinsic Motivators

In contrast to social psychological theories that depict rewards as harmful to the innate motivation for competence and self-determination, social learning theory holds that aspects of personal agency (e.g., self-motivation and self-directedness) arise, in part, from external influences. That is, social learning theory rejects the appeal to innate sources of motivation and contends that personal competencies (and other aspects of self-regulation) are developed with the aid of external incentives. Bandura indicates that

Many of the activities through which competencies are built are initially tiresome and uninteresting. As piano players, and the much larger ranks of former piano players, will attest, there is little joy in practicing the rudiments of the keyboard, especially when one's peers are at play. It is not until some proficiency is acquired that the activity becomes rewarding. Without the aid of positive incentives during the early phases of skill acquisition, potentialities are likely to remain undeveloped.[7]

Bandura's point is that external social rewards build initial interest and accomplished performance until natural consequences take over. Once skillful performance produces its own reward (e.g., the melodious sounds of musical performance), social incentives can be slowly withdrawn. A person with this kind of reward pattern pursues the activity seemingly "for its own sake" and enjoys doing it.

Bandura makes a useful distinction between extrinsic and intrinsic motivators, based on a consideration of the reward contingency and the locus of the rewarding effects. A reward contingency can be arbitrary or natural.[8] Also, the locus of reward can be external or internal. When the reward contingency is arbitrary and the rewarding effects are external to the person, the activity is said to be extrinsically motivated. Working for pay, solving puzzles for approval, practicing a musical instrument for time with friends, or doing mathematics problems to gain privileges are examples of behavior that is extrinsically motivated. In each case, the reward contingency is arbitrary and the source of reward is external to the person.

With extrinsic motivators, the rewards for behavior are socially arranged. When socially arranged rewards are removed, Bandura indicates that the behavior declines unless it produces other rewarding effects (i.e., natural consequences). In social learning theory, the decline in behavior is said to be due to changes in expectations of reward. Notice that the decrease in behavior is not assigned to a permanent loss of innate energy or drive. In other words, socially arranged rewards do not destroy innate motivation. If the behavior is socially important, arbitrary rewards can be reinstated to increase expectations of reward for the desired behavior. Once the person regains expectations of reward, rewards need be given only occasionally and slowly replaced by natural consequences.

For some people, the rewarding natural consequences of an activity may remain weak or ineffective. Thus, finding solutions to mathematical problems may remain a weak natural reward for many students. In these cases, socially arranged rewards (grades, praise and recognition) must remain in effect to maintain an appropriate level of mathematical performance. Many professional musicians, artists, and athletes perform at least partially for money, prestige, and recognition (e.g., awards like the Grammies and Oscars), even when more naturalistic rewards also regulate their behavior.

Bandura's analysis of reward contingency (arbitrary or natural) and locus of reward (external or internal) leads to different kinds of intrinsic motivators of behavior. One type of intrinsic motivator occurs when the rewarding effects are external but naturally related to behavior (i.e., external locus and natural contingency). Thus, touching a blanket produces tactile stimulation, striking guitar strings results in musical sounds, and looking through a microscope makes the unobservable world observable. In each of these instances, behavior produces natural, external sensory effects that increase or sustain the actions.

Another form of intrinsic motivator involves behavior that produces naturally rewarding effects internal to the person. Behavior that generates neurophysiological, neurochemical, or hormonal effects demonstrates this kind of intrinsic contingency. For example, food deprivation increases physical activity, which in turn is rewarded by the release of brain opiates (beta-endorphin) and neurotransmitters (dopamine). As physical activity increases to excessive levels, the reinforcing efficacy of eating (food intake) is reduced, perhaps due to the inhibitory effects of dopamine on peptides that control eating (e.g., Neuropeptide Y). This kind of intrinsic contingency could explain many cases of anorexia nervosa, in which patients exhibit excessive exercise, hyperactivity, and pacing, in conjunction with reduced food intake.[9]

The extrinsic and intrinsic reward contingencies identified by Bandura are not unique to social learning theory. Social learning theory requires that reward contingencies operate as incentives by activating thoughts about future outcomes. It is not clear how extrinsic and intrinsic motivators are distinguished in terms of expectations of reward and motivation. In fact, even though Bandura rejects the "response strengthening" effects of rewards advocated by behavior theory, his analysis is compatible with the behavioral principle of reinforcement. From a behavioral perspective, reward contingencies (both external and internal) select behavior for a given situation, thereby increasing forms of behavior that result in reinforcement and decreasing forms that are no longer rewarded (or are punished). Generally, social learning theory and behavior theory agree that consideration of reward contingencies in terms of the reward's source and contingencies are central to an analysis of human performance and interest.

Self-Regulation and Intrinsic Motivation

Social learning theory is distinguished from behavior theory by its attention to, and emphasis on, self-evaluative mechanisms. Self-evaluative processes constitute a third kind of intrinsic motivation involving internal (self-generated) rewards that are arbitrarily related to one's behavior (i.e., arbitrary contingency and internal locus). Bandura clarifies this kind of intrinsic motivation in the following passage.

In most activities from which people gain lasting enjoyment, neither the behavior itself nor its natural feedback is inherently rewarding. . . . It is people's affective self-reactions to their own performances that constitute the principal source of reward. To cite an uncommon example, there is nothing inherently gratifying about playing a tuba solo. To an aspiring tuba instrumentalist, however, a performance that fulfills a hoped-for standard is a source of considerable self-satisfaction that can sustain much tuba blowing. Improvements in intellectual, athletic, and artistic pursuits similarly activate self-reactions that provide a sense of fulfillment and create personal incentives for accomplishments. People differ widely in the pursuits in which they invest their self-evaluation. Hence, what is a source of self-satisfaction for one person may be devalued or of no consequence for another.[10]

In social learning theory, self-motivation by evaluation of one's own performance is a source of personal regulation (or agency) of behavior. That is, people are said to exert internal cognitive influences over their own behavior. The cognitions of self-motivation involve knowledge about how to sequence actions, set challenging standards for performance, and generate self-evaluations of performance accomplishments. Once this motivational system is in place, Bandura indicates, people will derive personal satisfaction from performances that meet or exceed their adopted standards.

In a behavioral view, self-generated rewards and the adoption of personal standards begin with (and are ultimately dependent on) socially arranged contingencies. Social contingencies relate behavior to rewards in arbitrary ways, which explains why self-generated rewards are also dispensed on an arbitrary basis. We propose that people learn from others, through social modeling and reinforcement processes, to sequence actions into skillful performances and to evaluate their performances against personal standards. Self-generated standards and evaluative reactions, from our perspective, are treated as part of behavior that is acquired and maintained by social modeling and reinforcement (external) contingencies. Self-regulatory behavior serves to guide and motivate actions, but it does not stand alone. In the long run, self-regulation depends on intermittent rewards from others and from the natural consequences of actions over time.

Social learning theory disputes whether any behavior occurs "for its own sake." The apparent motivation of behavior by an innate energy drive is rejected in a social learning analysis.[11] In social learning theory, performance and interest reside in the effects of extrinsic contingencies, intrinsic contingencies relating behavior to its natural effects, or intrinsic rewards based on the self-evaluation of personal accomplishments. For example, to the gymnast, the act of performing a balance beam routine is not innately satisfying. This kind of skillful performance is built up over time by corrective feedback from the coach, sensory feedback from the actions themselves, and the self-evaluation of performances that meet or exceed personal performance standards. Bandura asserts that it is the personal achievement of challenging goals that results in joy and interest. Without the personal challenges of performing a routine on the balance beam, it becomes a boring activity.

Rewards, Competence, and Interest

Bandura indicates that rewards given for achieving high levels of performance are controlling, in the sense that money, praise and recognition are only dispensed if a prescribed level of accomplishment is met. However, according to Bandura's analysis, this kind of reward system builds competence, self-efficacy, or beliefs about one's capabilities. In doing so, achievement-based rewards help people to develop personal control over outcomes, adopt challenging personal standards, and learn to make a positive self-evaluation of their accomplishments.

The competence feedback from external reward contingencies does not inevitably result in more interest in an activity. Social learning theory holds that rewards given for progress and graded achievements are likely to act as positive feedback for judgments of competence and, in doing so, to increase interest. In contrast, negative feedback from a reduction in rewards based on inadequate performance can decrease perceived self-efficacy, create obstacles to perceptions of personal control or self-determination, and thereby lower interest. Perceived competence mediates the effects of rewards on interest and motivation from a social learning perspective.[12]

A commonality exists between social learning and cognitive evaluation theory. Both theories claim that rewards can convey information about competence, which can, in turn, enhance intrinsic interest. Cognitive evaluation theory, however, has played down this aspect of reward contingencies, emphasizing instead the controlling effects of rewards in undermining self-determination and intrinsic motivation. This emphasis on control comes from the nativistic roots of the cognitive evaluation perspective. Because intrinsic motivation is said to be an innate energy source that drives human behavior, external sources of influence are cast as intrusions on autonomy, rather than sources of personal regulation. Bandura disagrees with the emphasis of cognitive evaluation theory on control and suggests that it leads to a strange paradox. He states:

On the one hand, intrinsic motivation is said to be the wellspring of motivity. On the other hand, it is contended that incentives, constraints, deadlines, and directives, all readily sap intrinsic motivation. If this were so, such a motivator would be thoroughly undermined by the countless extrinsic pressures impinging constantly on people in their daily lives. If intrinsic motivation is so easily wiped out by external influences, it could hardly function as a pervasive motivator of behavior.[13]

In contrast to cognitive evaluation notions, social learning theory suggests that extrinsic rewards can differentially affect the value of an activity. When others use rewards to convey the fact that an activity is uninteresting, people learn to devalue it. In contrast, when rewards are used to indicate proficiency, people learn to enjoy the activity for its own sake. From a social learning perspective, rewards have no inherent negative effects. It is the message conveyed by the use of rewards that results in different effects on interest and performance.

Non–Competency-Contingent and Competency-Contingent Rewards

In cognitive evaluation theory, Deci and his colleagues distinguished among task-, completion-, and performance-contingent rewards, emphasizing the controlling aspects of these reward contingencies. All these contingencies involve external rewards that are claimed to undermine self-determination and thereby produce negative effects on intrinsic motivation. In contrast to cognitive evaluation theory, Bandura's social learning theory distinguishes between non–competency-contingent rewards (rewards given without regard to mastery), and competency-contingent rewards (rewards for mastering activities or tasks). The emphasis in social learning is on how reward contingencies relate to perceived competence or self-efficacy rather than to perceived control and self-determination. Reward contingencies that enhance perceived competence or self-efficacy are expected to increase interest and performance of an activity.

Non–Competency-Contingent Rewards include rewards given for merely doing, completing, or repeating an activity. This type of reward contingency includes many of the studies that Deci and associates classified separately as task-, completion-, and performance-contingent rewards.[14] That is, most of the research on rewards and intrinsic motivation from a social learning view has involved rewards offered for engaging in an activity without regard to some standard or criterion of performance (mastery).

Extrinsic rewards given for merely doing an interesting activity repeatedly are most likely to reduce intrinsic interest. This kind of reward procedure, according to Bandura, imparts little indication of competency in that the rewards are only loosely tied to behavior. In a loose contingency, the rewards are allocated without regard to quality of performance. Bandura noted that a loose contingency of reward exerts weak influence over behavior, and as a result, other factors (or moderator variables) can readily alter or override the effects of the reward procedure.[15]

SOCIAL LEARNING AND NON–COMPETENCY-CONTINGENT REWARDS

Factors that moderate the effects of loose or non–competency-contingent rewards on intrinsic motivation include the level of initial task interest; ability on the task; the size, salience, and value of the rewards; the type of task; the age of the participants; and when and how intrinsic motivation is measured. Bandura argues that the analysis of non–competency-contingent rewards is

> of no great social import because rewards are rarely showered on people regardless of how they behave. Nor is there much call for incentive systems for activities people find highly interesting and thus readily pursue on their own without extrinsic motivators.[16]

The critical issue, according to Bandura, is how to cultivate interest and perceptions of personal efficacy through rewards based on performance. In social learning theory, performance-contingent rewards need to be separated into rewards given for task mastery (e.g., recognition for outstanding performance) and rewards given for routine activities (e.g., pay for each unit produced). A factory worker who is paid for each piece of leather cut to manufacture shoes (i.e., piece rate payments) is unlikely to derive much interest and satisfaction from the work.

Rewards given for mastery (i.e., achieving relatively challenging behavioral standards) are termed *competency-contingent rewards* and are the type of reward contingency that is said to develop perceptions of self-efficacy and task interest.[17] The cabinetmaker who is rewarded with recognition, praise, and money based on his or her woodworking skills and finely crafted product will probably develop beliefs in personal competency and enjoyment of the work. In this example, external rewards help to instill personal regulators of behavior (e.g., perceptions of competence and interest) rather than usurp intrinsic motivation.

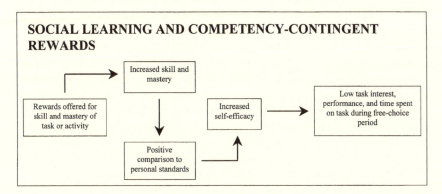

SOCIAL LEARNING AND COMPETENCY-CONTINGENT REWARDS

When rewards are given for mastering knowledge and subskills related to an individual's long-term goals, the person will gain a sense of competence. One researcher coming from this perspective found that for children who were poor at mathematics, incentives for mastering subskills raised mathematical performance and increased perceived competence at mathematics.[18] In a work setting, an employee who takes a series of training courses related to computers and accounting may receive praise, recognition, and monetary bonuses for daily and weekly accomplishments. This kind of reward system could promote the learning of career-oriented behavior and thereby enhance a person's self-assurance and career interest.

Rewards given for achieving relatively challenging standards are also indicative of competence.[19] Bandura notes that rewards given for meeting or exceeding a challenging criterion verify people's competence. When incentives are given for trying hard, people learn what skills they possess and what they are able to do.[20] Rewards tied to achieving performance objectives also cause people to care more about doing well at an activity and increase intrinsic interest more than positive performance feedback without reward.[21] Generally, when rewards are linked to overcoming challenges, these incentives help people develop a sense of self-efficacy, interest, and involvement in activities.[22]

Rewards and the Social Validation of Competence

In social learning theory, rewards can also serve as a social validation of one's competence. This is especially the case when people are unable to judge their competence from performance alone. When the magnitude of reward is tied to quality of performance, greater rewards can indicate that other people believe in the person's underlying abilities. Bandura explained that the competence-validation process is somewhat complex, involving the assessment of multiple behaviors. Thus, for example, baseball players must judge competencies from quality of batting, fielding, stealing bases, production of runs, and so on. A player's overall judgment of competence at baseball is based on the personal importance (subjective weighting) of each aspect of the game.

The ambiguity and uncertainty of this judgment process, according to Bandura, ensures that people look to others for indications of performance quality. In the search for social validation, the magnitude of the reward provides evidence of performance "worth" from which people make inferences of competence and self-efficacy. Research shows that the more the extrinsic reward for performance indicates competence, the greater the interest in an activity.[23]

An interesting aspect of social validation is that a person's talents and abilities (internal factors) are taken as the reasons for the rewards, rather than the rewards being seen as the cause of high-level performance.[24] Contrary to the claim that rewards are usually viewed as controlling, people often see themselves as controllers of the rewards (self-determined), especially when the rewards serve to validate competence.[25]

Temporal Lag and the Threshold between Competence and Interest

Bandura indicated that there is probably a delay between an increase in perceived self-efficacy and the cultivation of interest in an activity.[26] In the workplace, an incentive system that rewards improvement in job skills and knowledge, the overcoming of job-related challenges, and high quality of job performance is likely to build perceptions of personal competence over time. As a sense of efficacy develops, workers seek out additional mastery experiences that provide opportunities for positive self-evaluations. Self-evaluative reactions related to competence (or social feedback of competence) eventually lead to interest in an activity.

In addition to a time lag between perceived self-efficacy and intrinsic interest, Bandura speculates that personal competence must reach a moderate level (or threshold) before self-efficacy can uphold interest in an activity. In this scenario, an incentive system based on performance accomplishments builds beliefs in personal competency to the threshold level. At this point, people become highly interested in a task or activity. One study showed that children's moderate to high beliefs in personal competency predicted high intrinsic interest in an activity, regardless of the goals they had set for themselves.[27]   As people become highly confident in their abilities, they may find less and less challenge in an activity and lose intrinsic interest. Bandura's analysis therefore suggests that an inverted-U relationship exists between self-efficacy and intrinsic interest. At low levels of perceived competency, interest is minimal. As competency rises to moderate levels through the use of mastery-based rewards, people find high interest in an activity. Finally, at extreme levels of self-assurance, intrinsic interest drops again—the activity is no longer viewed as challenging and self-satisfying.

In conclusion, social learning theory views external rewards as an essential component in the development of self-regulation. Rewards given for the mastery of challenging tasks help to build beliefs in personal competency. As a person gains a sense of self-efficacy based on performance accomplishments, activities that held little initial interest begin to take on personal value or satisfaction. Thus, rewards contingent on quality of performance and mastery of difficult tasks do not directly increase interest in the activity. Only when a reward procedure instills (or increases) self-assurance will the activity take on (or gain) in interest. From a social learning perspective, then, a perception of personal competency is the central mediator of performance and interest in an activity.

BEHAVIOR THEORY, REWARDS, AND MOTIVATION

Social learning theory emphasizes cognitive mediators of behavior (self-efficacy, personal standards of performance, and self-evaluation) in the analysis of rewards, performance, and human motivation. Behavior theory agrees that rewards and other behavioral consequences are central to an analysis of human motivation; however, the behavioral approach does not posit beliefs about the self as the reasons for human conduct and motivation. From a behavioral perspective, people learn the contingent relationships between actions and consequences without cognitive mediators. Actions that are successful become more frequent over time; actions that are less successful decrease and eventually are extinguished. From a behavioral perspective, behavior is not driven by internal motives or thoughts; it is selected by its consequences.[28]

Behavioral researchers have argued for the basic and applied importance of the law of reinforcement and other principles of behavior. Several behavior analysts have reviewed the literature on reward and intrinsic motivation, offering analyses and evidence compatible with the principles of behavior. The general tenor of these behavioral explanations is that rewards are basically helpful (e.g., increasing desired behavior) but unusual conditions can arise that lead to a decline in behavior following the removal of reward. When these conditions are identified and corrected, rewards may be used in everyday settings without detrimental effects.

Behavior Analysis, Rewards, and Intrinsic Motivation

One issue of contention among behaviorists, cognitive evaluation theorists, and attribution theorists is the analysis of the behavior-environment relationships attributed to intrinsic interest or motivation. Behavioral researchers make a distinction between the automatic or natural consequences of behavior and the consequences of behavior arranged by other people.[29] The difference between natural and social consequences is seemingly at the heart of the controversy involving intrinsic versus extrinsic motivation. Cognitive evaluation researchers turn intrinsic (or natural) consequences of action into an innate energy source (intrinsic motivation) that is undermined by extrinsic (social) consequences. From this nativistic perspective, extrinsic rewards are given to strengthen desired behavior (i.e., reinforcement) but ultimately subvert people's natural interest in activities. In contrast, behaviorists argue that both the intrinsic and extrinsic consequences of behavior obey the law of reinforcement. Any decline in performance is a result of conditions that are fully explained by the principles of reinforcement rather than by a loss of innate energy or motivation.

Doing Things for Natural Rewards

An activity may appear to be done "for its own sake" when the behavior is, in fact, maintained by natural consequences. Studies conducted in the 1950s by Harry Harlow and his colleagues illustrate the operation of natural consequences.[30] Harlow and his associates reported that monkeys solved complex puzzle problems without food rewards; puzzle solving increased and decreased in an orderly fashion, based on the natural consequences of "finding a correct solution." Thus, Harlow showed that learning could take place with only natural rewards.

An important aspect of Harlow's experiment is the distinction between intrinsic and extrinsic rewards. According to Harlow, there were two types of rewards. The monkeys were solving puzzle problems for intrinsic, or natural, rewards, which acted much like extrinsic rewards such as food. That is, the learning of monkeys using natural rewards was similar to the learning of other animals using food rewards. Puzzle solving by the animals did not involve an innate interest but resulted from its natural consequences. These automatic, or natural, rewards strengthened behavior as expected by the law of effect. That is, natural and extrinsic rewards follow the same laws of reinforcement.

In everyday life, there are a variety of consequences that affect behavior. Some of these consequences are natural in the sense that they automatically occur when we do something. These are the rewards that Harlow identified in the studies of puzzle solving by monkeys. These are also the rewards that presumably underlie human activities apparently done for their own sake. Other consequences are socially arranged, as when a teacher grades a paper or an employee gets paid for work.

From a behavioral perspective, behavior is always a function of its consequences, whether those consequences are natural or social. It is confusing and deceptive to talk about intrinsic motivation and extrinsic rewards. Behavior that appears to be intrinsically motivated may in fact be due to its natural consequences. Consider the following questions: How long would a child play the piano if no sound came from it? How long would one solve puzzles if a solution never occurred? How long would one read a book if the text were word salad? The point is that behavior that looks intrinsically motivated is actually regulated by its natural consequences. That is, puzzle solving, musical sounds, and a good story are natural consequences of these activities that result in interest and enjoyment. The natural consequences reside in the environment, although other people do not arrange them. Generally, people do things for reasons, some of which are the natural consequences of their behavior.

Doing Things for Natural and Social Rewards

There are also consequences of behavior that are provided by others. Rewards such as gold stars, money, praise, corrective feedback, and recognition are consequences that can be socially arranged when the natural consequences of behavior are weak. People say "good," "right," "correct," or "excellent," to help a person build skillful performance. People also give nonverbal rewards such as smiles, winks, thumbs-up signs, hugs, congratulatory handshakes, pats on the back, or applause. At other times people give certificates, candy, prizes, and even money as rewards for accomplishments. These are the social reasons why people do what they do.

Social rewards are often used to supplement weak natural consequences or to build skillful actions that will eventually result in natural rewards. This is why people often use social rewards in everyday life. For example, for the beginning golfer, the first natural consequence is to hit the ball. That is, the person must swing the club in such a way that it contacts the ball. Many first-time golfers have great difficulty doing this and take a lot of air shots. The golf professional uses demonstration and corrective social feedback to shape effective swinging of the golf club. Eventually, the person consistently hits the ball and this part of the golf game no longer requires the socially arranged consequences of the professional.

At this point, the trainer concentrates on providing corrective feedback for distance and accuracy. Again, once distance and accuracy have been obtained, the professional goes on to teach the use of different clubs, how to make approach shots, how to get out of bunkers, how to putt, and so forth. This process continues until the person has learned the game. Once the game has been learned, the natural rewards of sinking the ball with a few good shots keep the person going. In addition, learning the game produces new social consequences. The golfer is now able to play the game with others, who supply social interaction, praise for good shots, and conversation about the game at the clubhouse. The golfer is now able to play in tournaments and reap the rewards of recognition and status.

The point is that learning to play the game of golf (or any other complex activity) involves the arrangement of both natural and social rewards. Without both sources of consequences, a person would never learn the game or find any interest or enjoyment in playing it. To say that the golfer is intrinsically motivated is misguided; most behavior is acquired and maintained by a combination of natural and social rewards.

Doing Things When Reward Is Intermittent or Delayed

Although many human actions appear to occur in the absence of any obvious or apparent extrinsic rewards, they may, in fact, be due to intermittent or infrequent consequences. In the golf example, an important part of the interaction between the golfer and the professional is that the social rewards given by the trainer become less and less frequent as the golfer gains proficiency. Even when the golfer has achieved a high level of accomplishment, the professional may intermittently reward aspects of the game.

In a classroom situation, a teacher may provide rewards dependent on the level of a child's proficiency at a particular subject. During the initial phases of learning, rewards from the teacher may be frequent and consistent. Later, as the child gains skill in the academic subject, the teacher provides rewards only occasionally. This practice involves good economics: that is, one should frequently reward weak behavior and infrequently reward strong behavior. It turns out that skillful performance is better maintained by intermittent reward than by continuous reward. When rewards are given infrequently, it is tempting to call the behavior intrinsically motivated. To an outside observer, the golfer and the student may appear to be intrinsically motivated. However, it is the intermittent rewards that account for the behavior.

Behavior that is regulated by its long-term consequences is also mistakenly attributed to intrinsic motivation. In such cases, the use of the term *intrinsic motivation* serves only to conceal a more in-depth analysis of human performance. For some activities, such as playing the piano or painting a picture, it takes considerable time and effort to become proficient enough to obtain the long-range effects. These activities are usually arranged in a series of progressive steps, with the effects of improved performance supporting behavior at each level. As part of this process, self-evaluative reactions bridge the gap between behavior and its long-range effects. For many activities in which people engage, the natural consequences are not yet rewarding. As previously noted, Bandura pointed to people's self-evaluative reactions to their behavior as the principal source of reward.[31]

From a behavioral perspective, self-evaluative reactions themselves are acquired and maintained by social rewards that reside outside the individual. People learn to set standards of performance for themselves and to evaluate these performances. The social consequences of judging one's performance and the actual attainment of skillful performance give self-evaluative reactions their value. Thus, the tuba player has learned to identify improvements in performance and to describe this improvement as positive. Self-evaluation bridges the steps between learning to play the tuba and the long-range skillful performance of a musical symphony. In other words, far more is involved in an account of musical performance than to say it is intrinsically motivated behavior.

Behavior Analysis, Rewards, and the Disruption of Performance

An implication of the behavioral argument is that researchers who use the term *intrinsic motivation* confuse behavior with the effects of that behavior. The effects of behavior involve rewards that are natural or socially arranged, and which may be intermittent or delayed. Labeling behavior as intrinsically motivated makes none of these distinctions. Once it is clear that people engage in actions for natural and social rewards, the claim that rewards are generally harmful is empty.

Behavioral psychologists acknowledge that it is possible to disrupt or subvert behavior through extrinsic social rewards; but it is just as plausible that behavior being maintained by social consequences is occasionally disrupted or subverted by natural rewards. The effective use of rewards is a tricky business, and side effects from a reward procedure are always possible.

People take medicine for sickness, and some medicine has unwanted side effects. These side effects do not usually stop us from taking medicine, although we would like to know about them and avoid them if possible. In a similar vein, natural and socially arranged rewards may sometimes create unwanted side effects. There is no need, however, to banish rewards from our schools and workplaces, especially when these consequences are the primary way to establish learning and promote persistence in an activity. Instead, we must identify and correct the possible side effects of reward contingencies, and at the same time stipulate how to use rewards effectively.

In this regard, it is informative to reconsider the research on rewards and intrinsic motivation. Recall that behaviorists insist that behavior is always due to its consequences and that it obeys the principles of reinforcement. Given this reality, how can we understand disruptions in performance that researchers report in the experiments on reward and intrinsic motivation? The answer lies in a detailed analysis of the experimental procedures and how aspects of the experimental arrangements affect the behavior of participants. Most important, decremental effects of reward found in studies are due to factors other than a decline in innate intrinsic motivation. Instead, such effects result from well-known behavioral processes associated with the presentation and subsequent withdrawal of reward.

Behaviorists have argued that when a reward is promised or presented only once, as in the studies conducted by Deci (1971, 1972b) and Lepper and his colleagues (Lepper, Greene, and Nisbett, 1973), performance may be strongly influenced by the individual's interpretation of task instructions and reinforcement history. For example, the effect on performance of promising a child a monetary reward for working on a puzzle may be influenced by whether previous promises by authority figures have been met and by previous ways in which puzzles have been rewarded. To differentiate the effects of current reinforcement conditions from prior learning, many behavior analysts favor the use of repeated reward sessions followed by repeated sessions after the reward has been removed. The early study by Feingold and Mahoney was conducted using this procedure, and no negative effects of reward were found on measures of intrinsic motivation.[32]

Differential Effects of Tangible Rewards and Praise

Carton addressed the differential effects of tangible rewards and praise from a behavior analysis perspective.[33] Carton noted that praise usually increases or leaves measures of intrinsic motivation unaffected; in contrast, an offer of a tangible reward for an activity often reduces these measures. Rather than claim that praise has informational properties about competence that enhance intrinsic motivation, whereas tangible rewards are controlling and decrease intrinsic interest, a behavior analysis points to procedural differences in studies that use praise versus tangible rewards. The proximity of reward to the target behavior, the number of reward administrations, and the stimuli or events associated with reward availability frequently differ between experiments that use tangible rewards and those that use praise. These procedural differences could account for the apparent loss of intrinsic motivation with tangible rewards and the increase (or absence of effect) with praise.

An examination of the literature indicates that tangible rewards and praise are delivered differently in experiments on intrinsic motivation. One difference concerns the temporal proximity of rewards and the target behavior. In a typical experiment using a tangible reward like money, payment is given to the experimental participants following the reward phase (the control group does not receive any payment). In some experiments, the tangible reward is delivered following the free-choice period, and in a few studies, the reward delivered only after a period of weeks. The basic issue is that the delivery of tangible rewards often involves a delay between doing the requisite behavior and receiving the reward. On the other hand, praise is usually delivered throughout the reward phase, immediately following the target behavior. Thus, any difference in intrinsic motivation between tangible rewards and praise could be due to a variation in delay between behavior and its consequences (as opposed to the relative degree of control of these rewards).

A related issue concerns the number of occurrences of reward in studies of intrinsic motivation using praise and tangible rewards. As explained in the discussion of operant or single-subject designs, repeated rewards given for behavior are likely to act as reinforcement, increasing the target response (this is discussed further in the next section). In many studies using tangible rewards, the rewards are given only once, at the end of the reward phase. A single reward administration is most characteristic of studies that offer tangible rewards for doing or engaging in a task. The bulk of these studies find negative effects of rewards on measures of intrinsic motivation (see our meta-analysis in Chapters 8 and 9). In contrast, experiments concerned with praise and intrinsic motivation typically administer the verbal rewards multiple times following the requisite behavior. Most of these studies find positive effects of praise on intrinsic motivation. One possibility is that the differential effects of praise and tangible reward on intrinsic motivation are due, in part, to the number of reward administrations rather than the nature of these rewards (i.e., controlling versus informational).

Another concern of behavioral researchers regarding praise and tangible-reward studies is the difference in stimuli that signal the availability (and withdrawal) of rewards. In general, in studies of praise and intrinsic motivation, participants are not told that the praise has stopped before the free-choice phase. In contrast, experimenters using tangible rewards often signal the availability of these consequences during the reward phase and the unavailability of reward during the free choice period. For example, in many tangible reward studies, the experimenter leaves the room before the free-choice period, signaling that the rewards, such as money, are no longer available.[34] In some tangible-reward studies before the free-choice phase, explicit statements are given to indicate that rewards have stopped.[35] The difference in stimuli that signal reward availability could account for the reduced free time spent on task for tangible rewards and the continued (or increased) engagement in the task when praise is used.

Consider machines that dispense soft drinks when people insert coins. Getting drinks from these dispensers typically reinforces the behavior of "inserting a coin and pressing a button for the desired drink." This behavior reliably occurs when the machine flashes the sign (stimulus), "Insert coins here." Thus, signals of reward availability play a role in keeping the behavior going. But what will happen if the soft-drink dispenser is broken and the machine operator places an "out of order" sign on the unit? The sign will usually act as a stimulus that indicates the unavailability of reward (i.e., no soft drinks), and most people will not insert money into the machine or press the buttons. The point is that a stimulus change from reward availability to reward unavailability can shift the probability of behavior from high to low. This kind of stimulus change and shift to a low probability of response should occur more often in studies of tangible reward and intrinsic motivation than in studies of praise.

PROCEDURAL DIFFERENCES IN STUDIES OF INTRINSIC MOTIVATION USING PRAISE VERSUS TANGIBLE REWARDS

1. *Immediacy of reward and target behavior*
   - Compared with tangible rewards, praise is more immediate.
2. *Number of reward administrations*
   - Compared with a single administration of tangible reward, praise involves repeated presentations of reward over time.
3. *Signals of reward availability*
   - Compared with studies using praise, experiments with tangible reward often signal the availability of reward.

Reinforcing versus Nonreinforcing Rewards

A decline in task performance during the free-choice phase could reflect participants' attempts at countercontrol, deliberate noncompliance, and feelings of control generated by the offer of rewards.[36]

That is, participants respond to the offered rewards as controlling and, when given a choice to do more of the task, actually do less, as a reaction to perceived control by the experimenter. The behavioral hypothesis of countercontrol induced by promises of reward is seemingly related to cognitive evaluation theory's emphasis on the controlling nature of rewards. A major difference, however, is that behavioral theory separates rewards into nonreinforcing and reinforcing consequences, both of which are controlling, but with different behavioral effects. In a behavioral view, rewards that are nonreinforcing are more likely to be perceived as controlling and more likely to generate deliberate noncompliance. These are the rewards used in the bulk of the intrinsic motivation studies. In contrast to the negative impact of nonreinforcing rewards, reinforcing rewards (i.e., rewards that increase performance) are less likely to seem controlling and less likely to induce countercontrol by participants. Skinner addressed this issue in the following passage.

The fact that positive reinforcement does not breed countercontrol has not gone unnoticed by would-be controllers, who have simply shifted to positive means. Here is an example: A government must raise money. If it does so through taxation, its citizens must pay or be punished, and they may escape from this aversive control by putting another party in power in the next election. As an alternative, the government organizes a lottery, and instead of being *forced* to pay taxes, the citizen *voluntarily* buys tickets. The result is the same: the citizens give the government money, but they feel free and do not protest in the second case. Nevertheless they are being controlled.[37]

Skinner's analysis, when applied to intrinsic motivation experiments, suggests that the nonreinforcing rewards given for doing a task act like demands. Participants view these nonreinforcing rewards as attempts to force them to behave in a given way and to react against the experimenter's control by showing deliberate noncompliance (i.e., reducing time and behavior on the task in the free choice phase). Behavioral researchers, on the other hand, have ensured that reinforcing rewards are used in their experiments. Presumably, participants regulated by positive reinforcement (reinforcing rewards) perceived their behavior as voluntary, felt free, and did not show deliberate noncompliance. This difference between nonreinforcing and reinforcing rewards could explain why behavioral experiments on reward and intrinsic motivation have not found detrimental effects of rewards and why nonbehavioral experiments have.

OFFERS OF NONREINFORCING REWARDS CAN INDUCE DELIBERATE NONCOMPLIANCE (REFUSAL TO ENGAGE IN TARGET ACTIVITY)

Compared with reinforcing rewards, noncompliance (refusing to choose the target activity in the free-choice period) is greater with nonreinforcing rewards.

Associating Rewards with Failure

Another possible explanation for the negative effects of reward is that the reward procedures in intrinsic motivation experiments are often aversive rather than nonreinforcing. From this perspective, participants' behavior is "punished by rewards," in the sense that the rewards have been tied to failure, used in a coercive manner, or correlated with the loss of social reinforcement.[38] For example, rewards are sometimes tied to the achievement of performance standards, and experimental participants may fail to meet these standards and thus not be able to obtain maximum reward. In this context, failure could act as a conditioned punisher and temporarily decrease task performance during the free-choice period.[39] Also, because failure is paired with the natural rewards of performing the activity or task, the intrinsic rewards could decrease in value (at least temporarily). Repeated encounters with failure could, in this way, undermine motivation.

In contrast, when rewards are given for meeting or exceeding a performance standard or group norm, they are said to be success contingent (maximal reward). From a behavioral view, rewards that are programmed for success are not expected to have detrimental effects on free-choice performance. In fact, even strong opponents of contingent rewards seem to recognize that success-contingent rewards do not have harmful effects. Deci and Ryan acknowledged the potential benefits of success-based rewards in their discussion of information and reward:

The important point is that rewards, like feedback, when used to convey to people a sense of appreciation for work well done, will tend to be experienced informationally and will maintain or enhance intrinsic motivation, but when they are used to motivate people, they will surely be experienced as controlling and will undermine intrinsic motivation.[40] . . . [R]ewards that are appropriately linked to performance, representing positive feedback in an informational context, ought not to be detrimental. The cost to the system, however, in signifying good performance through the use of performance-contingent rewards is that many people end up receiving the message that they are not doing very well and this is likely to be amotivating.[41]

When performance standards are graded, reasonable, and attainable, rewards are expected to have positive effects on motivation. On the other hand, rewards given for generally unattainable levels of performance ensure failure and reduce motivation to perform at school or at work. The general point is to tie rewards to success rather than failure.

REWARDS ASSOCIATED WITH FAILURE REDUCE FREE-CHOICE INTEREST AND PERFORMANCE

- Less than maximum reward is usually associated with failure; people who receive less than maximum reward for the target behavior will be less interested in the activity in a free-choice period.
- Achieving maximum reward at a task can indicate success; rewards based on achieving a criterion and rewards based on achieving a criterion and rewards obtained for surpassing a normative standard can also indicate success.

Rewards Used as a Form of Coercion

Rewards are often used to induce people to do things that they do not want to do. That is, rewards that are used to motivate people could involve a form of coercion.[42] In everyday settings, social agents (e.g., parents, managers, teachers, etc.) often use rewards only because they can be removed for instances of noncompliance. That is, children, workers, and students "behave well" in order to avoid the loss of promised rewards, impending punishment, or threats of punishment arranged by others. One way to test whether rewards are being used as positive reinforcement or coercion is to ask who benefits from the reward procedure. Rewards used to the advantage of the social agents are usually coercive, whereas rewards given to benefit the recipient often act as positive consequences.[43]

In terms of experiments on reward and intrinsic motivation, behavior analysts point to participants' pre-experimental history and the coercive use of rewards.

They note that most participants have experienced offers of reward to engage in activities that were later followed by loss of reward, punishment, or the threat of punishment. In this way, offers of reward (especially for doing some activity) come to act as conditioned aversive stimuli. In the context of the laboratory, these verbal statements induce experimental participants to engage in the designated task. At the same time, the offers of reward, when paired with the intrinsic rewards of the task, reduce the value of the target activity. The result is a decrease in task performance in the free-choice phase, in comparison to a control group that does not receive the offer of reward.

Alternatively, performance in the free-choice phase could decline due to deliberate noncompliance as a reaction to the coercive offer of reward by the experimenter. In this scenario, participants identify sources of coercion and react against them (again because of a pre-experimental history).[44] Because the offered reward has been tied to a designated activity, participants can show their noncompliance by refusing to engage in the activity during the free-choice period. Dickinson explained that "during reward administration, the rewards may maintain behavior; however, when they are no longer available, behavior that has irritated or inconvenienced coercers may be momentarily strong."[45]

REWARDS BECOME PUNISHERS THAT SUBVERT THE NATURAL CONSEQUENCES OF ACTIVITIES AND LEAD TO REDUCED INTRINSIC MOTIVATION

Offers of reward given "to motivate" people (given for the benefit of the social agent) are usually backed up by punishment or threat of punishment. These incentives become conditioned punishers, which, when associated with the natural rewards of the target behavior, decrease performance during free-choice.

OFFERED REWARDS CAN INDICATE COERCIVE CONTROL BY THE REWARD GIVER AND PEOPLE WILL REACT WITH DELIBERATE NONCOMPLIANCE

People react with countercontrol measures to those who use control. People will act in ways that upset or inconvenience the source of coercive control. In the laboratory, people react against the coercive influence of the experiment by refusing to engage in the target behavior.

Social and Cultural Issues

Another, more complex analysis involves the cultural practice of withholding approval, praise, and credit for behavior that is explicitly rewarded (e.g., behavior done for money). Behavior is said to be artistic, original, creative, or intelligent when its occurrence is unrelated to explicit consequences such as offers of money, grades, or gold stars. For example, a solution to a problem is admired as original if there has been no explicit training (i.e., coming from the person), but it is considered less worthy if it is due to obvious social influence. These contingencies could extend to explicit reward and offers of reward. Explicit reward would indicate that behavior did not emanate from the person and was not as worthy of social recognition. People who are reinforced by approval, praise, and credit could learn to act in ways that minimize the appearance of control by explicit rewards.

One response to minimize the appearance of control is refusal to engage in the rewarded activity. Noncompliance with the offered reward indicates weak external control, strong intrinsic motivation, and behavior worthy of social recognition and approval. In addition, such noncompliance will seem even more praiseworthy if the person claimed personal motivation or interest in the activity. Thus, the alcoholic who declines an offer of a drink seems more deserving of credit than the social drinker. In terms of experiments on rewards and intrinsic motivation, these cultural contingencies ensure that many participants will show a decrease in the free time on task (i.e., noncompliance) and, at the same time, claim a strong interest in the rewarded activity.[46]

CONCLUDING REMARKS

A behavior analysis of rewards and intrinsic motivation involves a series of hypotheses concerning the variables that change the probability of behavior from high to low. Behavioral researchers argue that well known processes of stimulus control, punishment, and reinforcement account for differences in free-choice performance in studies of intrinsic motivation.

According to Carton, there are three advantages to behavioral accounts of reward and intrinsic motivation: (1) parsimony, (2) falsifiability, and (3) external validity.[47] Behavioral hypotheses are said to be more parsimonious than cognitive theories (e.g., cognitive evaluation theory) because only a few variables, such as reward availability and frequency, rather than many, are used to account for differences in free-choice performance over studies. Reference to a variety of internal mediators such as self-determination and perceived competence is not required from a behavioral viewpoint.

Also, behavioral accounts or hypotheses are claimed to be more readily falsified than theories that rely on unobservable motivational constructs and innate sources of energy for explanation. That is, experiments can be arranged to control for, or manipulate, the reinforcement variables that are said to affect free-choice behavior. Thus, explicit procedures can be used to investigate whether changes in stimuli signaling reward availability actually explain differences in free-choice performance.[48]

A third advantage is the claim that behavioral accounts have greater external validity than cognitive evaluation theory in terms of implementing reward programs in applied settings. From the perspective of cognitive evaluation theory, it makes sense to offer a tangible reward to people for merely engaging in some activity, administer the reward only once, and then withdraw all rewards for the activity (producing the purported detrimental effect on intrinsic motivation). In everyday life, parents, teachers, and administrators would seldom (if ever) use such a reward system. Most reward systems in applied settings use repeated rewards tied to specific behavior, procedures that are closer to the ones suggested by reinforcement principles.

As a final comment, it is noteworthy that most studies on rewards and intrinsic motivation have used college students and involved contingencies of grades and credits. That is, students were required to participate in an experiment in order to fulfill their course obligations in introductory psychology. This means that both the experimental and control participants were extrinsically motivated to do the target activity before rewards such as money were offered to the experimental group. One interpretation of this is that much of the research on the topic actually concerns offers of extrinsic rewards for behavior that is already extrinsically motivated rather than the effects of extrinsic rewards on intrinsically motivated behavior.

NOTES

1. The "rewarding" aspects of musical sounds may depend on a learning history as different listeners and musicians will prefer different musical sounds, including classical, jazz, rock, and other genres.

2. For example, negative contrast, see Williams, 1983.

3. A difference between social learning theory and a behavioral approach is that from a social learning perspective, thoughts and beliefs about rewards are seen as the major determinants of human behavior and the interaction of human behavior with actual reward contingencies is downplayed.

4. Bandura, 1986, 1997.

5. Bandura, 1986, p. 228.

6. Recent evidence about human sensitivity to reinforcement seems to contradict Bandura's claims that awareness (i.e., verbalization of reward contingency) is necessary for rewards and other consequences to affect behavior. In an experiment conducted by Svartdal (1992), human participants showed sensitivity to reinforcement when awareness (and, presumably, expectancy) was reduced by a distraction procedure. Using a complex discrimination task as a distractor, the researcher provided reinforcement based on the force of a key-pressing response. Participants increased or decreased the force of their key pressing in accord with the requirements for reinforcement.

Sensitivity to the reinforcement protocol occurred even though participants were unaware of the link between force of response and reinforcement. In addition, greater distraction (i.e., complexity of the discrimination task) increased the control by the reinforcement contingency. Overall, the data from Svartdal (1992) support a behavioral view, indicating that reinforcement has direct effects on human behavior. Moreover, awareness seems to interfere with, rather than promote, the regulation of human behavior by reinforcement.

7. Bandura, 1986, p. 240.

8. Note that the distinction between natural and arbitrary consequences comes from behavioral psychology, as does the notion of automatic reinforcement.

9. See Epling and Pierce, 1991/1992.

10. Bandura, 1997, p. 219.

11. Bandura, 1986, p. 241.

12. See Eisenberger, Rhoades, and Cameron, 1999, for evidence on the mediation hypothesis.

13. Bandura, 1986, p. 245.

14. Deci, Koestner, and Ryan, 1999.

15. Also see Rosenfield, Folger, and Adelman, 1980.

16. Bandura, 1986, p. 246.

17. Harackiewicz and Sansone (2000) present a theoretical analysis of reward and intrinsic motivation that is similar to Bandura's (1986) analysis of competency-contingent reward. Harackiewicz and Sansone argue that when rewards are offered to meet a performance standard, they may "generate positive motivational processes as individuals approach and perform activities eager to attain competence" (p. 87). Such rewards are said to lead to feelings of accomplishment and pride. Under these conditions, the reward signifies the value of competence in the situation. Rewards that symbolize higher levels of achievement are expected to generate greater positive motivation. A reward offered and given for placing first in a golf tournament is said to symbolize higher levels of competence than a reward given for finishing the tournament in the top three. From this perspective, the same reward will have greater value in a national golf tournament than in a local one. In contrast to the predictions of cognitive evaluation theory, Harackiewicz and Sansone (2000) suggest that some types of rewards lead to greater intrinsic motivation.

18. Schunk, 1983.

19. Bandura, 1997.

20. Bandura, 1986, p. 246.

21. See Harackiewicz, Manderlink, and Sansone, 1984.

22. Bandura, 1997, p. 222.

23. Enzle and Ross, 1978.

24. Karniol and Ross, 1977.

25. Eisenberger, Rhoades, and Cameron, 1999.

26. Bandura, 1997, p. 220.

27. Bandura and Schunk, 1981.

28. Skinner, 1969.

29. Dickinson, 1989; Horcones, 1983, 1987; Vaughan and Michael, 1982.

30. Harlow, 1950; Harlow, Harlow, and Meyer, 1950.

31. Bandura, 1986.

32. Feingold and Mahoney, 1975.

33. Carton, 1996.

34. Taking the experimenter out of the setting is not an explicit signal of reward withdrawal, and the interpretation of the stimulus change could vary over participants and experiments.

35. Cognitive evaluation theory requires that there be no expectation of rewards during the free-choice period. Thus, in some studies, participants are told that rewards are no longer forthcoming.

36. Dickinson, 1989.

37. Skinner, 1974, p. 219; italics in the original.

38. See Kohn, 1993a, who argues that rewards are necessarily punishers.

39. Dickinson, 1989.

40. Deci and Ryan, 1985, p. 300.

41. Ibid., p. 310.

42. Sidman, 1989.

43. Skinner, 1953, p. 321.

44. This argument concerning freedom and dignity is based on Skinner (1971).

45. Dickinson, 1989, p. 6.

46. Other behavioral explanations for the reward and intrinsic motivation effects have been offered by a variety of researchers. One behavioral effect that could be mistaken for a change in intrinsic interest involves negative behavioral contrast (Balsam & Bondy, 1983; Dunham, 1968; Williams, 1983). If the decline in performance during a free-choice period is a contrast effect, the effects of reward should be a temporary reaction to the reward's removal (Daly, 1969a, 1969b; Flora, 1990; White & Cameron, 2000).

Another alternative is that offered rewards interfere with task motivation by eliciting competing responses (Reiss & Sushinsky, 1975, 1976). Competing responses may include perceptual or cognitive distraction, excitement related to anticipated rewards, or frustration due to delay of reward. These responses could interfere with task motivation. Recall that experiments using repeated rewards did not find a loss of intrinsic motivation. One way to explain this finding is in terms of the reduction, through habituation, of competing responses elicited by offered rewards as the rewards are presented repeatedly.

A learned helplessness explanation has also been offered for the detrimental effects of reward (Eisenberger & Cameron, 1996). Learned helplessness theory assumes that uncontrollable negative consequences result in generalized motivational and emotional deficits (Maier and Seligman, 1976; Overmier and Seligman, 1967; Overmier, 1985; Seligman, 1975). The theory has been applied to rewards and noncontingent reward presentations and has been found to produce performance deficits in children (Eisenberger, Kaplan, and Singer, 1974; Eisenberger, Leonard, Carlson, and Park, 1979). When applied to rewards and intrinsic motivation, the learned helplessness hypothesis states that when rewards are offered unrelated to any performance standards, people learn that the delivery of the reward has nothing to do with their performance and so give up on the task.

47. Carton, 1996.

48. See Carton and Nowicki, 1998.

PART IV

THE EMPIRICAL EVIDENCE FOR THE IMPACT OF REWARDS ON INTRINSIC MOTIVATION

Chapter 6

An Overview of the Experiments on Rewards and Intrinsic Motivation

Following the work of Deci and Lepper and his associates,[1] many researchers set out to test the hypothesis that rewards produced decremental effects on people's intrinsic motivation. Since 1971, almost 150 controlled experiments have been conducted on the topic. In this section of the book, we examine this large body of empirical research. In this chapter, we outline the various research paradigms used to assess the effects of rewards on intrinsic motivation and describe different conditions that have been investigated as potential moderators of reward effects. In Chapter 7, we evaluate meta-analytic reviews of the literature. A meta-analysis based on our recent work is presented in Chapter 8.[2] Our meta-analysis is designed to update and improve on previous reviews of the literature. Theoretical and practical implications of our findings are presented in Chapter 9.

The majority of studies on rewards and intrinsic motivation have used a between-groups design similar to the designs used in the original studies described in Chapter 2. The bulk of the between-group experiments have been designed from an overjustification or cognitive evaluation theoretical perspective. The focus of these studies has been to show when rewards produce decrements in intrinsic motivation. A few researchers have investigated the topic with single-subject designs like that of Feingold and Mahoney (outlined in Chapter 3).[3] These studies were designed to assess whether repeated presentations of reward followed by repeated assessments of intrinsic motivation following the removal of reward would result in decrements in intrinsic motivation. What follows is a brief description of these different research designs and a discussion of reward conditions that have been found to produce varying effects.

BETWEEN-GROUP DESIGNS

The vast majority of studies designed to assess the effects of reward on intrinsic motivation have been conducted in a laboratory setting using a between-group design.[4] In a typical study, participants are presented with a task (e.g., solving and assembling puzzles, drawing with magic markers, playing word games). Experimental participants are rewarded with money, grades, candy, praise, opportunity to engage in a preferred activity, good player certificates, and so forth for performing the activity. Rewards are either tangible (e.g., money, candy, gold stars) or verbal (e.g., praise, approval, positive feedback). In addition, the rewards may be offered beforehand (expected reward) or presented unexpectedly after the activity (unexpected reward). In some experiments, reward is offered simply for doing an activity; in other studies, the rewards are given for completing a task or for each puzzle or other unit solved. In a number of experiments, the rewards are offered for meeting or exceeding a specific standard.

Participants in a control condition engage in the activity without receiving a reward. The reward intervention is usually conducted over a ten-minute to one-hour period. Rewarded and nonrewarded groups are then observed during a nonreward period (typically, anywhere from two minutes to one hour), in which participants are free to continue performing the target task or to engage in some alternative activity. The nonreward period usually occurs immediately after the experimental session, although some researchers have observed participants several weeks later. The time participants spend on the target activity during this nonreward phase, their performance on the task during the free-choice period, or self-reported task interest are used as measures of intrinsic motivation. If rewarded participants spend less free time on the activity, perform at a lower level, or express less task interest than nonrewarded participants, reward is said to undermine intrinsic motivation.

The Impact of Moderator Variables

The findings from the between group-design studies have been mixed (positive, negative, and no effects have been reported). From the beginning, when Deci and Lepper and his associates conducted the initial studies on the topic, it was clear that rewards had different effects depending on how they were administered.[5] Specifically, verbal rewards were found to increase measures of intrinsic motivation, and tangible rewards produced negative effects only when they were offered beforehand and not contingent on a specified level of performance.

As research on the topic was amassed, other conditions were found to influence the impact of rewards. A number of reviews appeared on the topic; their aim was to assess the adequacy of different theoretical accounts and to identify conditions under which rewards produce decrements and increments in intrinsic

TYPICAL BETWEEN-GROUP DESIGN ON REWARDS AND INTRINSIC MOTIVATION

Participants randomly assigned

Experimental Group	*Control Group*
Participants asked to perform task	Participants asked to perform task (no offer of reward)
Participants work on task	Participants work on task
Reward delivered; Participants told that they have a free-choice period	No reward delivered; Participants told they have a free-choice period
Free-choice period; Participants can work on task or other activities	Free-choice period; Participants can work on task or other activities
Measure intrinsic motivation for task	Measure intrinsic motivation for task

motivation.[6] Next we describe some of the conditions thought to be critical in determining the impact of rewards.

MODERATOR VARIABLES FOR THE IMPACT OF REWARDS ON INTRINSIC MOTIVATION

- Reward type (verbal or tangible)
- Reward expectancy (expected or unexpected)
- Reward contingency
    Cognitive evaluation theory
        Task-noncontingent
        Task-contingent
        Completion-contingent
        Performance-contingent
    Social learning theory
        Non–competency-contingent (loose)
        Competency-contingent (specific)
- Maximum versus less than maximum reward
- Reward salience
- Initial task interest
- Interpersonal context

Type of Reward

In the intrinsic motivation literature, rewards are defined as verbal or tangible. Verbal rewards (praise, positive feedback) have generally been found to increase measures of intrinsic motivation. In one of the original experiments, Deci examined the effects of verbal rewards and found that participants who were praised for doing a task spent more time on the activity after the praise was no longer available than nonrewarded participants.[7] According to cognitive evaluation theory, all rewards are experienced as controlling by individuals, but verbal rewards provide an informational function that overrides the feelings of control. In the most recent statement of cognitive evaluation theory, Deci and his colleagues suggest that verbal rewards do not always result in increases in motivation.[8] Specifically, the researchers suggest that verbal rewards are more effective for adults than for children and that verbal praise presented in a controlling manner will reduce the informational function of the reward and lead to a decrease in intrinsic motivation.

Rewards classified as tangible include money, candy, gold stars, good player awards, theater tickets, opportunities to engage in preferred activities, and so on. The results of studies using tangible rewards are mixed; some studies found positive effects, whereas others found negative or no effects. An examination of the studies using tangible rewards indicates that the effects of tangible rewards depend on other conditions such as the reward expectancy or contingency.

Reward Expectancy

In the intrinsic motivation studies, rewards are classified as expected or un-expected; these terms refer to whether the research participants are promised the reward prior to its delivery. For example, in some experiments, rewarded participants are offered money before they engage in the experimental activity and the reward is delivered after they have worked on the task. In other studies, the participants are given the reward after they have engaged in the task but are not offered it prior to their involvement. Rewards that are promised to participants are referred to as "expected" rewards; "unexpected" rewards are those delivered at the end of the experimental session but not promised beforehand.

As described in Chapter 2, in the early study by Lepper and his associates, only expected tangible rewards were found to produce a negative effect on the free-time measure of intrinsic motivation; unexpected reward had no impact.[9] Both cognitive evaluation theorists and those who support the overjustification hypothesis suggest that unexpected rewards do not affect feelings of competence, self-determination, or locus of control because the controlling process only takes place when the rewards are in progress. With unexpected rewards, individuals do not know that they will receive a reward, and thus, intrinsic motivation will not be affected.

Following Lepper and his associates' finding with regard to unexpected rewards, few studies have been conducted to examine the impact of this type of reward. Instead, the focus has been on expected tangible reward. From the perspective of cognitive evaluation theory, expected tangible rewards decrease people's intrinsic motivation by undermining feelings of competence and self-determination. Proponents of the overjustification hypothesis claim that expected tangible rewards decrease intrinsic motivation by deflecting the source of motivation from internal to external causes. From both these viewpoints, expected tangible rewards are predicted to reduce intrinsic interest. Moreover, most between-group design studies have found negative effects of expected tangible reward. However, a few researchers have shown that when the rewards are tied to performance standards, intrinsic motivation increases.[10] The implication of this finding is that not all expected tangible rewards produce negative effects; the outcome depends on the contingency.

Reward Contingency

A contingency of reward states the basis on which rewards are delivered (arrangement of rewards). For example, rewards may be given for attaining a specific score on a task, completing a puzzle, or simply doing an activity.

The classification of reward contingencies has been somewhat confusing in the intrinsic motivation literature. The difficulty is that some researchers have used the same label to describe different contingencies or different labels to describe the same contingencies. For example, in one study the researchers describe a procedure whereby participants are paid to participate in a task as non-contingent;[11] the same procedure is labeled as contingent in other studies.

Using cognitive evaluation theory as their framework, in 1983, Ryan and his colleagues developed a taxonomy of reward contingencies that, they suggested, could bring order to the empirical data regarding expected tangible rewards.[12] In a slight alteration of this taxonomy, Deci, Koestner, and Ryan classified expected tangible rewards into four categories: task-noncontingent, engagement-contingent, completion-contingent, and performance-contingent rewards.[13] Task-noncontingent rewards are defined as "those given without specifically requiring the person to engage in the activity;"[14] engagement-contingent rewards are those offered to participants for engaging in a task without a requirement to complete the task, do it well, or reach some standard. Rewards categorized as completion contingent are those offered and given for completing a task, and performance-contingent rewards are defined as those "offered dependent upon the participants' level of performance."[15]

According to Deci and his associates, negative effects should be detected when the expected tangible rewards are contingent (only task-noncontingent rewards are predicted to produce no effect). As indicated in Chapter 4, engagement-contingent, completion-contingent, and performance-contingent rewards are said to be controlling; people receiving these types of rewards will feel a loss of autonomy. Their self-determination will diminish, and this, in turn, will lead to a loss of intrinsic motivation. Completion-contingent and performance-contingent rewards may provide information about competence, but according to cognitive evaluation theory, reductions in self-determination will override any increases in feelings of competence. Thus, each of these reward contingencies is expected to result in a loss of intrinsic motivation.[16]

Although Deci and his associates made these predictions, it is important to note that several studies using completion-contingent and performance contingent rewards did not result in decreases in measures of intrinsic motivation.[17] Even Deci himself used a completion-contingent reward condition in his early studies and found no significant negative effects of expected tangible reward.[18]

A different conceptualization of reward contingencies is suggested by social learning theory.[19] As outlined in Chapter 5, Bandura's social learning theory distinguishes between non–competency-contingent rewards (rewards given without regard to mastery), and competency-contingent rewards (rewards given for mastering activities or tasks). In contrast to cognitive evaluation theory, in which the emphasis is on control and perceived self-determination, social learning theory emphasizes how reward contingencies relate to perceived competence or self-efficacy. Reward contingencies that enhance perceived competence or self-efficacy are expected to increase interest and performance of an activity.

Non–competency-contingent rewards are those given for merely doing, completing, or repeating an activity and are most likely to reduce intrinsic interest. From the perspective of social learning theory, in this kind of loose reward procedure, the rewards do not convey competency to an individual. In a loose contingency, the rewards are given without regard to quality of performance, and as such, they exert a weak influence over behavior. Thus, other factors are expected to moderate the effects of loose (or non–competency-contingent) rewards, including the level of initial task interest, ability on the task, value of the rewards, type of task, age of the participants, and when and how intrinsic motivation is measured.

Competency-contingent rewards, on the other hand involve rewards given for mastery (i.e., achieving relatively challenging standards). This type of reward contingency is said to develop perceptions of self-efficacy and task interest. Rewards given for achieving challenging standards are also indicative of competence. Thus, according to social learning theory, when rewards are linked to attaining challenging performance standards, these incentives help people develop a sense of self-efficacy, interest, and involvement in activities.

Almost all the between-group design studies on rewards and intrinsic motivation have used non–competency-contingent rewards. Many of the experiments that Deci and associates classified separately as task-contingent, completion-contingent, and performance-contingent rewards would be classified in the non–competency-contingent category according to social learning theory. Only a handful of studies have used what Bandura has referred to as competency-contingent reward; in these types of studies, participants are rewarded for meeting or exceeding a specific performance standard. To date, no studies on the topic have examined the impact of reward given for meeting increasingly more difficult standards and attaining mastery on a task. Thus, from the perspective of social learning theory, research on the effects of rewards on intrinsic motivation has focused almost exclusively on the effects of non–competency-contingent rewards, with no systematic investigation of the types of reward procedures that lead to increased performance and motivation.

Maximal versus Less Than Maximal Reward

A further potential moderator of reward concerns whether participants receive the maximum amount of reward possible in the experiment. In studies of maximum reward, participants are offered rewards graded in terms of meeting a criterion or performance standard; all meet the criterion and receive the full amount of reward. Less than maximum reward occurs in studies where there is a time limit, such that some participants are unable to meet all the requirements in the time allotted and are given less than the full reward. For example, Deci's original experiment involved less than maximum reward.[20] Participants were offered $1 for each of four puzzles solved within a 13-minute time limit. Not all participants were able to solve the puzzles within the time limit, and therefore, not all received the full reward.

Although maximum versus less than maximum reward has not been a focus of theoretical predictions in this literature, the difference between these two conditions may lead to different effects on intrinsic motivation.[21] One way to understand these conditions is to consider what less than maximal reward signifies to participants. If people are told that they can obtain a certain level of reward but are given less than that level, they have received feedback information that indicates failure. In other words, this type of situation may represent failure feedback, not reward. On the other hand, if people receive the full reward, the reward signifies success at the task. Advocates of cognitive evaluation theory and overjustification theory do not make differentiated predictions about the effects of these different conditions.[22] For social learning theorists, on the other hand, failure at a task should reduce interest, whereas success should increase feelings of competence, self-efficacy, and interest.[23]

Reward Salience

The overjustification hypothesis proposes that when individuals are rewarded for engaging in an interesting activity, their perceptions shift from accounting for their behavior as self-initiated to accounting for it in terms of external rewards. Lepper, Greene, and Nisbett (1973) suggested that expected tangible rewards are especially detrimental to intrinsic motivation when they are particularly conspicuous or salient. The issue of salient versus nonsalient reward was addressed in a study by Ross in the mid-1970s.[24] When rewards were made conspicuous to participants (children), those who were offered the reward showed a decrease in intrinsic motivation, whereas rewards that were not salient led to an increase. In most between-group design studies, the rewards are made salient to the participants.

Level of Initial Task Interest

A major issue in the rewards and intrinsic motivation experiments concerns whether the tasks used in the studies are interesting to the participants. From the perspective of cognitive evaluation theory and the overjustification hypothesis, the effect of rewards on people's intrinsic motivation is only relevant if the activities the participants engage in are of high initial interest (see the discussion in Chapter 4). That is, the concern is that if individuals are given rewards for tasks that they already enjoy doing, removal of the rewards will cause them to be less motivated and less interested in the task than they were before the rewards were introduced. In terms of initial task interest, Deci and his associates have suggested that the undermining phenomenon is relevant only to interesting tasks because there is no intrinsic motivation to undermine with tasks of low initial interest.[25]

Social learning and behavioral investigators, on the other hand, are interested in the effects of rewards on motivation and performance when people are rewarded to engage in tasks with low levels of initial interest. From a social learning perspective, rewards can be used to cultivate task interest and to build competence and self-efficacy.[26]

The issue of initial task interest is of particular relevance to the practical application of reward. In the laboratory experiments, negative effects of reward have only been found when participants engage in activities that are of high initial interest. When the tasks are not initially interesting, it appears that the introduction of rewards either has no effect or else enhances measures of motivation and performance. In educational settings, teachers usually use reward and incentive systems to instill interest in academic subjects in which students have little initial interest. Evidence from laboratory experiments suggests that rewards are not harmful in this type of situation. Rewards have only been found to produce negative effects for tasks of high interest. As noted by several researchers, teachers are not likely to set up reward systems for activities that students already enjoy.[27]

Interpersonal Contexts

Cognitive evaluation theorists state that the effects of rewards (both verbal and tangible) depend on the interpersonal context (the atmosphere in classrooms, work environments, etc.).[28] When people feel pressured or controlled by the context, the view is that rewards will undermine intrinsic motivation. In contrast, if those who administer rewards do so in a noncontrolling style, the rewards are said to be experienced as more informational and to lead to less of a loss of intrinsic motivation.

Other Variables That Moderate the Impact of Rewards

Several other variables have been hypothesized to affect the impact of rewards on measures of intrinsic motivation. Researchers have investigated the effects of reward magnitude,[29] whether the rewards are attractive to participants,[30] whether the rewards are endogenous or exogenous to an activity,[31] whether there are norms about payment,[32] and whether participants are told prior to the measurement of intrinsic motivation that reward is no longer available.[33] Presently there are few studies that have systematically studied these variables; thus, conclusions about their impact at this point in time would be premature.

Measures of Intrinsic Motivation

Researchers investigating the effects of rewards have used a variety of measures to index intrinsic motivation. The main measures have included time on task during a nonrewarded free-choice period; performance on the task during the free-choice period; questionnaire measures of task interest, enjoyment or satisfaction; and participants' willingness to volunteer for future studies without reward. Some researchers have used a "free-choice" measure, which includes time on task as well as performance on the task during the free-choice session. On each of these measures, rewarded participants are compared to nonrewarded individuals. If rewarded participants spend less free time on the activity, report less task interest, perform at a lower level during the free-choice period, or are less willing to return for future studies than the control group, reward is said to undermine intrinsic motivation.

MEASURES OF INTRINSIC MOTIVATION

- Free time on task
- Performance on task in free-choice period
- Task interest, enjoyment, or satisfaction
- Willingness to volunteer for future studies without reward
- Free-choice measure—a combined measure based on free time and performance during free-choice period

---

Several researchers have noted that the results across different measures of intrinsic motivation are not consistent. For example, in many experiments a negative effect of reward was found on the free-time measure of intrinsic motivation but not on questionnaire measures of task interest.[34] Such results indicate that there are problems in defining (operationalizing) the construct of intrinsic motivation. One implication of this is that future research needs to focus on clarifying the concept of intrinsic motivation and developing suitable measures. Presently, the studies show that different results are obtained with different measures of intrinsic motivation.

SINGLE-SUBJECT DESIGNS

The impact of a variety of moderator variables on the effects of rewards on people's intrinsic motivation has been investigated with between-group designs. One criticism of this design, however, is that researchers employing it often refer to their reward manipulation as a reinforcement procedure. As discussed in Chapter 3, by definition, a reinforcer is an event that increases the frequency of the behavior it follows. However, in most of the between-group design studies on intrinsic motivation, the researchers did not demonstrate that the events used as rewards increased the frequency of the behavior studied. In addition, critics have suggested that the measurement phases in the between-groups design research are too brief to detect any temporal trends and transition states.[35] In order to address these issues, a few studies have been conducted using a repeated measures, single-subject design.

In the single-subject design, participants serve as their own controls. Measures such as time on task are taken over a number of sessions in a baseline phase before presentation of the reward. Reinforcement procedures are then implemented for repeated sessions, and finally, the reward is withdrawn and time on task is assessed on repeated occasions. Any change in intrinsic motivation is indexed by a difference in time spent on the task between the baseline and postreinforcement phases.

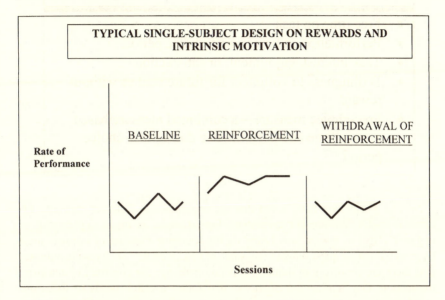

The advantage of the single-subject designs is that the researcher can determine whether the rewards being used are actual reinforcers—that is, whether behavior increases during the reinforcement phase. Statements can then be made about the effects of *reinforcement* rather than *reward*. In addition, the repeated use of reward followed by extended task performance without reward is more characteristic of the natural environment than the typical short-term experimental procedure used in the between-group designs.

Five studies employing a single-subject design with various types of tangible reward contingencies reported that participants' performance on the task during the postreward phase either exceeded or remained at the same level as performance in the prereward sessions.[36] These findings indicate that when rewards are shown to function as reinforcement and multiple-trials procedures are used, there is no evidence of a decremental effect of reward.

SUMMARY

A great deal of research has been conducted using a between-groups design to investigate negative effects of rewards on people's intrinsic motivation. Since the initial studies in the early 1970s, the findings have indicated that not all rewards lead to negative effects. Results from the experimental literature suggest that negative effects depend on the reward type, the reward expectancy, the reward contingency, whether participants receive maximum or less than maximum reward, level of initial task interest, the interpersonal context in which rewards are delivered, and how intrinsic motivation is measured.

Findings from single-subject designs further suggest that negative effects do not occur when the rewards that are used function as reinforcement and when repeated presentations of reward are followed by repeated assessments of measures of intrinsic motivation. That is, negative effects are found to be temporary.

A close inspection of all the studies on rewards and intrinsic motivation reveals contradictions. Not all studies of verbal reward have produced positive effects; not all studies have shown no effects of unexpected rewards, and not all studies of expected tangible reward contingencies have produced negative effects, as predicted by cognitive evaluation theory and the overjustification hypothesis. In addition, Deci and his colleagues have not accepted the findings of the single-subject designs and instead have suggested that the negative effects of reward are enduring rather than temporary.[37]

Given the diverse predictions and findings concerning rewards and intrinsic motivation, a number of reviewers have attempted to delineate the specific conditions under which rewards are either harmful or beneficial.[38] In addition, a few researchers have used meta-analytic techniques to assess the literature. In the next chapter, we provide a critical examination of meta-analyses on this topic.

NOTES

1. Deci, 1971, 1972a, 1972b; Lepper, Greene, and Nisbett, 1973.
2. Cameron, Banko, and Pierce, 2001.
3. Feingold and Mahoney, 1975.
4. Researchers using a between-groups design typically employ one of two methods: a "before-after" design or an "after-only" design. The before-after design involves a three-session paradigm, in which a baseline measure of intrinsic motivation on a particular task is taken. This entails measuring time on task in the absence of extrinsic reward, usually from a session of short duration (e.g., ten minutes). Participants are then assigned to either a reward or no-reward (control) condition, and an intervention with extrinsic rewards is carried out. Following this, the reward is withdrawn and time on task is again measured. The procedure is identical for both groups except that control participants do not experience the reward intervention in the second session. Mean differences in time on task between pre- and post-intervention are calculated for each group, and the scores for the experimental and control participants are then statistically compared. Any difference between the two groups is considered evidence of the effects of withdrawal of reward.

Most researchers have used an after-only design, in which no baseline measure of intrinsic motivation is taken. Experimental participants are presented with a task and rewarded for performing the activity; no reward is offered or given to control participants. All groups are then observed during a nonreward period. If experimental participants spend less time on the task (during the postreward observation) than the controls, reinforcement/reward is said to undermine intrinsic motivation.

5. Deci, 1971, 1972a, 1972b; Lepper, Greene, and Nisbett, 1973.
6. Bates, 1979; Bernstein, 1990; Dickinson, 1989; Flora, 1990; Morgan, 1984.

7. Deci, 1971, Experiment 3.

8. Deci, Koestner, and Ryan, 1999.

9. Lepper, Greene, and Nisbett, 1973.

10. For example, see Eisenberger, Rhoades, and Cameron, 1999.

11. Hamner and Foster, 1975.

12. Ryan, Mims, and Koestner, 1983.

13. Deci, Koestner, and Ryan, 1999.

14. Ibid., p. 636.

15. Ibid.

16. Ibid.

17. For example, see Harackiewicz, Manderlink, and Sansone, 1984.

18. Deci, 1971, 1972b.

19. Bandura, 1986.

20. Deci, 1971.

21. Deci, Koestner, and Ryan (1999) analyzed some studies that used less than maximum versus maximum rewards. Their findings indicated that expected tangible rewards produced large negative effects on measures of intrinsic motivation only when participants received the less than maximum reward.

22. Lepper, Keavney, and Drake (1996) suggested that there may be different effects on motivation depending on whether people are successful at obtaining the reward (see the discussion of this issue in Chapter 4). They did not, however, make any specific predictions; instead, their theoretical position was in accord with cognitive evaluation theory, which predicts negative effects for all the contingent reward conditions studied in this literature (task contingent, completion contingent, and performance contingent).

23. Dickinson (1989) also points out that negative effects are not found when rewards are tied to success.

24. Ross, 1975.

25. Deci, Koestner, and Ryan, 1999, p. 633.

26. Bandura, 1986.

27. For example, see Dickinson, 1989.

28. Deci, Koestner, and Ryan, 1999.

29. See Newman and Layton, 1984.

30. Williams, 1980.

31. Kruglanski, Riter, Armitai, Margolin, Shabatai, and Zaksh, 1975.

32. Staw, Calder, Hess, and Sandelands, 1980.

33. Carton and Nowicki, 1998.

34. For example, see Wicker, Brown, Wiehe, and Shim, 1990.

35. Feingold and Mahoney, 1975; Mawhinney, 1990.

36. Davidson and Bucher, 1978; Feingold and Mahoney, 1975; Mawhinney, Dickinson, and Taylor, 1989; Skaggs, Dickinson, and O'Connor, 1992; Vasta, Andrews, McLaughlin, Stirpe, and Comfort, 1978.

37. Deci, Koestner, and Ryan, 1999.

38. Bates, 1979; Bernstein, 1990; Carton, 1996; Dickinson, 1989; Flora, 1990; Morgan, 1984; Notz, 1975.

Chapter 7

A Critique of Meta-analyses of the Effects of Rewards on Intrinsic Motivation

Over the past three decades, a large body of experimental research has accumulated on the effects of rewards on people's intrinsic motivation. Although many researchers continue to argue that rewards produce pervasive negative effects, an examination of the literature indicates a mixed set of findings. As described in Chapter 6, many different variables impact the effect of rewards. In an attempt to make sense of the diverse results, some researchers have used meta-analytic techniques to evaluate the literature. Meta-analysis is a statistical technique for combining the results from a large number of studies on the same topic. It involves the statistical analysis of a large collection of results from individual studies to integrate the findings. In this chapter, we describe the logic and procedures of meta-analysis and discuss and evaluate findings from different meta-analyses on the topic of rewards and intrinsic motivation.

THE TECHNIQUE AND LOGIC OF META-ANALYSIS

In many areas of the social sciences, dozens of studies have been conducted to investigate a single issue. Rather than conduct additional studies, several researchers have pointed out that what is needed is a way to organize and make sense of the vast amounts of data that have been amassed on a topic.[1] In recent years, researchers have used meta-analysis as a way to organize and understand an area in which a large amount of data have been collected.

Normally, in an individual study, a researcher conducts an experiment and compares the results with what would be expected by chance. The difference between the result and chance is known as the deviation. If there is an effect, the deviation is large enough to reject chance. The size of the deviation (called the *effect size*) depends on the size of the sample. A small effect size in a large sample may be informative, but the same effect size in a small sample may not. Meta-analysis assesses the effect sizes over many studies on the same topic that differ in sample size. It involves a collection of statistical techniques designed to quantitatively summarize a body of data from conceptually related studies.

The term *meta-analysis* was coined by Gene Glass in the 1970s; Glass used the technique to organize and analyze a large number of studies conducted in psychotherapy and education.[2] Since the 1980s, meta-analysis has rapidly increased in importance in the behavioral and social sciences. Over the past 30 years, research summaries based on meta-analyses have become valued sources of information for both policy makers and researchers.

Quantitative analyses similar to meta-analysis have been conducted on single-subject designs;[3] however, meta-analysis is typically used with between-group designs in which a treatment group (e.g., rewarded group) is compared to a control group (nonrewarded group) on a common dependent measure (intrinsic motivation). The goals of a meta-analysis are to establish the relationship between independent and dependent variables (in this case, the relationship between rewards and intrinsic motivation) and to determine what factors moderate or alter the magnitude of the relationship (e.g., type of reward, reward contingency, etc.). Conducting a meta-analysis entails specifying the research questions, delineating the criteria for including and excluding studies, collecting all experiments that meet the criteria, coding the studies, and calculating effect sizes for each study.

STEPS INVOLVED IN A META-ANALYSIS

- Specify the research questions
- Outline criteria for including and excluding studies
- Collect all experiments that meet the inclusion criteria
- Code studies for various reward characteristics
- Calculate an effect size for experimental versus control groups for each study
- Conduct a meta-analysis to assess whether there is a statistically significant difference between experimental and control conditions
- Conduct moderator analyses to clarify under what conditions the experimental and control groups differ on effect size

---

In a meta-analysis, the effect size from each study becomes the unit of analysis, rather than the individual participants within a study. If the effect sizes from all the studies present a random pattern, they will hover around zero, indicating no evidence for an effect. On the other hand, the effect sizes may cluster in a positive or negative direction, indicating the presence of an effect. A positive pattern indicates that rewards produce increases in intrinsic motivation measures; a negative pattern supports the claim that rewards undermine intrinsic motivation.

META-ANALYSES OF THE EFFECTS OF REWARDS ON INTRINSIC MOTIVATION

Rummel and Feinberg (1988): Effects of Controlling Rewards

The first meta-analysis on the effects of rewards on intrinsic motivation was conducted by Rummel and Feinberg in 1988.[4] The purpose was to assess the claim of cognitive evaluation theory that "controlling" rewards lead to decreased intrinsic motivation. Forty-five studies were included, in which participants who received rewards that were defined by Rummel and Feinberg as conveying "controlling" information were compared to groups receiving other types of reward or no reward. Intrinsic motivation was indexed as both free-time measures and self-reports of task interest and satisfaction. These measures were included together in the meta-analysis. The researchers concluded that their meta-analytic results provided support for cognitive evaluation theory. Specifically, they argued that controlling extrinsic rewards have a detrimental effect on intrinsic motivation.

An Assessment of Rummel and Feinberg's Meta-analysis

Rummel and Feinberg's analysis was limited to what they defined as the effects of controlling rewards. The investigators did not include moderator analyses, such as the effects of different reward types, expectancies, contingencies, and so on. Verbal rewards and tangible rewards were combined, and different reward expectancies and contingencies were aggregated. In addition, the researchers combined free time and self-report measures. (As indicated in Chapter 6, these measures do not produce consistent findings, and thus should be analyzed separately.) By collapsing across different reward conditions and different measures of intrinsic motivation, Rummel and Feinberg's analysis produced an overall effect of reward, but no analyses were conducted to show how reward impacts intrinsic motivation measures under different conditions.

A further difficulty is that many of the effect sizes that Rummel and Feinberg used were not based on a comparison of a reward group to a control group on a measure of intrinsic motivation. Instead, many of the effect sizes used in the analysis involved comparisons among types of rewards. The problem with this technique is that it does not allow one to make a conclusion with regard to the effects of rewards versus no rewards.

A major difficulty with Rummel and Feinberg's analysis is that rewards were defined as controlling after the fact. When a reward was found to produce a negative effect, it was classified as controlling and the study was selected for the analysis. That is, the rewards were defined as controlling or informational after their effects on performance had been measured. This is not only an issue in Rummel and Feinberg's analysis; it exemplifies a major overall difficulty with cognitive evaluation theory. The problem is that "controlling" rewards are not defined in the literature; instead, they are inferred from the behavior they supposedly cause.

Cognitive evaluation theory proposes that changes in feelings of competence and self-determination are the causes of changes in intrinsic motivation, but these constructs are not typically measured. Changes in perceptions of competence and self-determination are assumed to be operating because behavior changes. In other words, the existence of competence, self-determination, and intrinsic motivation is inferred from the very behavior they supposedly cause. In cognitive evaluation theory and Rummel and Feinberg's analysis, rewards are defined as controlling if measures of intrinsic motivation decrease, and rewards are defined as informational when the dependent variable indexes an increase in motivation.

Thus, the findings and conclusions of the first meta-analysis on the topic are difficult to interpret because (a) no moderator analyses were conducted, (b) different measures of intrinsic motivation were combined, (c) many effect sizes included in the analysis were not based on a comparison of a reward group to a control group, and (d) rewards were defined as controlling after the effects on behavior were observed.

Wiersma (1992): The Measurement of Intrinsic Motivation

In 1992, Wiersma addressed the issue that the effects of reward depend on how intrinsic motivation is measured.[5] Wiersma's meta-analysis included 20 intrinsic motivation studies from work and organizational psychology journals. Only studies that used tangible rewards were included. Studies were divided into those with free-time measures of intrinsic motivation and those that measured performance on a task during the experimental phase of the study (the rewarded period).

The findings indicated that rewards enhanced performance measures but undermined free-time intrinsic motivation. Wiersma concluded that the finding that rewards reduced task behavior as measured in a free-time period supported cognitive evaluation theory but that the theory was not supported when task performance was measured while the extrinsic reward was in effect.

An Assessment of Wiersma's Meta-analysis

Deci and his colleagues suggested that performance measures taken when the reward contingency is in effect are not good indicators of intrinsic motivation because such a measure will reflect both intrinsic and extrinsic motives.[6] In addition, Wiersma's analysis is less than conclusive because only a small sample of the available studies was included, some studies did not include no-reward control groups, and no moderator analyses were conducted.

Tang and Hall (1995): The Overjustification Hypothesis

In a meta-analysis of 50 studies on rewards and intrinsic motivation, Tang and Hall tested several propositions of the overjustification hypothesis.[7] Specifically, they assessed the hypotheses that expected, tangible rewards would produce negative effects for tasks of high initial interest when the rewards were task contingent (what Deci and his associates later referred to as engagement contingent and completion contingent) and when the rewards were performance contingent. They further evaluated the hypotheses that negative effects would not occur for verbal rewards, unexpected rewards, task-noncontingent rewards, and rewards given for tasks of low initial interest.

For each of their analyses, Tang and Hall assessed the effects of reward on six different measures of intrinsic motivation (free time on task, task enjoyment ratings, quantity of performance during the reward phase, quality of performance during the reward phase, rating by others, and time waited to initiate the task in a free-choice session).

Generally, the results supported the hypotheses. Expected tangible rewards were found to decrease measures of intrinsic motivation on high-interest tasks when the rewards were task contingent and performance contingent. Task-noncontingent rewards did not affect measures of intrinsic motivation. Contrary to the predictions of the overjustification hypothesis, unexpected rewards led to increases on some of the measures of intrinsic motivation and verbal rewards led to decreases.[8]

An Assessment of Tang and Hall's Meta-analysis

Although Tang and Hall's analysis was more comprehensive than the previous two analyses described here, several shortcomings make their results difficult to interpret. First, several measures of intrinsic motivation were included that have been criticized as poor measures of the construct. For example, Tang and Hall included measures such as task enjoyment ratings and quantity and quality of performance during the reward phase. Deci and his colleagues have suggested that such measures are not pure measures of intrinsic motivation because they reflect a mix of intrinsic and extrinsic motivation.[9]

In addition, some studies in Tang and Hall's meta-analysis did not include no-reward control groups, several studies that were published prior to their meta-analysis were not included, a few studies were miscategorized, and some basic statistical assumptions were violated.[10] Overall, however, Tang and Hall's results supported the hypothesis that expected tangible rewards decrease measures of intrinsic motivation on high-interest tasks.

Cameron and Pierce (1994) and Eisenberger and Cameron (1996): The First Hierarchical Meta-analysis

In 1994, our research team published the first hierarchical meta-analysis of the literature (we added additional analyses in 1996).[11] The sample was made up of 96 studies. In our hierarchical meta-analysis, all studies were first included in an analysis of the overall effects of rewards. We then searched for moderator variables. The studies were broken out by one key moderator, then another, and so on. The moderators that we examined were based on theoretical considerations and sufficient replication in the studies (reward type, expectancy, and contingency). Our analysis included between-group designs in which rewarded participants were compared to nonrewarded control groups on measures of intrinsic motivation. The effects of rewards were analyzed separately for free-time measures of intrinsic motivation and self-reported attitudes toward the task.

Our results indicated that overall when all types of reward were aggregated, rewards did not negatively affect intrinsic motivation on either of the measures. When rewards were subdivided into reward type (verbal, tangible), expectancy (expected, unexpected), and contingency, the findings demonstrated that people who received a verbal reward spent more time on a task once the reward was withdrawn; they also reported more interest and enjoyment than nonrewarded persons.

Tangible reward produced no decrements in intrinsic motivation when it was received unexpectedly. Expected tangible rewards produced differing effects depending on the manner in which they were administered. Individuals who received an expected tangible reward for solving or completing a task, or achieving a specific level of performance did not spend less time on the task than controls once the reward was withdrawn. They did, however, report more interest, satisfaction, and enjoyment of the task when the reward was given for a certain level of performance.

Detrimental effects of reward appeared only when tangible rewards were offered to people simply for engaging in a task, independent of successful performance. Under these conditions, once the reward was removed, individuals spent less time on the task than controls; they did not, however, report a less favorable attitude toward the task.

In addition to our analysis of the group-design studies, we also provided a separate analysis of the single-subject designs. No undermining effects of reward were detected. Based on our results, we argued that there is no inherent negative property of rewards. We concluded that negative effects of reward are minimal, temporary, and easily preventable in applied settings.

An Assessment the Meta-analyses of Cameron and Pierce and of Eisenberger and Cameron

Our research and recommendations created considerable debate and furor.[12] Our critics suggested that our findings were invalid due to intentional bias, deliberate misrepresentation, and inept analysis. The popular writer Alfie Kohn commented that

a closer look at their [Cameron and Pierce's] review—and at the empirical literature as a whole—reveals that there is more than adequate justification for avoiding the use of incentives to control people's behavior, particularly in a school setting.[13]

Lepper and his colleagues stated that the procedures used by us were akin to turning silk purses into sow's ears. They suggested that our analysis was comparable to putting a beautiful dessert into an industrial blender and liquefying the entire concoction.[14] Ryan and Deci described our analysis as "an attempt to defend their [Cameron and Pierce's] behavioral turf [rather] than a meaningful consideration of the relevant data and issues."[15]

Further debate ensued in an issue of the *American Psychologist* following Eisenberger and Cameron's publication of the meta-analysis.[16] Although our findings supported many of the predictions made by cognitive evaluation theory and by the overjustification hypothesis (see predictions in Chapter 4), proponents of these theories (e.g., Deci, Lepper and colleagues) would not accept the results.[17]

Our findings were clearly contentious and of great concern to those who argue that negative effects of reward are substantial, generalized, and prevalent across many conditions.[18] In recent articles on the topic, Deci and his colleagues suggested that our work was seriously flawed and that rewards do substantially undermine people's intrinsic interest.[19] They suggested that our failure to detect more pervasive negative effects in our meta-analysis was due to a number of methodological inadequacies. Specifically, they criticized us for the following: (a) collapsing data across tasks with high and low initial interest in our overall analysis and omitting a moderator analysis of initial task interest, (b) including a study that used an inappropriate control group,[20] (c) omitting studies or data as outliers rather than attempting to isolate moderators from them, (d) omitting studies that were published during the period covered by our meta-analysis, (e) omitting unpublished doctoral dissertations, and (f) missclassifying studies into reward contingencies, as defined by cognitive evaluation theory.

Deci, Koestner, and Ryan (1999): A New Hierarchical Meta-analysis

Spurred by our research, in a 1999 issue of *Psychological Bulletin*, Deci, Koestner, and Ryan presented a new hierarchical meta-analysis that claimed to support the view that rewards have pervasive negative effects on intrinsic motivation.[21] They outlined a number of concerns that they had with previous meta-analyses; their meta-analysis was designed to address these concerns, test cognitive evaluation theory, and provide a more comprehensive review of the literature.

Their findings supported cognitive evaluation theory, and generally, rewards were found to have a substantial negative effect on people's intrinsic motivation. The reviewers concluded that "although rewards can control people's behavior—indeed, that is presumably why they are so widely advocated—the primary negative effect of rewards is that they tend to forestall self-regulation."[22]

Deci and his colleagues identified 128 experiments on rewards and intrinsic motivation, including 20 unpublished studies from Ph.D. dissertations. To rectify concerns that they had with our previous work, Deci and associates excluded studies deemed to have inappropriate control groups, included studies that were missed in previous meta-analyses, and also included unpublished doctoral dissertations. Their primary meta-analysis focused on reward effects on high interest tasks. Studies or conditions within studies were included only if the tasks used were measured or defined to be interesting; studies or conditions within studies were excluded if the tasks used were measured or defined as uninteresting. Thus, their primary meta-analysis began with the overall effects of rewards on intrinsic motivation for high-interest tasks only.[23]

The effects of reward were analyzed separately for measures of self-reported task interest and free-choice intrinsic motivation. The free-choice measure included time spent on a task after rewards were removed. When a time measure was not reported in a study, the reviewers used measures of task persistence during the free choice period (e.g., number of trials initiated in a game, number of balls played on a pinball machine, number of successes on a task). Hence, Deci's analysis of the free-choice measure was broader than our previous analyses, which used only studies that assessed time measures.

On high-interest tasks, Deci's findings indicated a significant overall negative effect of reward on the free-choice measure and a nonsignificant negative effect of reward on the self-report measure. In terms of moderator analyses, verbal rewards were found to increase free-choice intrinsic motivation for college students (a nonsignificant effect was found for children) and to enhance task interest for both children and college students. Tangible rewards were divided into unexpected and expected rewards; there were no reliable effects when the rewards were unexpected. Based on cognitive evaluation theory, expected tangible rewards were further subdivided into task-noncontingent, engagement-contingent, completion-contingent, and performance-contingent rewards. The results showed no reliable negative effects for task-noncontingent rewards, whereas engagement-contingent rewards produced significant negative effects on both free-choice intrinsic motivation and self-reported task interest. Completion-contingent and performance-contingent rewards also resulted in significant negative effects on the free-choice intrinsic motivation measure.

Additionally, Deci and his colleagues provided a breakdown of performance-contingent rewards into studies of "maximum" and "not-maximum" reward. A large negative effect was found for the six studies identified as involving not-maximum reward. (In this type of study, some participants failed to attain the criterion and were given less than maximum reward.)

As a supplementary analysis, Deci, Koestner, and Ryan analyzed studies with children in which the free-choice assessment of high-interest activities was conducted immediately following the removal of reward, within a week, and after a week. The results showed negative effects of reward at each time of assessment; the reviewers argued that these results indicate that the undermining effect is not a transitory phenomenon.

All in all, Deci, Koestner, and Ryan's meta-analysis of the effects of rewards on intrinsic motivation produced numerous negative effects of expected tangible rewards under the various reward contingencies. They claimed that their findings supported each of the predictions made by cognitive evaluation theory.

An Assessment of Deci, Koestner, and Ryan's Meta-analysis

Although Deci and his colleagues' analysis included more studies than any other meta-analyses prior to their publication, there are several shortcomings in their work. One issue concerns the overall effects of rewards across all types of tasks. Deci and his associates did not conduct a primary analysis of the overall effects of reward. Instead, they argued that the more theoretically relevant question concerns the effects of rewards on high-interest tasks. In terms of initial task interest, Deci's research team noted that

the field of inquiry has always been defined in terms of intrinsic motivation for interesting tasks and the undermining phenomenon has always been specified as applying only to interesting tasks insofar as with boring tasks there is little or no intrinsic motivation to undermine.[24]

Given that cognitive evaluation theory has little to say about the effects of rewards on low interest tasks, Deci, Koestner, and Ryan's primary meta-analysis focused on reward effects on high-interest tasks.

We contend that an analysis of the overall effect of reward is central to an understanding of this complex area of research. On a practical level, many educators, parents, and administrators have taken the position that rewards and incentive systems are harmful. The view is that rewards negatively affect students' intrinsic interest across all types of activities (e.g., reading, math, science, computer games, etc.); no distinction is made between low and high initial levels of task interest.

Writers who caution against the use of rewards and reinforcement frequently use examples to illustrate their point. More often than not, activities such as reading, lawn mowing, and mathematics are cited as activities in which people will lose interest if they are given rewards for performing the activity. Most of these activities are not ones that individuals begin doing with high levels of initial interest. Importantly, policy makers who adopt the view that rewards are harmful rarely distinguish between high- and low-interest tasks. Because of this, an analysis of the overall effects of reward is warranted. It is our contention that a more complete analysis of the effects of rewards on intrinsic motivation should begin at the level of all rewards over all types of tasks. Following this, a breakdown of reward effects on high- and low-interest tasks would be appropriate.

Another concern is that for some studies included in their analysis of high-interest tasks, Deci and his colleagues omitted conditions that were relevant to their analyses.[25] In addition, they also missed a few experiments that met their inclusion criteria and were published during the period covered by their meta-analysis. As well, several studies using high-interest tasks that measured self-reported task interest were either excluded or inadvertently omitted from the analyses. Many of these studies found positive effects on the self-report measure of task interest. Each of these issues is thoroughly documented in a set of appendices in our updated review of this literature.[26]

The major area of disagreement between Deci and his colleagues' work and our previous meta-analyses concerns the classification of expected, tangible reward into various reward contingencies. As indicated, Deci and his colleagues used cognitive evaluation theory to guide their classification of studies. They established the categories of task-noncontingent, engagement-contingent, completion-contingent and performance-contingent reward.

Although this categorization system may be informative for cognitive evaluation theory, the problem is that the categories are too broad. Studies that used very different procedures were pooled into overall categories of engagement-contingent, completion-contingent and performance-contingent reward. For example, experiments in which participants were offered a reward either for doing well, for each problem/unit solved, for obtaining a certain score, or for exceeding a norm were all categorized as performance contingent by a cognitive evaluation theory framework.

In a response to the work of Deci and his associates, Eisenberger, Pierce, and Cameron examined some of these diverse reward procedures and found very different effects on measures of intrinsic motivation.[27] Their findings indicated that when tangible rewards were offered for meeting or exceeding a specific criterion or surpassing the scores of others, measures of intrinsic motivation increased. Presently, it is difficult to reach a definitive conclusion about the effects of different reward contingencies. Studies using different procedures and producing different results need to be analyzed separately and not lumped into overall categories.

One way to resolve this issue is to return to the Methods section of the original studies, write down the precise statement of the reward contingency used by the researchers, and code the studies according to the procedures actually employed in the experiment. By categorizing studies in terms of the actual contingencies used rather than by those presumed to be an effect by any theoretical perspective, practitioners can determine whether the reward procedures used in the laboratory experiments are comparable to those used in applied settings. Furthermore, a procedural categorization allows for a test of cognitive evaluation theory and also provides a test of alternative accounts of the effects of rewards on intrinsic motivation.

The literature on rewards and intrinsic motivation is fraught with competing theories (e.g., cognitive evaluation theory, the overjustification hypothesis, social cognitive theory, general interest theory, the competing response hypothesis, behavioral theory). The problem with organizing studies according to a particular theoretical stance is that each theory could be used to organize the literature and, using categories appropriate to the theory, could thus gain support. Using a theoretical approach to guide the classification of the reward procedures does not provide a definitive answer about the effects of reward contingencies on measures of intrinsic motivation. Instead, we propose that a procedural description of reward contingencies, not only allows us to assess where we stand in terms of the effects of the actual reward contingencies, but also provides us with a test of alternative accounts of the effects of rewards on intrinsic motivation.

Researchers using a single-subject design found that when rewards were delivered repeatedly and repeated assessments of performance on the task were taken without reward, detrimental effects were not evident. Deci and his colleagues did not provide an analysis of these studies. Instead, they argued that results from such studies are not generalizable because too few participants are studied in any one experiment. They further argued that in the single-subject designs, there is no group that performs the activity without reinforcement; thus, one cannot know if there is an undermining effect relative to a control group. Hence, the conclusions reached by Deci and associates concerned results from the between-group design studies only.

Finally, we should point out that although Deci and his colleagues claimed that their findings support cognitive evaluation theory, they did not provide any test of the mediators (feelings of competence and self-determination) that are thought to be critical to producing changes in people's intrinsic motivation. Instead, Deci and his associates used evidence of decreases in measures of intrinsic motivation to infer the controlling nature of rewards. However, Eisenberger, Pierce, and Cameron showed that rewards offered for doing, completing, or meeting a performance criterion often increased people's perceived freedom and independence (autonomy).[28] This evidence suggests that rewards may not be viewed by people as controlling or restrictive to their sense of freedom. At present, cognitive evaluation theorists have not provided any evidence to indicate why people show a loss of intrinsic motivation on expected tangible-reward contingencies.

**PROBLEMS WITH DECI, KOESTNER, AND RYAN'S (1999)
META-ANALYSIS OF REWARDS AND INTRINSIC
MOTIVATION**

- No primary analysis of the overall effects of rewards
- No primary analysis of the effects of rewards for both high- and
  low-interest tasks
- Omitted conditions within studies that were relevant to the
  analyses
- Excluded experiments that met the inclusion criteria and were
  published during the period covered by the meta-analysis
- Omitted studies that met the inclusion criteria and showed
  positive effects of reward
- Collapsed data across different reward procedures that could have
  different effects on measures of intrinsic motivation

In sum, Deci, Koestner, and Ryan's meta-analysis on the effects of rewards on intrinsic motivation was broader than previous meta-analyses, but there are problems that make their conclusions less than satisfactory. Specifically, the researchers (a) did not include an analysis of the overall effects of rewards across all types of tasks,[29] (b) omitted conditions within studies that were relevant to their analyses, (c) missed experiments that met their inclusion criteria and were published during the period covered by their meta-analysis, and (d) omitted several studies that met their inclusion criteria and showed positive effects of reward on task interest measures. In addition, by organizing studies according to the cognitive evaluation framework rather than the actual procedures used in the studies, Deci and his colleagues collapsed data across distinct reward procedures. This strategy resulted in a finding of pervasive negative effects of reward when, in fact, many of the studies showed that rewards increased measures of intrinsic motivation. The point is that studies using different procedures that produce different results need to be analyzed separately and should not be combined into overall categories.

SUMMARY

Over the past 30 years, a large body of research has been devoted to assessing the effects of rewards on peoples' intrinsic motivation. More than 100 experiments have been conducted using a between-groups design in which rewarded participants are compared to nonrewarded participants on various measures of intrinsic motivation. The findings have been mixed. Meta-analytic reviews of the literature suggest that negative effects occur when the rewards are tangible and expected but that different effects occur under different contingencies.

In contrast to the typical use of a single pairing of task performance with reward followed by a single session of unrewarded task performance, five studies have compared repeated task performance before and after repeated-reward presentations. The results of these single-subject designs show no negative effects of reward. These findings suggest that when repeated trials procedures are used, rewards do not result in decremental effects.

Presently, it is difficult to make many definitive statements about the variables that affect the influence of rewards on intrinsic motivation measures. In 1994, we published a meta-analysis of this literature and concluded that negative effects of reward were circumscribed and easily avoidable (Cameron and Pierce, 1994). In contrast, a more recent meta-analysis by Deci, Koestner, and Ryan (1999) shows pervasive negative effects of expected tangible-reward contingencies.

Our examination of meta-analyses on the topic shows that different conclusions reached by different reviewers are a result of conceptual and methodological shortcomings. In the next chapter, we reanalyze the data on rewards and intrinsic motivation. The purpose of our analysis is to address shortcomings in previous meta-analytic reviews while drawing on their strengths.

NOTES

1. See Hunter and Schmidt, 1990.
2. Glass, 1976.
3. For example, see Kollins, Newland, and Critchfield, 1997.
4. Rummel and Feinberg, 1988.
5. Wiersma, 1992.
6. Deci, Koestner, and Ryan, 1999, p. 635.
7. Tang and Hall, 1995.
8. See Tang and Hall, 1995, pp. 380–381, Tables 7 and 8.
9. Deci, Koestner, and Ryan, 1999, p. 632.
10. See the comments in Cameron and Pierce, 1996. Also see the comments in the "Notes" section of Appendix 8A.
11. Cameron and Pierce, 1994; Eisenberger and Cameron, 1996.
12. Cameron and Pierce, 1996; Lepper, Keavney, and Drake, 1996; Kohn, 1996; Ryan and Deci, 1996.
13. Kohn, 1996, p. 3.
14. Lepper, Keavney, and Drake, 1996, pp. 25–26.
15. Ryan and Deci, 1996, p. 34.
16. Eisenberger and Cameron, 1998; Hennessey and Amabile, 1998; Lepper, 1998; Sansone and Harackiewicz, 1998.
17. Hennessey and Amabile, 1998; Lepper, 1998; Sansone and Harackiewicz, 1998.
18. See the comments by Cameron and Pierce (1996) and Eisenberger and Cameron (1998), who responded to criticism of their research.

19. Deci, Koestner, and Ryan 1999, 2001.

20. Specifically, Deci, Koestner, and Ryan (1999) were concerned because we had included a study by Boal and Cummings (1981). This study was slightly different from other included studies. Instead of taking place in a laboratory, the study was conducted in a workplace. The participants were employees, and all were paid on the job. During the reward intervention, the experimental participants were paid extra; control participants were not. Deci et al.'s (1999) concern was that because all participants were receiving pay, there was no nonrewarded control group.

21. Deci, Koestner, and Ryan, 1999, p. 633.

22. Ibid., p. 659.

23. An additional analysis of the effects of rewards on low-interest tasks was conducted by Deci, Koestner, and Ryan (1999); no reliable effects were detected. A problem with this analysis, however, is that several studies that used low-interest tasks were excluded (e.g., Freedman and Phillips, 1985; Overskeid and Svartdal, 1996).

24. Deci, Koestner, and Ryan, 1999, p. 650.

25. For example, in an experiment by Wilson (1978), one group was offered $.50 to engage in the target activity, a second group was offered $2.50 for the same task, and a control group performed the task without the offer of reward. In Deci, Koestner, and Ryan's (1999) analyses, only one of the rewarded groups was included. For other studies that used more than one level of reward magnitude (e.g., Earn, 1982; McLoyd, 1979; Newman and Layton, 1984), Deci et al. included all reward conditions. The omission of certain conditions within studies does not appear to be systematic (for example, reward magnitude was not examined by Deci et al. as a moderator), yet there are a number of different types of cases where this occurred.

26. Cameron, Banko, and Pierce, 2001.

27. Eisenberger, Pierce, and Cameron, 1999.

28. Ibid.

29. Deci, Koestner, and Ryan (1999) did conduct a supplemental analysis of the overall effects of rewards across high- and low-interest tasks. The problem, however, is that many studies that used low-interest tasks (which were excluded from their primary analysis of high-interest tasks) were not included in their overall analysis (e.g., Freedman and Phillips, 1985; Phillips and Freedman, 1985).

Chapter 8

A Meta-analysis of the Effects of Rewards on Intrinsic Motivation

In this chapter, we present an updated meta-analysis of the experimental studies on the effects of rewards on people's intrinsic motivation.[1] The purpose of our current meta-analytic review is to (a) resolve differences between previous meta-analytic findings, (b) provide a meta-analysis of rewards and intrinsic motivation that allows for tests of competing theoretical explanations, and (c) provide educators, managers, and other practitioners with a clear understanding of what they can extrapolate from the laboratory investigations of rewards and intrinsic motivation to applied settings.

Our reanalysis is informed by a consideration of decisions and procedures used in the previous meta-analyses. In addition, the concerns raised in Chapter 7 about prior meta-analyses (including ours) are addressed. Our analysis is not guided by any particular theory; instead, we categorize studies in order to test different theoretical predictions. Based on our findings, in the next chapter we evaluate the adequacy of cognitive evaluation theory, the overjustification hypothesis, social learning theory, and behavioral explanations for the effects of rewards on intrinsic motivation.

We begin with a description of the procedures used in the current meta-analysis and then present our results. Next, we provide a review of studies assessing long-term effects of reward as well as an examination of studies that have assessed mediational processes of reward. Technical aspects of our meta-analysis and a detailed statistical description of our findings are presented in Appendix 8A, at the end of the chapter.

THE PRESENT META-ANALYSIS

The purpose of the present meta-analysis was to make a causal statement about the effects of extrinsic rewards on intrinsic motivation. This analysis was designed to address a number of concerns. Of major importance is whether the bulk of evidence suggests that extrinsic rewards produce decrements in intrinsic motivation. If so, what is the size of any relationships being uncovered? Also, do different patterns emerge with different types of tasks (high or low levels of initial task interest), different reward types (e.g., tangible or verbal rewards), reward expectancies (expected, unexpected), reward contingencies (e.g., rewards delivered for engaging in a task, completing or solving a task, or meeting a specified level of performance), and so on? In order to address these issues, our analysis focused on results from between-group design studies. Our goal was to assess how reward affects measures of free-choice intrinsic motivation[2] and self-reported task interest.

Research Questions

There are several steps to conducting a meta-analysis that were used in the current research. The first step was to specify the research questions. The following questions were addressed in the present meta-analysis:

1. Overall, what is the effect of reward on intrinsic motivation? Our analysis begins with an assessment of the overall effects of reward. Studies were included in which participants who received a reward were compared to a nonrewarded control group. The purpose of this analysis was to assess the effects of rewards across all types of tasks and over different reward types.

2. Under what conditions do rewards lead to decreased or increased intrinsic motivation? As discussed in Chapters 6 and 7, several moderator variables interact with reward to produce increments or decrements in intrinsic motivation. Specifically, our meta-analysis is designed to investigate the following:

    a. the effect of reward on intrinsic motivation when the tasks used are of either high or low initial interest.

    b. the effect of reward type on intrinsic motivation (i.e., whether rewards are verbal or tangible);

    c. the effect of reward expectancy on intrinsic motivation (i.e., whether rewards are expected—promised and delivered to participants—or unexpected—delivered to participants but not promised);

    d. the effect of reward contingency on intrinsic motivation (i.e., whether rewards are delivered for participating in an experimental session regardless of what participants do, for engaging in a task, for completing or solving a task, etc.);

    e. the effect of delivering maximum or less than maximum reward.

All analyses performed on these features were conducted with between-group design studies in which a rewarded group was compared to a nonrewarded control group. Separate analyses were conducted on the free-choice and task interest measures. These analyses were designed to lead to a greater understanding of the specific conditions under which reward affects intrinsic motivation.

Sample of Studies

Studies included in the present analysis incorporated the databases from prior meta-analyses.[3] In addition, in a search of the PsycINFO database (of the American Psychological Association), we located a few new studies and a few studies that were inadvertently missed in previous meta-analyses. The criteria for including a study in a sample were: a rewarded group was compared to a non-rewarded group, the rewards were distinguished as verbal (praise, positive feedback) or tangible (e.g., money, candy, good player awards), and intrinsic motivation was indexed as free-choice behavior (time spent on the task following the removal of reward or performance on the task during the free-choice period) or by self-reported measures of task interest (task liking, enjoyment, satisfaction or task preference).

In addition to including published work, and in keeping with Deci, Koestner and Ryan's (1999) analysis of this literature, we included unpublished doctoral dissertations.[4] The resulting sample consisted of 145 independent studies (21 of the experiments were from unpublished doctoral dissertations). A total of 115 studies included a free choice measure of intrinsic motivation and 100 studies included a self-report measure of task interest. A list of the studies included in our meta-analysis can be found in the Reference section of this book.

Classification and Coding of Studies

All studies were first coded for initial levels of task interest.[5] If a measure of initial task interest was reported in the article, the study was classified as a low-interest task if the average on that measure was below the midpoint of the scale for the activity and a high-interest task if the average was at or above the midpoint. Studies without preinterest measures were classified as high or low interest depending on how the researcher defined the task or whether the task had been described as interesting or uninteresting in prior experiments.

Studies were also classified according to reward type (tangible, verbal), expectancy (expected, unexpected), and contingency. Tangible rewards were money, tickets to a theater, candy, toys, and so on; verbal rewards involved giving participants praise or positive feedback on the experimental task. In terms of reward expectancy, expected rewards were those offered to participants prior to engaging in the activity; the rewards were delivered after they had worked on the task. Unexpected rewards were those delivered at the end of the experimental session but not offered beforehand.

Table 8.1
Description of Expected Tangible Reward Contingencies

Reward Contingency	Description
Task noncontingent	—reward is offered for agreeing to participate, for coming to the study, or for waiting for the experimenter —offer of reward is unrelated to engaging in the task
Rewards offered for doing well	—reward is offered for doing well on the task or for doing a good job —no specification is given as to what it means to do a good job or to do well
Rewards offered for doing a task	—reward is offered to participants to engage in the experimental activity —no instructions are given about how well participants must perform or whether they must complete the task
Rewards offered for finishing or completing a task	—reward is offered to finish an activity, complete a task, or get to a certain point on the task —reward is not related to quality of performance
Rewards offered for each unit solved	—reward is offered for each unit, puzzle, problem, etc., that is solved
Rewards offered for surpassing a score	—reward is offered for surpassing a particular specified score (absolute standard) —in some cases, the better the score, the higher the reward
Rewards offered for exceeding a norm	—reward is offered to meet or exceed the performance of others on the task (relative standard)

For reward contingency, rather than classify studies according to a cognitive evaluation theory framework (as was done by Deci and his colleagues) or in accord with any other theoretical framework, we categorized reward contingency in terms of the actual procedures used in the studies. This procedure allowed us to test a variety of theoretical predictions.

To classify studies by reward contingency, we went back to the original studies, read the precise procedures used for reward delivery, and recorded what was said to the participants and how the reward was delivered. We then organized the studies into seven main categories of reward contingency: rewards delivered regardless of task involvement (task noncontingent); for doing a task; for doing well; for finishing or completing a task; for each problem, puzzle, or unit solved; for achieving or surpassing a specific score; and for meeting or exceeding the performance of the others. A definition of each of the reward contingencies is presented in Table 8.1.[6]

Finally, we identified studies that involved either maximum or less than maximum reward. Such studies involved offering participants a reward for doing well, finishing a task, each problem/unit solved, surpassing a score, or exceeding a norm. As discussed in Chapter 6, studies were labeled "maximum" reward if participants in the reward condition met the performance requirements and received the full reward. "Less than maximum" reward occurred when there was a time limit such that some participants were unable to meet all the requirements in the time allotted and were given less than the full reward.

Calculation and Analysis of Effect Sizes

After all studies were coded, we calculated effect sizes for each comparison of a rewarded group to a nonrewarded group on the free-choice and self-report measures of intrinsic motivation. In the present meta-analysis, positive effect sizes indicate that the reward produced increases in intrinsic motivation, negative effect sizes support the claim that rewards undermine intrinsic motivation, and zero effects indicate no evidence for an effect of reward. A list of studies used in each of the analyses, the classification and coding of each study, and effect sizes are presented in Appendix 8B, at the end of this chapter. After all the effect sizes were calculated, statistical analyses of the effect sizes were performed using a computer program called META.[7]

Procedures Used in Our Hierarchical Analysis

We conducted a hierarchical analysis that began at the level of all rewards across all types of tasks. We then examined the effects of different moderator variables. Our first breakdown was in terms of high and low initial task interest. It is important to recognize that this is not the only way in which a hierarchical meta-analysis on this topic could proceed. As we pointed out in Chapter 7, Deci, Koestner, and Ryan's focus on high interest tasks is based on their theoretical position—cognitive evaluation theory.[8] However, the field is not unified theoretically. Thus, one can imagine that researchers from other theoretical positions would begin a different moderator analysis. For example, a researcher with an overjustification viewpoint might select for reward salience and subdivide studies into those with high and low reward salience. A social-cognitive investigator might focus solely on the effects of rewards on low interest tasks because rewards can be used to cultivate task interest and to build competence and self-efficacy. A behavioral researcher, on the other hand, might wish to break studies into those in which the rewards are shown to function as reinforcement and those in which they are not. The point is that if there were enough studies in each of these categories, the choice of which moderator to emphasize would vary depending on one's theoretical stance.

Because Deci and his colleagues focused their analysis on the effects of rewards on high-interest tasks, we chose high and low initial task interest as our first breakdown. Subdividing the studies by high and low initial task interest allowed us to directly compare our findings with those of Deci and his associates. In doing so, we favor cognitive evaluation theory. On the other hand, failure to find pervasive negative effects even with high-interest tasks favors the conclusion that reward contingencies do not destroy interest. In other words, the strongest way to test Deci, Koestner, and Ryan's claims was to use their requirement that tasks used in the studies must be broken out by high or low initial interest.

Few studies used tasks of low initial interest, and thus, no further breakdown of these studies was carried out. On tasks of high initial interest, however, studies were subdivided by reward type (verbal, tangible); tangible rewards were further broken down by reward expectancy (expected, unexpected), and the effects of expected tangible rewards were assessed by the reward contingency. At the final level of analysis, studies were analyzed that used maximum versus less than maximum reward.

RESULTS

Overall Effects of Reward

Our first set of analyses concerned the overall effects of reward on free-choice intrinsic motivation and self-reported task interest. Free-choice intrinsic motivation was measured as time spent on the task after the reward was withdrawn or performance on the task during the free-choice period. Task interest was assessed by questionnaire measures of participants' task interest, enjoyment, or satisfaction. These analyses included studies with both high- and low-interest tasks as well as studies that used verbal or tangible rewards. That is, all studies were included in these analyses.

On the free-choice measure of intrinsic motivation, the statistical test showed that there was no significant effect of reward. In terms of self-reported task interest, the meta-analysis revealed a small but significant positive finding. That is, overall, individuals reported greater task interest when they received a reward. These findings suggest that the evidence does not support the claim that rewards have general detrimental effects. The results indicate that when rewards are collapsed across different task and reward types, overall, rewards do not significantly undermine intrinsic motivation as measured by free-choice and self-report measures.[9]

Effects of Reward on Low- and High-Interest Tasks

Although the analysis shows that rewards do not have generalized negative effects, several researchers have suggested that level of initial task interest is of prime importance. The claim from cognitive evaluation theory is that if people enjoy, and are highly interested in, an activity, the introduction of reward will destroy their intrinsic interest. Cognitive evaluation theory has little to say about the effects of rewards on low-interest tasks. On the other hand, from the perspective of social learning theory, rewards can be used to enhance interest and performance on tasks in which people are not initially interested. Thus, our next analysis concerns the effects of rewards on low-interest versus high-interest tasks.

For the analysis of the effects of reward on low-interest tasks, 12 studies used a free-choice measure of intrinsic motivation and 11 studies measured task interest. The meta-analysis revealed a statistically significant positive effect on the free-choice measure; there was no reliable effect on self-reported task interest.[10] These findings indicate that when a task is not initially interesting, rewards enhance time and performance on the task but do not enhance verbal expressions of task interest.

The bulk of studies used tasks that were of high interest to participants. A total of 114 studies used high-interest tasks and measured the effects of reward on free-choice intrinsic motivation, whereas 98 studies used self-report measures. For high-interest tasks, on free choice, the meta-analysis showed a small but significant negative effect. The mean effect size (average) for self-reported task interest was significant; it was small, but in a positive direction. Thus, for high-interest tasks, rewards were found to undermine free-choice intrinsic motivation but rewarded participants reported greater task interest.

Breakdown of Reward Effects on High-Interest Tasks

Given the large number of studies that used high-interest tasks, it was possible to examine aspects of the reward procedures that could lead to increments or decrements in intrinsic motivation. Specifically, the concern was when, and under what conditions, reward procedures produce positive or negative effects on free-choice intrinsic motivation and self-reported task interest.

Effects of Reward Type

One possibility is that different types of rewards may have different effects. To assess this possibility, studies that used either verbal or tangible rewards were evaluated. Verbal rewards included praise or positive feedback; tangible rewards were money, toys, gold stars, and so on.

One way to visually compare the results of many studies involves the use of funnel diagrams. Funnel graphs are used to plot effect size (x axis) against sample size (y axis) for each study. The advantage of a funnel display is that it capitalizes on a well-known statistical principle: the larger the sample, the closer the effect size will come to represent the true underlying effect size. Smaller samples are more prone to sampling error and are likely to deviate considerably from the true mean effect size. For these reasons, the distribution is expected to take the shape of an inverted funnel; the tip of the funnel will hone in around the true effect size.

Figure 8.1 presents the pattern of effect sizes on high-interest tasks for verbal and tangible reward on free-choice intrinsic motivation.[11] Each data point rep-

Figure 8.1
Funnel Distribution of Effect Sizes on High-Interest Tasks for Verbal and Tangible Rewards on Free-Choice Intrinsic Motivation

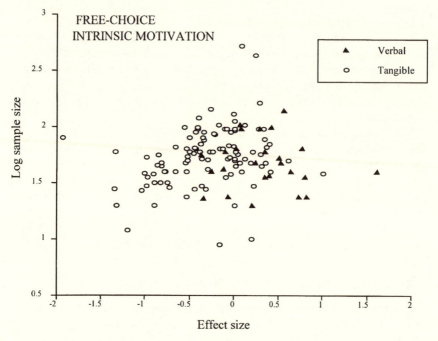

rooontr the effect size from an individual study. Studies falling to the left of zero are consistent with the view that reward decreases intrinsic motivation. Those on the right of zero indicate increases in the measure of intrinsic motivation.

Considering the results of verbal and tangible reward separately, visual inspection of the graph suggests some tendency for tangible rewards (open circles) to reduce free-choice intrinsic motivation. Verbal rewards (closed triangles) appear to have produced a positive effect. In other words, verbal rewards (praise and positive feedback) increased free-choice performance while tangible rewards reduced free-choice intrinsic motivation. Meta-analyses showed that these effects were statistically significant.

On the task-interest measure, an inspection of the funnel graph presented in Figure 8.2 indicates that positive effects emerge from verbal reward studies, whereas tangible rewards hone in around zero. The meta-analytic results showed a positive effect for both verbal and tangible rewards; however, the mean effect for tangible rewards was very small. These differences suggest that the effects of reward depend on the type of reward.

Figure 8.2
Funnel Distribution of Effect Sizes on High-Interest Tasks for Verbal and
Tangible Rewards on Self-Reported Task Interest

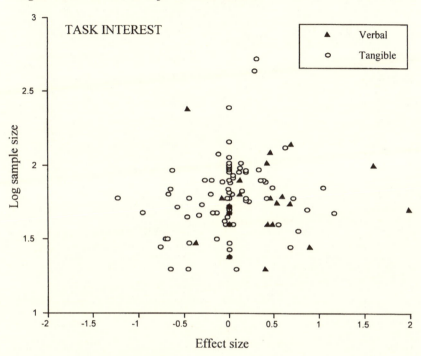

Effects of Reward Expectancy

In experiments involving the use of tangible rewards, the procedures for administering and delivering such rewards varied.[12] One procedure was whether the rewards were expected (promised before participants engaged in the experimental activity) or unexpected (delivered but not promised beforehand). Thus, the next breakdown in our analysis involved assessing the effects of different reward expectancies.

Tangible rewards were subdivided into unexpected and expected categories. No significant effects were detected for unexpected tangible rewards on either measure of intrinsic motivation. That is, if participants were given a tangible reward but not offered it prior to engaging in the experimental activity, intrinsic motivation was not altered. Expected tangible rewards produced a significant negative effect on the free-choice measure and a reliable positive effect on the self-report measure.

Effects of Reward Contingency

At the next level of analysis, expected tangible rewards were subdivided into various reward contingencies. The studies were classified into seven categories

Table 8.2

High-Interest Tasks: The Effects of Tangible Expected Reward Contingencies

FREE-CHOICE INTRINSIC MOTIVATION

Expected Reward Condition	Number of Studies	Mean Effect Size	Change in Intrinsic Motivation
Task noncontingent	7	-0.10 (n.s.)	No change
For doing well	11	-0.31*	Decrease
For doing task	50	-0.30*	Decrease
For finishing task	6	-0.24 (n.s.)	No change
For each unit solved	20	-0.16*	Decrease
For surpassing a score	11	0.02 (n.s.)	No change
For exceeding others	11	0.18	Increase

SELF-REPORTED TASK INTEREST

Expected Reward Condition	Number of Studies	Mean Effect Size	Change in Intrinsic Motivation
Task noncontingent	6	0.17 (n.s.)	No change
For doing well	6	0.04 (n.s.)	No change
For doing task	38	-0.13*	Decrease
For finishing task	6	0.32*	Increase
For each unit solved	20	0.15*	Increase
For surpassing a score	11	0.24*	Increase
For exceeding others	14	0,14*	Increase

Note: * = significant at $p < .05$, n.s. = not significant. Positive effect sizes indicate higher intrinsic
motivation for rewarded groups compared to non-rewarded groups. Negative effect sizes indicate lower intrinsic motivation for rewarded groups

of reward contingency: rewards delivered regardless of task involvement (task
noncontingent); for doing a task; for doing well; for finishing or completing a
task; for each problem, puzzle, or unit solved; for achieving or surpassing a
specific score; and for meeting or exceeding others.

The results of our analyses are presented in Table 8.2., which presents the
number of studies included in each analysis, the mean effect size for each reward
contingency, and an indication of whether or not the effect size was statistically
significant. An effect of around ±.20 is considered small, ±.50 is moderate,
and greater than ±.80 is large.[13]

On free-choice intrinsic motivation, no reliable effects were detected when the rewards were task noncontingent, offered for finishing or completing a task, or offered for attaining or surpassing a score. Table 8.2 shows significant negative effects on free choice when the rewards were offered for doing a task, for doing well on a task, or for each unit solved. A significant positive effect was found when the rewards were offered for meeting or exceeding the performance level of others.

For task interest, the analysis presented in Table 8.2 shows no reliable effect for task-noncontingent reward, a small but significant negative effect for rewards offered for doing, and significant positive effects for each of the other reward contingencies.

These findings indicate that when the reward contingency is defined in terms of the actual procedures used in the experiments, negative, neutral, and positive effects are obtained.

Effects of Maximum versus Less Than Maximum Reward

At the final level of analysis, we examined the effects of maximum versus less than maximum reward. Maximum reward refers to a procedure whereby all participants in the reward condition met the performance requirements of the study and received the full amount of reward. Less than maximum reward occurred when some participants were not able to fulfill the performance requirement and were given less than the full reward.

There was only one reward contingency—rewards offered per unit solved—that allowed for a comparison between maximum and less than maximum reward.[14] For other reward contingencies, too few studies involved less than maximum reward, and so a meta-analysis was not feasible. When rewards were offered for each unit solved, the findings on free-choice intrinsic motivation showed a nonsignificant effect in studies of maximum rewards and a significant negative effect in studies of less than maximum reward. These results suggest that the negative effect of reward per unit is associated with participants receiving less than maximum rewards.

SUMMARY OF OUR META-ANALYTIC FINDINGS

A summary of our meta-analytic findings is presented in Figure 8.3. The analyses are arranged hierarchically, with the more general procedural categories closer to the top of the diagram. First we present the overall effects of reward; studies are then broken down into subsets of different moderator variables. A positive effect (+) indicates that rewards enhanced the measure of intrinsic motivation relative to a control condition, a negative effect (−) indicates a decrease for the rewarded group, and a zero effect (0) indicates no reliable effect.

On the free-choice intrinsic motivation measure, in terms of the overall effects of reward, our meta-analysis indicates no evidence for a detrimental effect of reward. This finding is important because many researchers and writers espouse the view that rewards, in general, reduce motivation and performance. In addi-

Figure 8.3
**A Summary of the Meta-analysis Comparing Free-Choice Intrinsic Motivation
and Self-Reported Task Interest**

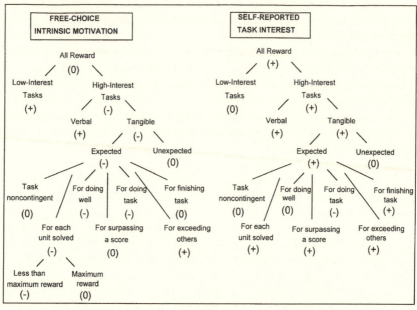

Note: (0) indicates no reliable effect; (−) indicates a statistically significant negative effect of
reward; (+) indicates a statistically significant positive effect of reward.

tion, many students of psychology and education are taught that rewards are
harmful and that reward procedures should be avoided in applied settings. Our
findings indicate that there is no inherent negative property of reward; instead,
our research demonstrates that rewards have either positive, neutral, or negative
effects, depending on how they are administered.

In Figure 8.3, the effects of all rewards are first broken into high- and low-
interest tasks. The findings concerning free-choice intrinsic motivation are interesting. When the tasks used in the studies are of low initial interest, rewards
increase free-choice intrinsic motivation. This finding indicates that rewards can
be used to enhance time and performance on tasks that initially hold little enjoyment. This result suggests that reward procedures are one way to cultivate
interest in an activity. In education, a major goal is to instill motivation and
enjoyment of academic activities. Many academic activities are not of high initial interest to students. An implication of our finding is that rewards can be
used to increase motivation and performance on low-interest academic activities.

On high-interest tasks, rewards produce a decrease in free-choice intrinsic
motivation. At first glance, this seems to provide support for popular assertions
about detrimental effects of reward. But as we proceed from the general clas-

sification of all rewards under high interest tasks to more specific classifications, we see that negative effects are conditional and specialized.

Verbal rewards are found to increase free choice. This finding replicates the results of previous meta-analyses. Most social interaction in business, education, and clinical settings involves the use of verbal praise and positive feedback from managers, teachers, and therapists. When praise and other forms of positive feedback are given and later removed, our finding indicates that people continue to engage in the activity and perform at a high level.

The effects of tangible reward on free-choice intrinsic motivation differ by reward expectancy. Expected rewards are those promised to participants before the experimental session. Unexpected rewards are delivered during or following the session but not promised beforehand. Tangible rewards alone have been so divided because in most studies the presentation of verbal reward was unexpected. At this level of analysis, the detrimental effects of reward on the free-choice measure are restricted to the influence of expected tangible reward. When rewards are delivered unexpectedly (without a description of the reward contingency), there is no evidence of a reliable effect. This suggests that it is not tangible rewards, per se, that undermine motivation; instead, the particular effect depends on instruction and the statement of contingency.

At the next level of analysis, in Figure 8.3, expected tangible rewards are categorized according to the description of the reward contingency. When the offer of reward is unrelated to task behavior (task noncontingent), there is no evidence for an effect of reward on the free-choice measure. On the other hand, when people are offered a tangible reward for doing a task or for doing it well, they choose to do the activity less in a free choice period. Generally, when the description of the reward contingency implies that rewards are loosely tied to performance, the evidence suggests that people show a small reduction in performance and interest.

Figure 8.3 shows that rewards offered for finishing or completing a task have a statistically nonsignificant effect on free choice. Because there were few studies in this category, drawing a firm conclusion about the effect is premature. A stronger conclusion can be drawn for the analysis of rewards offered for each unit solved. When participants are offered a reward for each problem, puzzle, or unit solved, our findings indicate a negative effect on free choice. At the final level of analysis, involving less than maximum reward and maximum reward, the results show that the negative effect on free choice occurs when participants obtain less than the full reward. In studies of less than maximum reward, participants are given a time limit to solve problems. Thus, the negative effect may be a result of time pressure rather than reward. Another way to understand this result is to consider what less than maximal reward signifies to participants. If people are told that they can obtain a certain level of reward but are given less than that level, they have received feedback information that indicates failure. In other words, this type of situation may represent failure feedback rather than reward. When participants are not under time pressure and are able to obtain the maximal reward, there is no reliable effect on the free-choice measure.

When rewards are offered for meeting or surpassing a score, we found no reliable effect on free choice (see Figure 8.3). However, when rewards are given for exceeding the performance level of others, the results show a significant positive effect on free choice.

The data concerning self-reported task interest provide little evidence for decremental effects of any type of reward. On high interest tasks, both verbal and tangible rewards had an overall positive effect. For tangible rewards, as we proceeded to subsequent levels of analysis, we determined that unexpected rewards did not alter task interest and expected rewards (a) had no effect when they were noncontingent or offered for doing well on a task, (b) produced a negative effect when they were offered for doing the task, and (c) led to increased expressed task interest when they were offered for finishing a task, for each unit solved, for surpassing a score, or for exceeding others.

Thus, on task interest, the only negative effect occurred when the rewards were tangible, expected, and given simply for engaging in an activity, without regard to any performance standards. No negative effect was detected when the rewards were offered for doing well. We should point out, however, that there were only six studies in the "doing well" category (see Table 8.2). Thus, it is possible that the true effect for this reward contingency may also be negative, but at this point in time, there are too few studies to yield a reliable estimate.

Overall, our meta-analysis showed that rewards can be used to produce both negative and positive effects on measures of intrinsic motivation. Rewards can be used to increase motivation and performance on tasks that are of low initial interest. On high-interest tasks, positive effects are obtained when participants are verbally praised for their work and when tangible rewards are offered and explicitly tied to performance standards and to success. Negative effects are produced when rewards signify failure or are only loosely tied to behavior.

DURABILITY OF REWARD EFFECTS ON INTRINSIC MOTIVATION

Deci and his colleagues claimed that negative effects of rewards are not temporary.[15] In a supplemental analysis, Deci and his research team examined studies of children in which the free-choice assessment was conducted both within one week following the removal of reward and after one week. Their analysis showed negative effects on free choice for each time of assessment. The researchers concluded that their results "indicate quite clearly that the phenomenon of extrinsic rewards undermining intrinsic motivation is not merely transitory."[16]

An examination of the studies included in Deci and his colleagues' supplementary analysis indicates that almost all the studies involved rewards offered for doing the task or for doing well. When the free-choice assessment was conducted within a week following the removal of reward, 10 of 12 studies involved rewards offered for doing well or for doing the task. Of 14 studies with assessments conducted more than a week later, 13 were concerned with rewards offered for doing well. Given this, our interpretation of Deci and his colleagues' findings is that it is tangible rewards that are offered for doing a task or for doing well on a task that continue to produce a negative effect on free-choice intrinsic motivation (even when the assessment of the free-choice measure is taken a week or more than a week later). There is no evidence to suggest that other reward contingencies (rewards offered for success, for meeting or surpassing a performance standard, or for exceeding others) produce negative effects over time.

An unresolved issue, however, is whether there is a change in free-choice intrinsic motivation over time. In most of the studies included in Deci and his research team's analysis of the durability of reward effects, the free-choice assessment was only measured at one time. That is, the free-choice assessment was done immediately following the experimental intervention, a week later, or more than a week later, but only at one of these times. We examined seven studies of rewards offered for doing the task that assessed whether negative effects were maintained over time.[17] These studies included two measures of free-choice intrinsic motivation, one after the removal of reward and a second measure done a few weeks later. Only two of the seven studies showed a significant negative effect on the second measure.[18] These results suggest that rewards offered for doing a task have transitory effects when multiple measures of free-choice motivation are used, but the small number of studies makes it difficult to draw a strong conclusion.

This conclusion is strengthened, however, by examining the results from studies using repeated presentations of reward followed by repeated assessments of intrinsic motivation measures following reward removal. As discussed in Chapter 6, some researchers tested the effects of rewards on intrinsic motivation by experimental designs in which the same individual was exposed to a baseline period, a reward intervention, and a return to baseline.[19] Participants were measured repeatedly during each phase of the experiment, and rewards were shown to increase measures of performance, indicating that the rewards functioned as reinforcement. The results of these experiments showed that participants spent as much (or more) time on the target activity in the postreward phase as they did in the initial, baseline period. These findings indicate that negative effects of reward do not persist when task performance is rewarded on repeated occasions.

Taken together, the results from group-design studies that provided more than one assessment of free-choice intrinsic motivation and the results from single-subject designs in which participants were rewarded over a period of time and repeated assessments of intrinsic motivation were taken suggest that the negative effects of rewards are, in fact, a transitory phenomenon.

ASSESSMENT OF MEDIATIONAL PROCESSES

In Chapters 4 and 5, we described a number of theories that make predictions and attempt to account for the effects of rewards on intrinsic motivation. Most tests of theoretical claims (e.g., cognitive evaluation theory, the overjustification hypothesis) consider the influence of reward on behavioral measures of intrinsic motivation (free choice) and attitudes toward the task (self-reported task interest) without attempting to directly assess presumed underlying psychological processes. However, a few studies have considered whether reward-produced changes of intrinsic motivation are mediated by changes in perceived self-determination or a change in the perceived locus of causality. In this section, we examine studies that have directly assessed proposed mediational processes.

Cognitive evaluation theory holds that verbal praise presented in a nonthreatening informational manner should enhance perceptions of competence without affecting perceived self-determination. Six studies have evaluated the effects of verbal praise on perceived competence. Perceived competence was indexed by participants' reports of (a) how competent they felt following their performance,[20] (b) whether feelings of competence influenced how hard they worked on the task,[21] and (c) how well participants thought they performed relative to others.[22] In all six experiments, verbal reward was found to increase feelings of competence relative to control participants who did not receive reward. However, the three studies that used causal modeling to assess the relationships among praise, competence, and intrinsic motivation produced mixed results. One study reported mediating effects of competence[23] whereas two studies did not find competence to have a reliable mediating effect.[24] Although additional replications are needed because of the mixed results, the findings suggest that verbal praise may increase feelings of competence but give little support to the view that intrinsic interest is mediated by enhanced perceptions of competence.

For contingent, tangible, expected rewards, cognitive evaluation theory invokes a loss of perceived self-determination as the underlying mechanism that leads to decreases in intrinsic motivation. In a 1999 article, Eisenberger, Pierce, and Cameron identified five studies that measured the effects of expected tangible rewards on perceived self-determination.[25] All five studies showed positive effects of reward on self-determination.[26] Contrary to the predictions of cognitive evaluation theory, the results indicated that rewards increased perceived autonomy. A meta-analysis of the results produced a statistically significant positive effect ($d+ = 0.37$).

The overjustification hypothesis also predicts negative effects of expected, tangible, contingent rewards on measures of intrinsic motivation. According to overjustification theory, tangible rewards lead people to view the reward, rather than their own interest, as the locus of causality for an activity. In two studies using expected tangible rewards, participants were asked to indicate whether they attributed their performance to intrinsic factors (e.g., ability and personal effort) or to extrinsic factors such as the reward. Contrary to the overjustification hypothesis, one of the experiments reported an increased attribution of perfor-mance to intrinsic factors;[27] the other experiment reported no reliable effect.[28]

Overall, and consistent with cognitive evaluation theory, all six studies of ver-bal reward reported increased perceptions of competence. However, two of three studies employing causal modeling failed to find a mediating effect of compe-tence. It is important to conduct additional causal modeling studies with verbal re-ward to provide more complete evidence on the mediating influence of competence. Of the five studies for which cognitive evaluation theory predicts a decremental effect on self-determination, all reported an incremental effect. These results do not support the assumption of cognitive evaluation theory that tangible, expected, contingent rewards reduce people's self-determination. In terms of evi-dence about mediational processes proposed by the overjustification hypothesis, at present, the evidence is too limited to draw definitive conclusions.

CONCLUDING REMARKS

Overall, the meta-analysis presented in this chapter shows that rewards can be used to produce either negative, neutral, or positive effects on measures of intrinsic motivation. Rewards can be used to increase motivation and perfor-mance on tasks that are of low initial interest. On high-interest tasks, positive effects are obtained when participants are verbally praised for their work and when tangible rewards are offered and explicitly tied to performance standards and to success.

Although several writers have argued that the negative effects of reward are pervasive and long-lasting, the results of our meta-analysis indicate that any detrimental effects of reward are limited. Specifically, negative effects are pro-duced on high-interest tasks when tangible rewards signify failure or are loosely tied to behavior. This effect does not appear to be long-lasting; in fact, when rewards are delivered repeatedly and intrinsic motivation is assessed on more than one occasion, the evidence suggests that the negative effects are fleeting and transitory.

In terms of mediational processes, we evaluated studies that examined the effects of mediators proposed by cognitive evaluation theory and the over-justification hypothesis to underlie changes in intrinsic motivation. At present, the best evidence is that rewards are not viewed by people as controlling or restrictive to their sense of freedom.

NOTES

1. This analysis is based on the work of Cameron, Banko, and Pierce, 2001.

2. In accord with the meta-analysis by Deci, Koestner, and Ryan (1999), our free-choice measure includes free time on task when the rewards were removed and, when time measures were not available, performance during the free-choice period. As did Deci et al., we combined performance and time measures to make up the free-choice

intrinsic motivation index (we found no significant differences in the analyses when only time measures were analyzed).

3. The databases of Cameron and Pierce (1994) and Deci, Koestner, and Ryan (1999) were included in the present meta-analysis.

4. The same dissertations included by Deci, Koestner, and Ryan (1999) were included in the present meta-analysis, and one additional dissertation (Adorney, 1983) was added.

5. To code for initial levels of task interest, we used the same procedures as Deci, Koestner, and Ryan, 1999.

6. Although all types of rewards were classified in terms of contingency, it was at the level of tangible expected reward that it became necessary to analyze studies in terms of the various reward contingencies.

7. The META program was developed by Schwarzer (1991); the meta-analytic method used in this analysis is based on the weighted integration method described in Hedges and Olkin (1985).

8. Deci, Koestner, and Ryan, 1999.

9. This analysis was not conducted by Deci, Koestner, and Ryan (1999). The results, however, are in accord with Cameron and Pierce (1994).

10. There were too few studies that used low-interest tasks to conduct meta-analyses of the separate effects of reward type, reward expectancy, and reward contingency. However we did examine whether there were any differences as a result of these moderators. On the free-choice measure, only one study included a condition that used a verbal reward (the effect was positive). For tangible reward, only one study included an unexpected reward condition (the effect was positive). All 12 studies with low-interest tasks included an expected tangible reward condition; compared with a nonreward control, the mean effect was significantly positive. Nine studies involved offering the tangible reward for doing the task; on the free-choice measure, the effect remained significantly positive. For self-reported task interest, no reliable effects were found under any of the conditions.

11. Because the sample sizes in the original studies ranged from as few as 10 participants to as many as 500, in Figures 9.1 and 9.2, sample size is represented in common logs. Log 1 indicates a sample size of 10, 2 indicates 100, and 3 indicates 1,000.

12. In most studies of verbal reward, the rewards were unexpected and the mean effect was positive; a positive effect was also found in the five studies that used expected rewards. In addition, verbal rewards were generally delivered simply for doing a task and were not contingent on any specific level of performance (again, the effects were positive).

13. Cohen, 1988.

14. Other contingencies that used maximum or less than maximum reward involved tangible rewards offered for doing well, for meeting or surpassing a specific standard, and for exceeding others. In each of these categories, the majority of studies used maximum reward. Thus, an analysis of maximum versus less than maximum reward could not be conducted in these categories.

15. Deci, Koestner, and Ryan 1999, 2001.

16. Ibid., p. 650.

17. Chung, 1995; Loveland and Olley, 1979; Morgan, 1983, Experiments 1 and 2; Ogilvie and Prior, 1982; Ross, 1975, Experiment 1; Shiffman-Kauffman, 1990.

18. Morgan, 1983, Experiments 1 and 2.

19. Davidson and Bucher, 1978; Feingold and Mahoney, 1975; Mawhinney, Dick-

inson, and Taylor, 1989; Skaggs, Dickinson, and O'Connor, 1992; Vasta, Andrews, McLanghlin, Stirpe, and Comfort, 1978.

20. Vallerand, 1983; Vallerand and Reid, 1984.

21. Shanab, Peterson, Dargahi, and Deroian, 1981.

22. Sansone, 1989; Sansone, Sachau, and Weir, 1989.

23. Vallerand and Reid, 1984.

24. Sansone, 1989; Sansone, Sachau, and Weir, 1989.

25. Eisenberger, Pierce, and Cameron, 1999.

26. Eisenberger, Rhoades, and Cameron, 1999, Experiment 1; Freedman and Phillips, 1985; Overskeid and Svartdal, 1996, Experiments 1 and 2; Shiffman-Kauffman, 1990.

27. Wimperis and Farr, 1979.

28. Arnold, 1985.

Appendix 8A: Technical Aspects of Our Meta-Analysis and Statistical Findings

In this section we provide a detailed description of the meta-analytic procedures we used to assess the effects of rewards on intrinsic motivation. In addition, we present statistical analyses of our results. Many of the issues discussed in this section are highly technical but nonetheless fundamental to an understanding of a meta-analysis of this literature.

OUR META-ANALYTIC PROCEDURES

Meta-analysis involves several steps, the first of which is to specify the research questions. Our meta-analysis was designed to address the following questions:

- Do rewards generally lead to a decrease in intrinsic motivation?
- Under what conditions do rewards lead to either decreased or increased intrinsic motivation?

Other steps in the meta-analysis involved specifying the criteria for including and excluding studies, collecting all experiments that met the criteria, reading and coding the studies, calculating effect sizes for each study, and performing statistical analyses of effect sizes.

Selection of Studies

Our meta-analysis included studies that were used in previous meta-analyses on the topic.[1] As well, a few other relevant studies were located through a search of PsycINFO. In addition, we included unpublished doctoral dissertations. The meta-analysis started with Deci's 1971 experiment[2] and includes research published before 1999.

The analysis entailed assessing the effects of reward from studies that used between-group designs. Criteria for including studies in the sample were that: (a) the study included an experimental manipulation of a reward condition and a nonrewarded control group, (b) any characteristic of rewarded participants was either held constant or varied and was represented identically for both rewarded and control groups,[3] (c) studies were written in English, and (d) studies assessed the effects of reward versus no reward on the two main measures of intrinsic motivation (free choice and self-reported task interest).

Intrinsic motivation has been measured in a variety of ways. Researchers have examined the effects of reward on measures such as quantity and quality of performance during a rewarded phase, participants' willingness to volunteer for future research, time spent on an experimental task in a free-choice period after reward is removed, performance during the free-choice period, and questionnaire measures of task interest. In Chapter 7, we described how researchers have found different effects of rewards depending on how intrinsic motivation is indexed.[4] Deci and his colleagues argued that a measure taken during a reward phase is not a pure measure of intrinsic motivation because it reflects both extrinsic and intrinsic motives.[5] Instead, they claimed that the best measures of intrinsic motivation are free-choice intrinsic motivation (time spent on the task following the removal of reward or performance on the task during the free-choice period) and self-reports of task interest (task liking, enjoyment, satisfaction, or task preference). Thus, for the present meta-analysis, studies were selected that used either the free-choice or self-report measures of intrinsic motivation.[6]

One criticism of the meta-analytic technique is that researchers often lump together different measures.[7] This has been referred to as the "apples and oranges problem," in that it is argued that logical conclusions cannot be drawn from comparisons of studies using different measures of the same construct (intrinsic motivation).[8] To avoid this problem, we conducted separate analyses for the effects of reward on free-choice intrinsic motivation and self-reported task interest. The overall sample consisted of 145 studies, of which 115 studies assessed the effects of reward on free-choice measures of intrinsic motivation and 100 included questionnaire measures of task interest.

Coding of Studies

Once all relevant studies had been collected, each study was read and coded. The following aspects of the studies were coded: (a) task type (high or low interest), (b) reward type (verbal or tangible), (c) reward expectancy (expected or unexpected), (d) reward contingency, and (e) whether participants received maximum or less than maximum reward.

The classification of studies by reward contingency has been somewhat controversial. In the most recent meta-analysis of this literature, Deci and associates (Deci, Koestner, and Ryan, 1999) used cognitive evaluation theory to guide their classification of reward contingencies. However, their categories were too broad. The problem is that studies using different procedures and producing different findings were pooled together, with the result that the effects were obscured when the results were aggregated. Our solution to this problem was to return to the original studies and code the contingency in terms of the actual procedures used. Using a procedural definition of reward contingencies, we identified seven different types of contingencies (task-noncontingent rewards—given regardless of task involvement—and rewards given for doing the task, doing well, finishing or completing a task, each problem or unit solved, achieving or surpassing a specific score, and meeting or exceeding the performance of others). A definition of each of these contingencies is provided in Chapter 8 in Table 8.1.

In some studies, there was not enough information to code specific characteristics of reward.[9] In addition, a couple of studies used a contingency that did not fit into any of the seven categories described here.[10] These studies were included in overall analyses of reward but were omitted from analyses designed to assess the effects of specific reward conditions. Descriptive characteristics and effect sizes of the reviewed studies are summarized in Appendix 8B.

Intercoder Reliability

To ensure reliability of coding, an independent coder was given the definitions for each contingency (Table 8.1) and a sample of 32 studies to code (each of the studies involved expected tangible rewards).[11] Reliability, calculated as percentage agreement, was 97 percent (31 of 32 studies). One study included a condition in which participants were offered a reward to take pictures.[12] The issue was whether this contingency involved reward simply for doing the task or for finishing the task. The second author was brought in to code the study; he pointed out that participants in the reward condition were not required to complete or finish the task in order to obtain the reward and that the author of the study stated that "the reward did not imply that the subject had done well on the task, only that s/he had engaged in it."[13] Hence, the reward contingency was classified as "reward offered for doing the task."

Computation and Analysis of Effect Sizes

The present meta-analysis was conducted by employing a hierarchical breakdown of the effects of rewards on intrinsic motivation. The procedures described here are based on the weighted integration method.[14]

Once all relevant studies had been identified, the statistical result of each study was transformed into an effect size by converting the findings from each study into a standard deviation unit. In the rewards and intrinsic motivation literature, the effect size from each study indicates the extent to which the experimental group (rewarded group) and the control group (nonrewarded group) differed in the mean scores on measures of intrinsic motivation (e.g., free-choice task interest). In its simplest form, the effect size (g) is the difference between the means of the rewarded group and the means of the nonrewarded control group divided by the pooled standard deviation of this difference.

For each study, we calculated effect sizes (g) for each comparison of a rewarded group to a nonrewarded group on free-choice and self-report measures of intrinsic motivation. Positive effect sizes indicate that rewards produced an increase in measures of intrinsic motivation relative to a control group, negative effect sizes denote a decrease, and an effect size of 0.00 indicates no difference.

One problem in meta-analysis arises when studies fail to provide enough information to calculate effect sizes. When means and standard deviations are not available, effect sizes can be calculated from t tests, F statistics, and p-level values.[15] However, in some cases, there may still be insufficient information to obtain an effect size. The meta-analyst can write to the researchers and try to obtain the missing data. When the data cannot be procured, the study can be excluded from the analyses or assigned an effect size of 0 (indicating no difference between the experimental and control groups).

It has been argued that including zero effect sizes is a conservative strategy; if a significant effect is detected in spite of the inclusion of zeros, the contention is that the results would not alter if missing data were available.[16] On the other hand, if one's bias is toward no effect (that is, we are satisfied if the treatment is not harmful), including zeros favors this conclusion. One strategy for dealing with this issue is to conduct the analyses with zeros included and excluded.[17]

When there was not enough information to calculate an effect size from a study, we attempted to contact the researchers. From a list of 22 researchers, we were able to locate e-mail addresses for 9. E-mail messages were sent requesting the missing data. Although 8 people replied, 6 could not locate the data and so only 2 provided us with data.[18] When we could not obtain missing data, we imputed an effect size of 0. Each analysis was conducted with zeros both included and excluded. We report the analyses with the zeros included. However, when mean effect sizes were altered to any extent by the inclusion of zeros, we report the analysis with and without zeros.

After effects sizes (g) were calculated for each relevant study, an overall mean effect size ($d+$) was obtained. First, gs were converted to ds by correcting them for bias (g is an overestimation of the population effect size, particularly for small samples).[19] The overall mean effect size is obtained by weighting each effect size by the reciprocal of its variance and averaging the weighted ds. This procedure gives more weight to effect sizes that are more reliably estimated. The calculation of mean effect sizes provides a significance test (whether the value differs significantly from 0) and a 95 percent confidence interval (when the confidence interval contains 0, the results suggest that there is no evidence of a statistically reliable effect).

Procedures in a Hierarchical Meta-analysis

In the present hierarchical meta-analysis, all studies were included in an overall analysis. We then searched for moderator variables. The studies were broken out by one key moderator, then another, and so on. The moderators that we chose to examine were based on theoretical considerations (e.g., levels of initial task interest, reward type, reward expectancy, and reward contingency).

Some meta-analysts recommend using homogeneity tests to ascertain whether a moderator analysis is necessary.[20] A homogeneity statistic is used to determine whether a set of effect sizes in a sample shares a common effect size (i.e., is consistent across studies). Essentially, the procedure is to use a chi-square statistic, Q, with $k - 1$ degrees of freedom, where k is the number of effect sizes.

The null hypothesis is that the effect sizes are homogeneous (i.e., effect sizes in a given analysis are viewed as values sampled from a single population; variation in effect sizes among studies is merely due to sampling variation). When Q is statistically significant, the implication is that moderator analyses should be conducted. The original set of studies is then broken into subsets until the chi-square statistics within the subgroups are nonsignificant.

At each level of our analysis, a homogeneity statistic (Q) was calculated to determine whether the set of effect sizes could be considered homogeneous. When Q was significant, we proceeded with further moderator analyses. In a few cases, homogeneity could not be obtained even after a thorough examination of potential moderators. In these cases, we conducted the analysis by removing outliers, as was done in previous meta-analyses.[21] Outliers were examined in an attempt to explain their extreme values. At each level of our analysis, we report mean effect sizes and 95 percent confidence-level intervals. However, we should point out that making conclusions based on heterogeneous samples may be misleading. In a hierarchical breakdown, interpretations should focus on the homogeneous effects at the bottom level of the analysis.[22]

For several studies in our analyses, more than one effect size was calculated. For example, if a single study assessed free choice and used two types of expected tangible rewards (e.g., rewards offered for doing the task and rewards offered for surpassing a certain score) plus a control group, two effect sizes were calculated. In order to satisfy the independence assumption of meta-analytic statistics, only one effect size per study was entered into each analysis.[23] When two or more effect sizes from one study were appropriate for a particular analysis, these effect sizes were averaged.[24] To illustrate, for the estimate of the overall effect of reward on the free-time measure of intrinsic motivation, some studies assessed the effects of several types of rewards. If a single study, for example, contained two or more reward groups (e.g., expected reward and unexpected reward) and a control condition, the two effect sizes were averaged so that the study contributed only one effect size to the overall analysis of reward.

For an analysis of the effects of expected reward on intrinsic motivation, only the one appropriate effect size from the study was used. This strategy retained as much data as possible without violating the assumption of independence.[25] Thus, subcategories (e.g., rewards offered for doing the task, for doing well, etc.) may contain more effect sizes than the superordinate category (expected tangible reward). For example, for all rewards on the free-choice measure (over both high- and low interest tasks), there were 126 effect sizes, but only 115 of these are independent (several are within the same study).

After all effect sizes were calculated, the present analyses were run on the META computer program.[26] The program converts gs (effect sizes) to ds; mean weighted effect sizes ($d+$s) are obtained; statistical tests are provided, 95 percent confidence-level intervals are constructed around the means, and a homogeneity statistic, Q, is computed.

STATISTICAL RESULTS OF OUR META-ANALYSIS

In Table 8A.1, we present the results for our meta-analysis up to the level of reward contingency. Table 8A.1 presents mean weighted effect sizes ($d+$s) and 95 percent confidence-level intervals for each analysis. Mean effects are considered statistically significant when the confidence interval does not include zero. In the present meta-analysis, positive effect sizes indicate that reward produces increases in intrinsic motivation, negative effect sizes support the claim that rewards undermine intrinsic motivation, and zero effects indicate no evidence for an effect of reward. An effect size of around $\pm$ .20 is considered small, $\pm$ .50 is moderate, and greater than $\pm$ .80 is large.[27]

All Rewards

First, the overall effects of reward were analyzed across all conditions and across high-and low-interest tasks. On the free-choice measure, Table 8A.1 indicates that there was no reliable effect ($d+ = -.08$, CI $= -.12$, .02). On the measure of self-reported task interest, a small, significant positive effect was detected ($d+ = .12$, CI $= .07$, .16).[28] On both the free-choice and self-report measures, however, the sets of studies were significantly heterogeneous, suggesting the necessity of a moderator analysis. Thus, at the next level of analysis, we divided studies into those with low- versus high-interest tasks.

The Effects of Rewards on Low-Interest Tasks

When reward effects were analyzed for tasks with low initial interest, (see Table 8A.1), we found a statistically significant positive effect on the free-choice measure ($d+ = .28$, CI $= .07$, .47); there was no reliable effect on self-reported task interest ($d+ = .12$, CI $= -.06$, .30). These findings indicate that when a task is not initially interesting, rewards enhance free-choice intrinsic motivation but verbal expressions of task interest do not.[29]

Although the studies in this analysis were considered homogeneous (that is, Q was not significant), we examined whether there were any differences among different types of rewards, expectancies, and contingencies. On the free-choice measure, only one study included a condition that used a verbal reward (the effect was positive). For tangible reward, one study included an unexpected reward condition (the effect was positive). All the 12 studies with low-interest tasks included an expected tangible reward condition; compared with a non-reward control, the mean effect was significantly positive ($d+ = 0.26$, CI $= .06$, .45). A total of 9 studies involved offering the reward for doing the task; on the free-choice measure, the effect remained significant ($d+ = .26$, CI $= .03$, .48). For self-reported task interest, no reliable effects were found under any of the conditions.

Table 8A.1
Hierarchical Analysis of the Effects of Rewards on Measures of Intrinsic Motivation

FREE-CHOICE INTRINSIC MOTIVATION

Analysis of the effects of reward	K	N	d+	95% CI
All reward[†]	115	8176	-0.08	-0.12, 0.02
Low initial task interest	12	429	0.28*	0.07, 0.47
High initial task interest[†]	114	7888	-0.09*	-0.14, -0.04
Verbal reward	25	1374	0.31*	0.20, 0.41
Tangible reward[†]	102	6942	-0.17*	-0.22, -0.12
Unexpected reward	9	375	0.02	-0.18, 0.22
Expected reward[†]	101	6703	-0.18*	-0.23, -0.13

SELF-REPORTED TASK INTEREST

Analysis of the effects of reward	K	N	d+	95% CI
All reward[†]	100	8028	0.12*	0.07, 0.16
Low initial task interest	11	503	0.12	-0.06, 0.30
High initial task interest[†]	98	7547	0.12*	0.07, 0.17
Verbal reward[†]	24	1584	0.32*	0.22, 0.43
Tangible reward[†]	83	6354	0.08*	0.03, 0.13
Unexpected reward	5	299	0.03	-0.20, 0.26
Expected reward[†]	81	6138	0.08*	0.03, 0.13

Note: Analyses marked with a † indicate that the sample of effect sizes was significantly heterogeneous. K = number of studies; N = total sample size; d+ = mean weighted effect size; effect sizes marked with an asterisk were statistically significant at p < .05; 95% CI = 95% confidence interval.

The Effects of Rewards on High-Interest Tasks

For high-interest tasks; the mean effect size on free choice (Table 8A.1) showed a small but significant negative effect ($d+ = -0.09$, CI $= -.14, -.04$); the set of effect sizes, however was heterogeneous.[30] The mean effect size for self-reported task interest was positive and small but significant ($d+ = .12$, CI $= .07, .17$); the sample of effect sizes was also heterogeneous.

Verbal Rewards

Table 8A.1 shows that verbal rewards were found to significantly enhance both free-choice intrinsic motivation ($d+ = .31$, CI $= .20, .41$) and self-reported task interest ($d+ = .32$, CI $= .22, .43$).[31] That is, when participants were given positive feedback or verbally praised, they spent more time on a task and performed at a higher level once the praise was no longer forthcoming than did a nonrewarded control group. They also expressed greater interest in the task.

On the free-choice measure, the set of effect sizes was homogeneous, suggesting that no further breakdowns were necessary. In most studies of verbal reward, the rewards were unexpected and the mean effect was positive; a positive effect was also found in the five studies that used expected rewards. In addition, verbal rewards were generally delivered simply for doing a task, not contingent on any specific level of performance (again, the effects were positive). When the effects of verbal reward on free choice were examined with children versus adults (mainly, college students), children showed a smaller positive effect ($k = 10$, $N = 320$, $d+ = .22$, CI $= .04, .39$) than adults ($K = 15$, $N = 844$, $d+ = .36$, CI $= .22, .49$).[32]

On the task-interest measure, the set of effect sizes for verbal reward was significantly heterogeneous. We conducted moderator analyses of children versus adults and expected reward versus unexpected. Mean effect sizes for each of these analyses remained significantly positive but homogeneity was still not obtained. In almost all the studies, the rewards were given for doing the task; hence, this reward contingency could not be a moderator.

To obtain homogeneity, three studies were removed from the analysis; these were the same outliers removed by Deci, Koestner, and Ryan (1999). Inspection of the outliers indicated that two of the studies produced large positive effects;[33] these studies did not differ in obvious ways from other studies in the sample except for their tendency to generate extreme values of effect size. The third outlier produced a negative effect ($-.46$).[34] In this study, control participants were compared to participants who were praised for their performance on the task as well as to another group whose members were also praised but also told that they should be doing well. The second verbal reward condition produced the negative effect and was different from verbal reward used in other studies; Deci and his colleagues have termed this a "controlling" reward.[35] When the outliers were removed from the analysis of verbal rewards on the task-interest measure, the set of studies was homogeneous and the mean effect remained significantly positive ($K = 21$, $N = 1,194$, $d+ = .32$, CI $= .21, .44$).[36]

Tangible Rewards

When the effects of tangible rewards on high interest tasks were analyzed, (see Table 8A.1), we found a small significant negative effect on the free-choice measure ($d+ = -.17$, CI $= -.22, -.12$) and a small, positive, reliable effect on self-reported task interest ($d+ = 0.08$, CI $= .03, .13$). Both these samples of effects sizes were significantly heterogeneous and required a further moderator analysis.

The Effects of Tangible Reward Expectancies. Tangible rewards were subdivided into unexpected (rewards delivered without a statement of the contingency) and expected (rewards delivered after a statement of contingency). No significant effects were detected for unexpected tangible rewards (see Table

Figure 8A.1

The Effects of Expected Tangible Reward Contingencies on Free-Choice Intrinsic Motivation under High Levels of Initial Task Interest

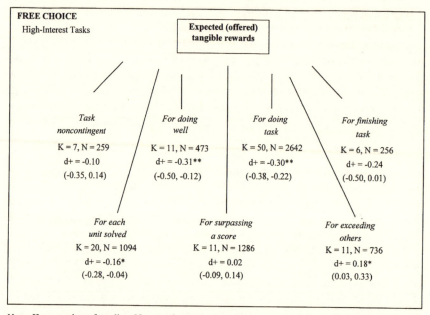

Note: K = number of studies; N = total sample size; d+ = mean weighted effect size; statistically reliable effect sizes are marked with an asterisk (* = p < .05; ** = p < .01). Positive effect sizes indicate higher intrinsic motivation for rewarded versus control group; negative effect sizes indicate lower intrinsic motivation for rewarded groups. Numbers in parentheses represent 95% confidence intervals. All effect sizes are based on homogeneous samples.

8A.1) and the samples were homogenous. Expected tangible rewards produced a negative effect on the free-choice measure ($d+ = -.18$, CI $= -.23, -.13$) and a positive effect on the self-report measure ($d+ = .08$, CI $= .03, .13$), but both these samples were significantly heterogeneous.

The Effects of Expected Tangible Reward Contingencies. For the next level of analysis, expected tangible rewards were subdivided into various reward contingencies.

Results of our analysis on the free-choice measure are presented in Figure 8A.1. No reliable effects were detected when the rewards were task noncontingent, offered for finishing or completing a task, or offered for attaining or surpassing a score. Figure 8A.1 shows significant negative effects when the rewards were offered for doing a task, for doing well on a task, and for each unit solved. A significant positive effect was found when the rewards were offered for meeting or exceeding the performance level of others.[37]

When rewards were offered for doing a task, the effect was significantly

Figure 8A.2
The Effects of Expected Tangible Reward Contingencies on Self-Reports of Task Interest under High Levels of Initial Task Interest

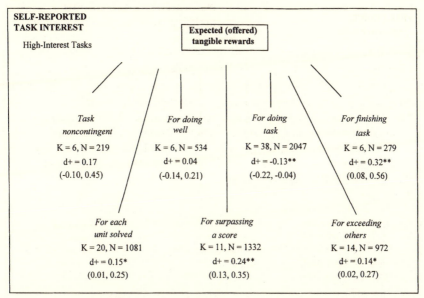

Note: K = number of studies; N = total sample size; d+ = mean weighted effect size; statistically reliable effect sizes are marked with an asterisk (*) = p < .05; ** = p < .01). Positive effect sizes indicate higher intrinsic motivation for rewarded versus control group; negative effect sizes indicate lower intrinsic motivation for rewarded groups. Numbers in parentheses represent 95% confidence intervals. All effect sizes are based on homogeneous samples.

negative ($K = 57$, $N = 2,910$, $d+ = -.35$, CI $= -.43, -.27$), but not homogeneous. Although we searched for moderators (salient versus nonsalient reward, children versus adults, and time of reward delivery), analyses of these variables did not result in homogeneous samples. As a result, outliers were identified and omitted. The mean effect size with outliers removed is presented in Figure 8A.1.[38]

Our findings for free choice indicate that when reward contingency is defined in terms of experimental procedures, negative, neutral, and positive effects are obtained. Our results for the task interest data are presented in Figure 8A.2. The analysis shows no reliable effect for task-noncontingent rewards; a small, reliable, negative effect for rewards offered for doing, and significant, positive effects for each of the other contingencies.[39] In one analysis, rewards offered for each unit completed, when all studies were included, the effect was positive ($K = 22$, $N = 1,161$, $d+ = .19$, CI $= .08, .31$), but significantly heterogeneous. Two studies had a large positive effect size; when these studies were omitted, homogeneity was attained.[40]

Maximum versus Less Than Maximum Reward. There was only one reward contingency (rewards offered per unit solved) that allowed for a comparison between maximum and less than maximum reward. For other reward contingencies, most studies involved maximum reward; a comparison with less than maximum reward would thus be unreliable. When rewards were offered for each unit solved, the findings showed a nonreliable negative effect for studies of maximum rewards ($K = 6$, $N = 345$, $d+ = -.03$, CI $= -.25$, $.18$) and a significant negative effect for studies of less than maximum reward ($K = 14$, $N = 749$, $d+ = -.22$, CI $= -.37$, $-.07$). These two sets of effect sizes were homogeneous. These results suggest that the negative effect of pay per unit is associated with participants receiving less than maximum rewards.

No analyses were conducted on differences between maximum and less than maximum rewards on the self-report measure. Most of the contingencies had too few studies that used less than maximum reward; for studies involving the offer of reward for each problem solved, there were too few experiments using maximum reward (see Appendix 8B).

NOTES

1. Studies identified by Cameron and Pierce (1994) and by Deci, Koestner, and Ryan (1999) were included in the present analysis.

2. Deci, 1971.

3. Two studies included in Cameron and Pierce's (1994) research were omitted in the present analyses. In one study (Boggiano and Hertel, 1983), the dependent measure was assessed before all participants worked on the task; in the other study (Boal and Cummings, 1981), all participants (including the control group) received monetary payments. These studies were also not included in Deci, Koestner, and Ryan's (1999) analyses.

4. For example, see Wiersma, 1992.

5. Deci, Koestner, and Ryan, 1999.

6. In accord with the meta-analysis by Deci, Koestner, and Ryan (1999), our free-choice measure includes free time on task when the rewards were removed and, when time measures were not available, performance during the free choice period. As did Deci et al., we combined performance and time measures to make up the free-choice intrinsic motivation index (we found no significant differences in the analyses when only time measures were analyzed).

7. Rummel and Feinberg (1988) combined free-time and questionnaire measures in their meta-analysis of the effects of rewards on intrinsic motivation.

8. See Glass, McGaw, and Smith, 1981.

9. For example, see Chung, 1995, Horn, 1987.

10. For example, Smith (1975) offered rewards to participants for showing signs of learning. This was the only study that used this type of reward contingency.

11. We would like to thank Katherine Banko for coding studies and doing reliability checks.

12. Goldstein, 1977.

13. Ibid., p. 30.

14. The meta-analytic procedures described and used in the current analysis are based

on Hedges and Olkin (1985); these were the basic procedures used by Cameron and Pierce (1994) and by Deci, Koestner, and Ryan (1999).

15. Hedges and Becker (1986) describe how to calculate effect sizes from t tests, F statistics, and p-level values. Cameron and Pierce (1994, p. 404) also provide formulas for these calculations.

16. For a discussion of this issue, see Light and Pillemer, 1984.

17. In Cameron and Pierce's (1994) meta-analysis, studies in which there was insufficient information to calculate effect sizes were not included; Deci, Koestner, and Ryan (1999) included such studies in their meta-analysis and imputed effect sizes of 0.00.

18. Wicker, Brown, Wiehe, and Shim, 1990; Dollinger and Thelen, 1978.

19. See Hedges, 1981.

20. Hedges and Olkin, 1985.

21. See Cameron and Pierce, 1994; Deci, Koestner, and Ryan, 1999.

22. See Hunter and Schmidt, 1990.

23. Hedges and Olkin, 1985.

24. Average effect sizes were obtained by weighting each g index by the number of participants on which it was based. See Cooper, 1989.

25. This procedure was used by Cameron and Pierce (1994) and by Deci, Koestner, and Ryan (1999). Hedges and Olkin (1985) discussed the independence assumption. It is important to point out that a serious statistical violation occurs when more than one effect size from an individual experiment is entered into a single meta-analysis. Typically, in such cases, a control group is compared with more than one experimental treatment within a study, several effect sizes are calculated, and each is entered into a single meta-analytic test. The major problem is that the effect sizes are not independent (errors among observations are correlated). Another problem is that a particular study will contribute more weight to the overall meta-analytic outcome than a study yielding only one effect size. Other meta-analyses of reward and intrinsic motivation have violated the independence assumption by entering several or many effect sizes from one study (sometimes over ten effect sizes) into a single meta-analytic test (e.g., Tang and Hall, 1995; Rummel and Feinberg, 1988). The implication is that conclusions based on these meta-analyses could be incorrect.

26. The META program was developed by Schwarzer (1991); the meta-analytic method used in this analysis is based on the weighted integration method described in Hedges and Olkin (1985).

27. Cohen, 1988.

28. These results are in accord with Cameron and Pierce (1994) and Eisenberger and Cameron (1996).

29. In Deci, Koestner, and Ryan's (1999) supplemental analysis of low-interest tasks (p. 651), fewer studies were included and no reliable effects were found on either the free-choice or the self-report measures of intrinsic motivation.

30. Deci, Koestner, and Ryan (1999) also reported a significant negative effect on the free choice measure for the effects of rewards on high-interest tasks but a nonreliable effect on the task interest measure. On the self-report measure, Deci et al. (1999) omitted or missed several self-report effect sizes.

31. These results were also obtained by Deci, Koestner, and Ryan (1999), who reported similar small to moderate positive effects of verbal rewards.

32. Deci, Koestner, and Ryan (1999) also reported a larger effect of verbal rewards

on free choice for adults but a nonsignificant effect for children. Our effect for children was statistically significant; however, we included more studies than Deci et al.

33. Butler, 1987; Vallerand, 1983.

34. Kast and Connor, 1988.

35. Deci, Koestner, and Ryan, 1999.

36. For high-interest tasks, in the data set for the effects of verbal reward on self-reported task interest, there were six studies that did not provide enough information to obtain an effect size estimate (these studies were assigned an effect size of 0.00). When these studies were removed the mean effect size for task interest showed a slight increase ($K = 15$, $N = 981$, $d+ = 0.40$, $CI = 0.27, 0.53$).

37. In the studies in which participants were offered a tangible reward for surpassing a score or for exceeding the performance of others, there were two possible types of control comparisons. In some studies, the control group was told the performance objectives and given performance feedback (complete control); in others, the control group was not told a performance objective and no feedback was given (partial control). Eisenberger, Pierce, and Cameron (1999) examined differences between these two types of comparisons (reward versus partial control and reward versus complete control). One small difference was detected on the free-choice measure. When rewards were offered to exceed others, reward versus a partial control condition resulted in a nonsignificant positive effect; the mean effect for reward versus a complete control was significantly positive (no other comparisons resulted in differences). Because this difference was small and both mean effects were in the same direction, in the present analyses we included studies with either type of control condition. If a study contained both types of controls (e.g., Harackiewicz, Manderlink, and Sansone, 1984), one effect size was calculated to compare the reward condition to both controls.

38. Two of the outliers produced positive effects; the only differences between these two studies and the majority of the studies were that the study by Tripathi and Agarwal (1988) was conducted in India and the study by Brennan and Glover (1980) was designed to assess the effects of rewards when the rewards were shown to function as reinforcement. Other outliers (Chung, 1995; Danner & Lonkey, 1981; Fabes, Eisenberg, Fultz, and Miller, 1988, Morgan, 1981, Experiment 1; Okano, 1981, Experiment 2) had large negative effects but revealed no common factor that could explain their extreme values.

39. In the analysis of rewards offered for doing the task on the task interest measure, 14 studies were given effect sizes of 0.00; when these studies were removed from the analysis, the negative effect increased from -0.13 to -0.22 ($K = 24$, $N = 1201$, $d+ = -0.22$, $CI = -0.33, -0.10$).

40. Kruglanski, Riter, Amitai, Margolin, Shabatai, and Zaksh, 1975, Experiment 1; Wimperis and Farr, 1979.

Appendix 8B: Studies Included in our Meta-Analysis

Studies Included in the Analysis of the Effects of Rewards on Intrinsic Motivation for Tasks with Low Initial Interest

Study	Reward Type	Reward Expectancy	Reward Contingency	N_E	N_C	Free-Choice Effect Size (g)	Self-Report Effect Size (g)
Calder & Staw (1975)	T	E	for finishing task	10	10	—	0.61
Chung (1995)	T	E	for doing task	5	5	1.93	—
	T	E	insufficient info	5	5	1.22	—
Crino & White (1982)	V	U	per unit sloved	10	5	—	-0.05
	V	U	yolked/per unit	10	5	—	0.32
Daniel & Esser (1980)	T	E	for doing quickly	16	16	-0.28	0.08
Eisenstein (1985)	T	U	for finishing task	6	6	0.62	—
	T	E	for finishing	16	6	0.22	—
Freedman & Phillips (1985)	T	E	per unit solved	24	25	—	0.24
	T	E	for finishing task	26	25	—	0.53
Griffith (1984) D	T	E	for doing task	44	44	0.25	—
Hamner & Foster (1975)	T	E	for doing task	16	15	—	-0.28
	T	E	per unit sloved	19	15	—	0.52
Hitt et al. (1992)	T	E	for doing task	30	15	0.57	-0.16
Loveland & Olley (1979)	T	E	for doing task	6	6	1.20	—
McLoyd (1979)	T	E	for finishing task	18	9	0.61	0.00
Mynatt et al. (1978)	T	E	for doing task	5	5	1.35	—
Newman & Layton (1984)	T	E	for doing task	20	10	0.41	—
Overskeid & Svartdal (1996) Exp. 1	T	E	for doing task	10	10	-0.29	0.39
Overskeid & Svartdal (1996) Exp 2	T	E	for doing task	64	32	—	-0.15
Phillips & Freedman (1985)	T	E	for finishing task	12	12	—	0.63
	T	E	per unit solved	12	12	—	-0.10
Smith (1980) D	T	E	for doing task	21	27	0.04	—
	V	U	for doing task	22	26	0.17	—
Wilson (1978) D	T	E	for doing task	46	23	-0.03	0.12

Studies Included in the Analysis of the Effects of Verbal Rewards on
Intrinsic Motivation for Tasks with High-Initial Interest

Study	Reward Expectancy	Reward Contingency	N_E	N_C	Free-Choice Effect Size (g)	Self-Report Effect Size (g)
Anderson & Rodin (1989)	U	for doing task	10	10	0.20	0.40
Anderson et al. (1976)	U	for doing task	18	19	0.40	—
Blanck et al. (1984) Exp. 1	U	for doing task	70	69	0.56	0.69
Blanck et al. (1984) Exp. 2	U	for doing task	12	12	0.73	0.00
Boggiano & Barrett (1985)	U	for doing task	18	18	0.35	—
Boggiano et al. (1988)	U	for doing task	66	34	0.42	—
Butler (1987)	E	for doing task	50	50	—	1.59 *
Cohen (1974) D	U	for doing task	52	52	0.07	0.42
Crino & White (1982)	U	per unit solved	10	5	—	0.05
	U	yolked/per unit	10	5	—	-0.79
Danner & Lonkey (1981)	U	for doing task	30	30	-0.10	-0.08
Deci (1971) Exp. 3	U	for doing task	12	12	0.82	0.00
Deci (1972a)	U	for doing task	48	48	0.29	—
Deci et al. (1975)	no info	no info	32	32	0.02	—
Dollinger & Thelen (1978)	E	for doing well	12	12	-0.07	0.00
Effron (1976) D	U	for doing task	15	13	—	0.89
Goldstein (1977) D	U	for doing task	32	32	0.77	0.12
Harackiewicz (1979)	U	for doing task	31	31	—	0.59
Hom (1987) Exp. 2	no info	no info	28	28	-0.37	—
Kast & Connor (1988)	U	for doing task	180	60	—	-0.46 *
Koestner et al. (1987)	U	for doing task	35	18	0.51	0.00
Orlick & Mosher (1978)	U	for doing task	11	12	-0.34	—
Pallak et al. (1982)	U	for doing task	16	12	-0.47	—
	E	for doing task	14	12	0.32	—
Pittman et al. (1980)	U	for doing task	24	12	0.80	—
Pretty & Seligman (1984) Exp 1	U	for doing task	30	30	0.35	0.46
Ryan et al. (1983)	E	for doing task	32	16	0.53	0.00
Sansone (1986)	U	for doing task	44	11	—	0.68
Sansone (1989)	E	for doing task	82	41	—	0.46
Sansone et al. (1989)	U	for doing task	40	40	—	0.12
Shanab et al. (1981)	U	for doing task	10	20	0.64	0.43
Smith, W.E. (1975) D	U	for learning	20	20	0.04	0.00
Smith, A.T. (1980) D	U	for doing task	21	27	0.24	—
Tripathi & Agarwal (1985)	E	for doing task	20	20	1.61	0.48
Vallerand & Reid (1984)	E	for doing task	28	28	—	0.53
Vallerand (1983)	E	for doing task	40	10	—	1.98 *
Zinser et al. (1982)	U	for doing task	64	32	0.08	—

Studies Included in the Analysis of Tangible Rewards on Intrinsic Motivation for Tasks with High-Initial Interest

UNEXPECTED TANGIBLE REWARDS—ALL REWARD CONTINGENCIES

Study	Reward Contingency	N_E	N_C	Free-Choice Effect Size (g)	Self-Report Effect Size (g)
Eisenstein (1985)	for finishing	10	10	0.46	—
Greene & Lepper (1974)	for doing well	26	15	0.14	—
Harackiewicz et al. (1984) Exp. 2	exceeding others	15	15	0.44[a]	0.15
Kruglanski et al. (1972)	for winning	36	33	—	-0.65
Lepper et al. (1973)	for doing task	18	15	0.12	—
Orlick & Mosher (1978)	for doing well	12	12	-1.28	—
Pallak et al. (1982)	for doing task	15	12	-0.43	—
Pretty & Seligman (1984) Exp. 1	for doing task	30	30	0.06	0.42
Pretty& Seligman (1984) Exp. 2	for doing task	30	30	0.06	0.38
Smith (1975) D	for learning	20	20	0.08	0.00

EXPECTED TANGIBLE REWARDS—LISTED BY REWARD CONTINGENCY

Task noncontingent

Study	N_E	N_C	Free Choice Effect size (g)	Self Report Effect size (g)
Dafoe (1985) D	25	28	-0.20	0.73
Deci (1972a)	24	16	0.08	—
Earn (1982)	40	20	-0.28	0.18
Kruglanski et al. (1971)	16	16	—	-0.69
Okano (1981) Exp. 2	11	11	-0.47	-0.27
Pittman et al. (1982) Exp. 1	10	10	0.26	0.00
Ross et al. (1976)	12	12	0.44	—
Swann & Pittman (1977) Exp. 1	20	20	-0.21	—
Wimperis & Farr (1979)	16	16	—	0.56

Rewards offered for doing task

Study	N_E	N_C	Free-Choice Effect Size (g)	Self-Report Effect Size (g)
Amabile et al. (1986) Exp. 1	56	57	0.00	0.00
Amabile et al. (1986) Exp. 3	30	30	—	0.00
Anderson et al. (1976)	36	19	-0.53	—
Arnold (1976)	17	36	—	0.00
Arnold (1985)	13	16	—-	-0.04
Boggiano & Ruble (1979)	20	20	-0.61	—
Boggiano et al. (1982)	81	84	0.28	—

Rewards and Intrinsic Motivation

Boggiano et al. (1985)	26	13	-0.79	—
Brennan & Glover (1980)	20	19	1.00*	—
Brewer (1980) D	24	24	-0.13	0.12
Chung (1995)	5	5	-1.61*	—
Danner & Lonkey (1981)	30	30	-1.33*	-1.23
DeLoach et al. (1983)	26	26	0.00	—
Dimitroff (1984) D	108	36	-0.27	0.00
Effron (1976) D	12	13	—	0.19
Fabes et al. (1986)	24	24	0.06	-0.14
Fabes et al. (1988)	14	14	-1.34*	-0.76
Fabes et al. (1989)	15	14	-0.73	—
Feehan & Enzle (1991) Exp 1	24	12	-0.97	—
Goldstein (1977) D	16	16	-0.99	-0.87
Greene & Lepper (1974)	15	15	-0.70	—
Griffith (1984) D	44	44	-0.23	—
Hamner & Foster (1975)	15	15	—	-0.14
Harackiewicz (1979)	31	31	—	-0.38
Hitt et al. (1992)	30	15	-0.82	-0.47
Hyman (1985) D	32	32	-0.42	—
Karniol & Ross (1977)	17	20	-0.08	—
Lepper et al. (1973)	18	15	-0.72	—
Lepper et al. (1982)	32	32	-0.13	—
Loveland & Olley (1979)	6	6	-1.20	—
Morgan (1981) Exp. 1	27	27	-0.98	-0.31
Morgan (1981) Exp. 2	20	20	-0.77	0.04
Morgan (1983) Exp. 1	40	40	-1.94*	
	40	20		-0.54
Morgan (1983) Exp. 2	20	20	-0.66	0.00
Mynatt et al. (1978)	5	5	0.19	—
Newman & Layton (1984)	20	10	-0.37	—
Ogilvie & Prior (1982)	26	26	-0.08	—
Okano (1981) Exp. 1	15	15	-0.99	-0.45
Okano (1981) Exp. 2	10	11	-1.31*	0.00
Patrick (1985) D	33	31	0.00	0.00
Perry et al. (1977)	32	32	-0.43	-0.21
Picek (1976) D	10	10	0.00	-0.65
Pittman et al. (1982) Exp. 1	10	10	0.17	0.00

Pittman et al. (1982) Exp. 2	27	27	-0.05	—
Pretty & Seligman (1984) Exp. 1	30	30	-0.75	-0.05
Pretty & Seligman (1984) Exp. 2	30	30	-0.13	-0.16
Reiss & Sushinski (1975)	16	16	-0.83	—
Ross (1975) Exp. 1	40	20	0.01	-0.45
Ross (1975) Exp. 2	52	14	-0.66	0.00
Ross et al. (1976)	12	12	-0.64	—
Ryan et al. (1983)	16	16	-0.35	0.00
Sarafino (1984)	85	15	-0.41	0.00
Shiffman-Kauffman (1990) D	20	20	0.06	-0.04
Smith (1980) D	21	27	--0.82	—
Swann & Pittman (1977) Exp. 1	20	20	-0.78	—
Swann & Pittman (1977) Exp. 2	26	13	-1.01	—
Thompson et al. (1993)	34	33	-0.003	0.14
Tripathi & Agarwal (1988)	20	10	0.34*	0.72
Tripathi (1991)	20	5	0.00	0.00
Weiner & Mander (1978)	30	30	-0.34	0.00
Williams (1980)	24	24	0.18	0.00
Wilson (1978) D	46	23	-0.06	-0.01
Yuen (1984) D	60	60	-0.40	-0.12

Rewards offered for "doing well" or "doing a good job" on the task

Study	Reward Delivery	N_E	N_C	Free-Choice Effect Size (g)	Self-Report Effect Size (g)
Brewer (1980) D	M	48	24	-0.08	0.12
Dafoe (1985) D	M	26	28	0.00	0.59
Dollinger & Thelen (1978)	L	36	12	-0.55	0.00
Enzle et al. (1991)	M	40	10	-0.53	—
Fabes (1987) Exp. 1	M	18	19	-0.87	
Goldstein (1977) D	M	16	32	-0.08	-0.48
Greene & Lepper (1974)	M	15	15	-0.57	—
Hyman (1985) D	M	16	16	0.11	—
Orlick & Mosher (1978)	M	14	12	-0.53	—
Pallak et al. (1982)	M	15	12	-0.17	—
Ryan et al. (1983)	M	32	32	-0.46	0.00
Taub & Dollinger (1975)	NI	124	124	—	0.00

Rewards offered for finishing or completing a task

Study	Reward Delivery	N_E	N_C	Free-Choice Effect Size (g)	Self-Report Effect Size (g)
Calder & Staw (1975)	M	10	10	—	-0.46
Eisenstein (1985)	M	18	10	-0.53	—
Fabes (1987) 1	M	19	19	-0.82	—
Fabes (1987) 2	M	14	14	-0.45	—
Freedman & Phillips (1985)	M	26	22	—	0.94
Griffith et al. (1984)	M	64	32	0.00	—
McLoyd (1979)	M	18	9	-1.04	0.00
Phillips & Freedman (1985)	M	12	12	—	0.74
Staw et al. (1980)	M	47	46	—	0.19
Tripathi & Agarwal (1985)	M	20	20	0.41	0.54

Rewards offered for each problem, puzzle, unit, etc. solved

Study	Reward Delivery	N_E	N_C	Free-Choice Effect Size (g)	Self-Report Effect Size (g)
Arkes (1979)	M	32	32	-0.16	0.03
Arnold (1985)	L	13	16	—	-0.05
Bartelme (1983) D	M	35	34	0.04[a]	0.03
Boggiano et al. (1985)	M	26	13	-0.10	—
Brockner & Vasta (1981)	L	26	26	-0.37	-0.58
Carton & Nowicki (1998) 1	L	44	22	0.36[a]	—
Carton & Nowicki (1998) 2	L	40	20	0.20[a]	0.71
Cohen (1974) D	L	52	52	-0.18	0.13
Deci (1972a)	L	64	32	0.33	—
Deci (1971) Exp. 1	L	12	12	-0.54	0.00
Effron (1976) D	L	43	28	—	-0.04
Feehan & Enzle (1991) Exp. 2	M	30	15	0.31[a]	—
Freedman & Phillips (1985)	L	23	22	—	1.12
Goldstein (1980) D	L	14	14	-0.32	0.68
Hamner & Foster (1975)	L	18	15	—	-0.21
Kruglanski (1975) Exp. 1	M	24	24	—	1.15*
Lee (1982) D	M	40	40	-0.36[a]	0.35
Liberty (1986) Exp 1 D	l	23	23	-0.86[a]	-0.34
Liberty (1986) Exp. 2 D	L	44	42	-0.22[a]	0.04
McGraw & McCullers (1979)	NI	20	20	—	-0.04
Phillips & Freedman (1985)	L	12	12	—	0.77

Porac & Meindl (1982)	L	20	20	-0.78	—
Shapira (1976)	L	30	30	—	0.41
Sorenson & Maehr (1976)	L	20	20	-0.54	—
Vasta & Stirpe (1979)	L	4	5	-0.16	—
Weiner & Mander (1978)	L	30	30	-0.54	0.00
Weiner (1980)	M	24	24	0.35	0.00
Wicker et al. (1990)	L	29	29	-0.46	0.18
Wimperis & Farr (1979)	NI	16	16	—	1.36*

Rewards offered for meeting a specific standard or surpassing a score

Study	Reward Delivery	N_E	N_C	Free-Choice Effect Size (g)	Self-Report Effect Size (g)
Adorney (1983) D	L	35	36	0.39	0.48
Bartelme (1983) D	M	35	34	0.19[a]	-0.03
Boggiano & Ruble (1979)	M	20	20	-0.17	—
Dafoe (1985) D	M	28	28	0.15	0.59
Eisenberger (1999)	M	214	316	0.08	0.31
Eisenberger et al. (1999) Exp.1	M	110	113	0.10	0.34
Harackiewicz et al. (1987)	M	13	25	—	-0.28
Hyman (1985) D	M	16	16	0.04	—
Kruglanski et al. (1975) Exp. 2	M	40	40	—	0.38
Patrick (1985) D	M	30	31	0.00	0.00
Pittman et al. (1977)	L	60	20	-0.50[a]	-0.20
Smith & Pittman (1978)	L	66	33	-0.56[a]	0.00
Tripathi (1991)	M	20	5	0.00	0.00

Rewards offered for meeting or exceeding others

Study	Reward Delivery	N_E	N_C	Free-Choice Effect Size (g)	Self-Report Effect Size (g)
Dafoe (1985) D	M	25	28	0.00	0.59
Eisenberger et al. (1999) Exp. 1	M	106	106	0.38	0.22
Harackiewicz (1979)	M	31	31	—	-0.87
Harackiewicz & Manderlink(1984)	M	47	47	—	0.33
Harackiewicz et al. (1984) Exp. 1	M	32	64	0.27	0.12
Harackiewicz et al. (1984) Exp. 2	M	15	15	-0.43[a]	-0.18
Harackiewicz et al. (1984) Exp. 3	M	26	52	0.34[a]	0.40
Harackiewicz et al. (1987)	M	11	29	—	0.12
Karniol & Ross (1977)	L/M	20	20	0.15	—
Luyten & Lens (1981)	L	10	10	-0.90	0.08

Rosenfield et al. (1980)	L/M	30	27	0.30	0.22
Salancik (1975)	M	38	39	-0.34	0.01
Shiffman-Kauffman (1990) D	M	20	20	0.35	0.00
Tripathi & Agarwal (1988)	M	20	10	0.87	1.01
Weinberg & Jackson (1979)	L	40	40	—	0.00

Studies or Conditions Within Studies Included in the Overall Analyses of Reward and Tangible Reward That Could Not Be Classified into Reward Contingencies

Study	Reward Contingency	N_E	N_C	Free-Choice Effect Size (g)	Self-Report Effect Size (g)
Chung (1995)	insufficient info	5	5	-1.02	—
Daniel & Esser (1980)	for doing quickly	16	16	-0.75	-0.71
Hom (1987) Exp. 1	no information	26	26	0.12	0.00
Hom (1987) Exp. 2	no information	28	28	-0.37[a]	—
Smith (1975) D	for showing learning	20	20	-0.56	0.00

Note: Studies followed by a "D" refer to unpublished doctoral dissertations. *For reward type*, T = tangible reward; V = verbal reward. *For reward expectancy*, E = expected (offered beforehand); U = unexpected (delivered but not offered). Reward contingency refers to what the participants were rewarded for. *For reward delivery*, M = maximum reward; L = less than maximum reward; NI = not enough information. N_E = sample size for experimental group (rewarded group); N_C = sample size of control group; g = effect size. Effect sizes listed under free-choice intrinsic motivation are based on the difference between rewarded and control groups on the amount of time spent on a task once the reward was removed; [a] in this column signifies effect sizes based on performance measures on the task during the free choice period (e.g., number of balls played in a pinball game, number of trials initiated in a Labyrinth game, number of words found in a word search game). Self-report effect sizes are based on questionnaire measures of task liking, satisfaction, enjoyment or task preference. Effect sizes marked with an asterisk (*) were outliers in the data set.

Chapter 9

Discussion and Implications of Our Meta-analytic Findings

Our meta-analysis of the empirical literature on the effects of rewards on intrinsic motivation (presented in Chapter 8), shows that there is no inherent negative property of reward. Our findings do not support the claim that rewards produce significant and substantial decreases in people's intrinsic interest.[1] In Chapters 2 and 3, an examination of the early studies on the topic showed that negative effects of reward were extremely limited. After 30 years of research and more than 100 experimental investigations on the topic, the findings continue to show that negative effects of reward occur under a highly circumscribed set of conditions. Importantly, our meta-analysis indicates that, when properly arranged, rewards can be used to enhance performance and motivation. In this chapter, we discuss our meta-analytic results and elucidate the theoretical and practical implications of our findings.

WHAT OUR META-ANALYTIC RESULTS REVEAL

In terms of the overall effects of reward, in accord with our earlier reviews,[2] our meta-analysis indicates no evidence for a general detrimental effect of reward on measures of intrinsic motivation. This finding is important. Over the years, many statements have appeared in newspaper articles, magazines, and academic texts condemning the use of all rewards. As a result, many practitioners have been concerned that the incentive systems that they have designed are actually more harmful than beneficial. In addition, many students of psychology and education are taught that, overall, rewards are harmful and should be avoided in applied settings. Our meta-analytic results suggest that the argu-

Table 9.1
A Summary of Our Meta-Analytic Findings on the Effects of Rewards on Measures of Intrinsic Motivation

	Change in Intrinsic Motivation	
Reward Condition	Free-Choice Behavior	Task Interest
All reward		
Low initial task interest	Increase	No change
High initial task interest		
Verbal reward	Increase	Increase
Tangible reward		
Unexpected reward	No change	No change
Expected reward (offered)		
Task noncontingent	No change	No change
Reward offered for doing task	Decrease	Decrease
Reward offered for doing well	Decrease	No change
Reward offered for finishing task	No change	Increase
Reward offered for each unit solved	Decrease	Increase
Maximum reward	No change	
Less than maximum reward	Decrease	
Reward offered for surpassing a score	No change	Increase
Reward offered for exceeding others	Increase	Increase

ment that rewards, in general, destroy people's intrinsic motivation is not supported by the empirical data.

Our finding of no overall effect of reward, however, must be treated with caution. In our meta-analysis, the overall reward category lacked homogeneity, indicating the appropriateness of a moderator analysis. In other words, the overall reward category is too inclusive; rewards have different effects under different moderating conditions.

In Table 9.1, we present a summary of our findings. The table shows which reward conditions produce increases or decreases in the two main measures of intrinsic motivation—free-choice behavior and self-reported task interest. Only results from categories that were considered homogeneous are presented. Other categories were too broad, suggesting that a further subdivision of rewards was necessary.

In Table 9.1, the effects of all rewards are first broken into high-and low-interest tasks. When the tasks used in the studies are of low initial interest, rewards increase free choice but do not affect self-reported task interest. This finding indicates that rewards can be used to enhance time and performance on tasks that initially hold little appeal. As noted in Chapter 5, Bandura pointed out that few tasks are initially interesting to people. But when individuals are given appropriate learning experiences, many activities can become interesting and important. Many of the tasks used in educational settings are not of high initial interest to students. Our results suggest that reward procedures are one way to cultivate interest in an activity.

On high-interest tasks, the effects of reward depend on the reward type, the expectancy, and contingency. Table 9.1 shows that verbal rewards significantly enhance both free-choice intrinsic motivation and self-reported task interest. These findings suggest that when praise and other forms of positive feedback are given and later removed, people continue to engage in the activity and also express high levels of task interest.

The effects of tangible rewards are found to differ by reward expectancy. When rewards are delivered unexpectedly (without a description of the reward contingency), there is no evidence of significant effects on either measure of intrinsic motivation. The findings from our meta-analysis indicate that only expected tangible rewards produce a decremental effect on intrinsic motivation and the effect of expected tangible rewards depends on the contingency.

In Table 9.1, expected tangible rewards are categorized according to the description of the reward contingency. The results indicate decreases in free-choice intrinsic motivation when rewards are tangible and offered simply for doing a task or for doing well. A negative effect is also found when participants are offered a reward for each unit or problem solved. However, the negative effect of reward offered for each unit solved does not hold if participants are given the maximum reward. That is, if people are offered a reward for each individual task that they solve, their motivation is not altered if they are successful at the task. A negative effect occurs if individuals are offered a reward for each problem solved but they are also given a time limit and are unable to obtain the maximum reward, a type of situation that represents the effects of failure feedback rather than the effects of reward. On the task-interest measure, only participants who are offered a reward for doing a task show a decrease in expressed task interest. No other negative effects on task interest were found.

Finally, the results in Table 9.1 show that when rewards are offered for meeting or surpassing a score, there is no significant effect on free choice but a significant positive effect on task interest. When rewards are given for exceeding the performance level of others, the results show a significant increase on both free-choice intrinsic motivation and self-reported task interest.

Our meta-analytic results suggest that the findings on rewards and intrinsic motivation have stood the test of time. Our review (Chapters 2 and 3) of the initial studies by Deci (1971, 1972b) and by Lepper and his colleagues (Lepper, Greene, and Nisbett, 1973) showed that obtaining a negative effect of reward required a particular combination of conditions. An evaluation of over 100 experiments on the topic shows that the negative effect continues to be highly circumscribed. To produce the phenomenon, the following must occur:

- The activity must be of high initial interest (using rewards with low-interest activities does not produce a negative effect).

- The delivery of rewards must be stated beforehand (unexpected rewards do not produce a negative effect).

- The rewards must be material or tangible (verbal rewards do not produce a negative effect).

- The reward contingency must be loose or vague (rewards given for success or for meeting a performance standard do not produce a negative effect).

- The reward must be delivered only once over a single reward session (the repeated delivery of rewards does not produce a negative effect).

- Intrinsic motivation must be indexed by free-choice behavior or self-reported task interest following the withdrawal of reward (measuring intrinsic motivation during the rewarded period does not produce a negative effect).

- Intrinsic motivation must be assessed only once following the removal or rewards (repeated assessments of intrinsic motivation measures following the removal of reward show no negative effects).

Clearly, one can see that it takes an unusual combination of conditions to produce a negative effect of reward in the laboratory. Of particular interest is the fact that the bulk of the between-group design experiments on the topic were primarily designed to detect negative effects. In spite of this, many of the studies showed that rewards can be used effectively to enhance or maintain motivation and interest.

Overall, in accord with our previous reviews,[3] our updated meta-analysis shows that rewards can be used to reduce, enhance, or have no effect on measures of intrinsic motivation.[4] Rewards increase motivation and performance on tasks that are of low initial interest. On high-interest tasks, positive effects are obtained when participants are verbally praised for their work and when tangible rewards are offered and explicitly tied to performance standards and success. Producing a negative effect of reward requires a particular combination of circumstances; negative effects are obtained primarily on high-interest tasks when tangible rewards signify failure or are loosely tied to behavior.

FINDINGS FROM 30 YEARS OF RESEARCH ON REWARDS AND INTRINSIC MOTIVATION

Conditions necessary to produce a negative effect of reward:

- Task is of high initial interest
- Reward is tangible or material
- Reward is offered beforehand (expected)
- Reward is offered and delivered without regard to success or to a specific level of performance
- Reward is delivered once over a single session
- Intrinsic motivation is indexed as free-choice behavior or self-reported task interest following the withdrawal of reward
- Intrinsic motivation is measured with a single assessment following the removal of reward

A COMPARISON OF OUR META-ANALYTIC FINDINGS TO THOSE OF DECI, KOESTNER, AND RYAN (1999)

Deci and his colleagues claimed that rewards have significant and substantial negative effects on peoples intrinsic motivation. Our analysis, on the other hand, shows that negative effects are limited. Given these discrepancies, in this section we compare our analysis and findings with the meta-analysis conducted by Deci and his research team.

First, it is important to point out that there are several areas of agreement between our current analysis, Deci, Koestner, and Ryan's (1999) meta-analysis, and our previous reviews. In each of these meta-analyses, verbal rewards are shown to increase measures of intrinsic motivation. The findings also show that unexpected tangible rewards do not affect measures of intrinsic motivation. In addition, when rewards are tangible, offered beforehand (expected), and not related to the task at hand (task noncontingent), intrinsic motivation is unaffected. Clearly, not all rewards inevitably result in a loss of intrinsic motivation.

Deci and his associates' claim that tangible rewards are generally harmful is based on their analysis of expected tangible reward contingencies.[5] Our pattern of findings for expected tangible reward contingencies differs from the results of Deci and colleagues' meta-analysis. In Figures 9.1 and 9.2, we compare our present analysis of expected tangible reward contingencies with the meta-analysis of Deci, Koestner, and Ryan. Figure 9.1 shows the effects of rewards

Figure 9.1
**A Comparison of Findings Using a Cognitive Evaluation Framework versus a
Procedural Analysis of the Effects of Expected Tangible Reward Contingencies on
Free-Choice Intrinsic Motivation for High-Interest Tasks**

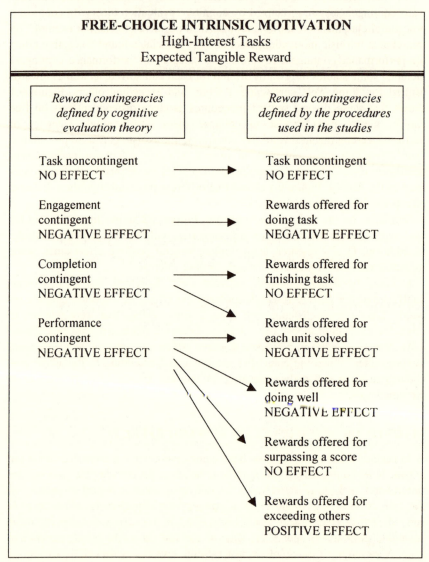

Note: In the cognitive evaluation classification, the completion-contingent and performance-contingent reward groupings contained studies that involved "reward offered for each unit solved."

on free-choice behavior when studies are classified according to cognitive evaluation theory versus a procedural classification of the contingencies. Figure 9.2 presents a comparison of the findings for self-reported task interest.

An examination of Figure 9.1 indicates pervasive negative effects when reward contingencies are organized by cognitive evaluation theory. In contrast, a procedural classification shows circumscribed negative effects. For example, on free-choice intrinsic motivation, Deci and his associates found a negative effect for performance-contingent rewards. The category of performance contingent included some studies of rewards offered for each unit solved, as well as rewards offered for doing well, surpassing a score, and exceeding others. Figure 9.1 shows that these diverse reward procedures produce different effects on free choice; hence, it is unwise to collapse them into a single category of performance-contingent reward. By combining these distinct reward procedures, Deci's research team obtained an overall negative effect for performance-contingent reward. In contrast, when contingencies are defined by the procedures used in the studies, Figure 9.1 shows that different procedures produce different effects on free choice.

Similarly, on the task-interest measure, Figure 9.2 shows that Deci and his associates collapsed data over reward categories, with similar problems resulting. In addition, Deci's research team omitted several positive effects that, when included, resulted in positive findings for task interest.

In sum, the major difference between Deci, Koestner, and Ryan's meta-analysis and our current research concerns the effects of expected tangible rewards. Deci's research team used reward contingencies that were relevant to cognitive evaluation theory but collapsed data over distinct reward procedures. This strategy resulted in pervasive negative effects of expected tangible reward contingencies. When the categories are organized according to the actual procedures used in the studies, negative effects are limited to a specific set of circumstances.

MAGNITUDE AND IMPACT OF REWARD EFFECTS

In each of the meta-analyses to date, a negative effect has been detected when a task is of high initial interest, when the rewards are tangible and offered beforehand, and when the rewards are delivered without regard to success on the task or to any specified level of performance. Specifically, when tangible rewards are offered simply for doing a task (or for doing well on it), some rewarded participants spend less time at the task in a free-choice period and report less interest than a nonrewarded group. Given that this effect was found to be statistically significant in each of the meta-analyses to date, it may be informative to consider how serious the negative effect is.

In all the studies involving reward offered for doing a task (or for doing well on it), time spent on the task during the free-choice period was the measure of free-choice intrinsic motivation. Using the free-time measure, one could ask how

Figure 9.2

A Comparison of Findings Using a Cognitive Evaluation Framework versus a Procedural Analysis of the Effects of Expected Tangible Reward Contingencies on Self-Reported Task Interest for High-Interest Tasks

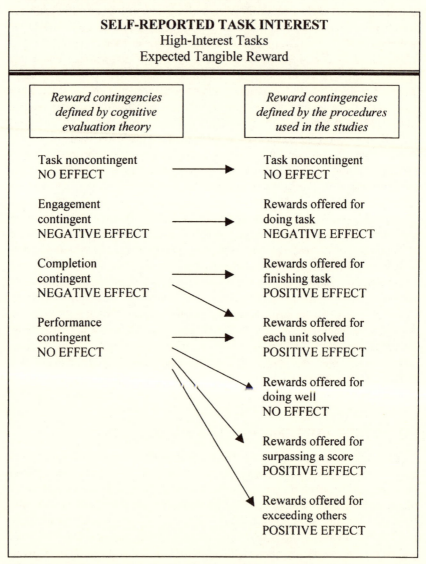

Note: In the cognitive evaluation classification, the completion-contingent and performance-contingent reward groupings contained studies that involved "reward offered for each unit solved."

much less time students would spend on high-interest tasks (e.g., art, music, reading, drama) if a teacher implemented a reward system for doing the task (or for doing it well) and then removed it. Results from our meta-analysis indicate that the average effect size for a comparison between students who receive this reward procedure and nonrewarded individuals on time on task following the withdrawal of reward is about −.30.

In the original experiments, free time on task was typically measured over an eight-minute period. In order to convert the effect size of −.30 to real time, one needs to know the pooled standard deviation of rewarded and nonrewarded groups. Because many researchers report only t or F statistics, which cannot be converted to the overall pooled standard deviation, we were unable to provide an estimate of this parameter. Instead, we used a well-designed study conducted by Pretty and Seligman in 1984 that provides a pooled standard deviation.[6] Pretty and Seligman conducted two experiments with large samples and readily available statistical information. Both experiments compared a condition of tangible rewards offered for doing a high-interest task (Soma™ puzzles) with a nonrewarded control group on eight minutes of free time. The pooled standard deviation was 2.6 minutes.[7]

Using 2.6 minutes as the estimate of error, we were able to convert the negative effect size from the meta-analysis into real time. An effect size of −.30 would mean that in an eight-minute period, the average individual who is offered a tangible reward for doing the task (or doing well) will spend about 47 seconds less time on the task when the reward is withdrawn than the average nonrewarded individual.

Given this result, what would happen if a teacher implemented this incentive procedure in a reading program (for children who already enjoy reading) and then removed it? According to this estimate, students who were offered gold stars for reading would spend about four minutes less time reading in a forty minute free-choice period than students not given the incentive. If we assume that students without reward spend about 30 minutes reading in the 40-minute free choice period, then rewarded students would spend about 26 minutes reading.[8] A four- to five-minute reduction in free-time reading could be behaviorally important if cumulated over many successive opportunities to read, but there are no studies that have addressed this issue. In fact, the few studies that have made repeated measures of intrinsic motivation (following the removal of reward) have found that, over time, participants' intrinsic motivation is not reduced.

A cautionary note is in order. Our example of reading and reward depends on the use of a standard deviation from a single, though well-designed study. It also depends on the ability to extrapolate from an eight-minute experimental period to longer ones. It is possible that the negative effects, such as they are, are evident only for a short time at the beginning of the free-choice period. That is, it may well be the case that if an hour of free choice were given, results might look very different. The point is that this is a hypothetical example. Further evidence is required to generalize the findings to experiments with longer free-choice periods or to everyday settings where choice is distributed over long periods of time.

Given the state of the literature, we conclude that the negative effect of tangible rewards offered for doing a high-interest task (or for doing it well) is statistically significant, but the size of the effect does not suggest a strong impact. Of course, our conclusion with regard to the magnitude of the negative effects of reward contingencies applies equally to positive effects. That is, while the positive effects are statistically significant, they, too, are small.

THEORETICAL IMPLICATIONS

How do the results of our meta-analyses square with the different theories that have been proposed to account for effects of rewards on intrinsic motivation? In Chapter 4 we described the basic tenets of cognitive evaluation theory and the overjustification hypothesis (attribution theory); both of these theories view rewards primarily as harmful. In Chapter 5, we examined social learning theory and behavioral accounts of rewards and intrinsic motivation; from these two perspectives, rewards can be used in helpful ways. In this section, we examine our meta-analytic results in light of the predictions made by these different theoretical positions.

Cognitive Evaluation Theory

According to cognitive evaluation theory, underlying intrinsic motivation are the innate needs for competence and self-determination.[9] Intrinsic motivation is said to be altered by changes in feelings of competence and self-determination. The effect of rewards on people's intrinsic motivation depends on how these events impact an individual's perceptions of competence and self-determination. Events that increase people's beliefs that they are skilled in performing a task and that their performance is based on personal choice will enhance intrinsic motivation. On the other hand, when events decrease self-determination and perceived competence, intrinsic motivation will be undermined. Cognitive evaluation theorists assert that rewards have two aspects: an informational function and a controlling aspect. The informational aspect conveys self-determined competence to an individual, and thus, intrinsic motivation is enhanced. On the other hand, rewards are also experienced as controlling, and hence, self-determination and intrinsic motivation will be reduced.

Cognitive evaluation theory accounts for the incremental effects of verbal praise on intrinsic motivation measures, as found in the meta-analyses to date, by claiming an informational role for verbal rewards. For Deci and his colleagues, verbal praise delivered in a "nonjudgemental" way contains positive informational feedback that serves to increase a person's perceptions of competence and self-determination, which in turn leads to increased intrinsic motivation.[10] As noted in Chapter 8, a few studies using verbal praise showed that feelings of competence increased. The mediating roles of competence and self-determination are less clear-cut, however.

Cognitive evaluation theorists argue that, in contrast to verbal rewards, tangible rewards elicit a strong perception of external control. However, because the cognitive evaluation process is said to take place while a rewarded activity is occurring, unexpected tangible rewards are not predicted to alter people's intrinsic motivation. On high-interest tasks, when tangible rewards are offered to people for doing a task, completing a task, or meeting a performance standard, cognitive evaluation theorists claim that the rewards will be experienced as controlling, and hence, an individual's sense of self-determination will be undermined. Although in some instances, contingent rewards may convey competence, the prediction is that the loss of self-determination will override feelings of competence and the net result will be a decrease in intrinsic motivation for engagement-contingent, completion-contingent, and performance-contingent rewards.

There are two problems with this prediction. First, when expected tangible rewards are classified according to the procedures used, no negative effects are detected on intrinsic motivation measures when the rewards are linked to success, surpassing a score, or exceeding others. A second difficulty concerns the effects of rewards on measures of perceived self-determination. As discussed in Chapter 8, Eisenberger, Pierce, and Cameron evaluated studies with measures of self-determination and showed that rewards offered for doing, completing, or meeting a performance criterion often increased people's perceived sense of freedom and autonomy.[11] These findings are in direct contrast to the predictions made by cognitive evaluation theory.

Our pattern of findings contradicts a strict application of cognitive evaluation theory. Cognitive evaluation theory emphasizes the controlling aspect of expected, contingent, tangible rewards in reducing personal autonomy or self-determination. The loss of perceived autonomy leads to a loss in intrinsic motivation. Our finding that rewards given for success or rewards specifically tied to level of performance (surpassing a score or exceeding others) do not undermine measures of intrinsic motivation is incompatible with the claims of cognitive evaluation theory.

Cognitive evaluation theory could handle the pattern of results if rewards offered for doing a task or for doing it well were shown to be controlling while rewards tied to performance level were shown to enhance perceptions of competency. This is one possible way to relate cognitive evaluation theory to the current results. Of course, the implication is that cognitive evaluation theory would require modification in order to handle positive effects of rewards tied to level of performance and the fact that reward contingencies can increase perceptions of self-determination.

The Overjustification Hypothesis

The predictions of overjustification theory regarding the effects of rewards on intrinsic motivation are essentially the same as those of cognitive evaluation theory.[12] Overjustification theory emphasizes the shift in attribution from internal to external sources that rewards are said to produce. From this perspective, people's perceptions about the causes of their behavior influence future motivation. Unexpected reward is not predicted to alter intrinsic motivation because an individual would have to know about the reward in advance in order to attribute his or her performance to it. Proponents of overjustification theory accept the assumption of cognitive evaluation theory that intrinsic interest will not be undermined by rewards that increase perceived competence without lessening perceived self-determination, such as verbal approval delivered in an uncontrolling manner.[13]

Decrements in intrinsic motivation are predicted to occur when there is a high degree of interest in an activity and when the extrinsic rewards are salient and offered beforehand (expected). Under these conditions, people's perceptions shift from accounting for their behavior as self-initiated to accounting for it in terms of external rewards. In accord with cognitive evaluation theory, expected tangible rewards contingent on doing a task, doing well on a task, completing a task, and meeting a performance standard are all expected to reduce people's intrinsic motivation. Thus, the predictions of the overjustification hypothesis are highly similar to those of cognitive evaluation theory and appear to greatly limit the differences between the two accounts.

The positive effects of verbal praise found in our meta-analysis and the negative effects of tangible rewards offered for doing a task or for doing it well are correctly predicted by the overjustification hypothesis. However, the overjustification hypothesis also predicts negative effects for other expected tangible reward contingencies, which was not supported by our meta-analytic results. In addition, at present, the evidence does not indicate that rewards cause people to attribute their performance to external rather than internal causes.

Social Learning Theory

Based on a procedural classification of reward contingencies, our meta-analytic findings are in accord with a social learning (social cognitive) perspective.[14] The emphasis in social learning is on how reward contingencies relate to perceived competence or self-efficacy. Reward contingencies that enhance perceived competence or self-efficacy are expected to increase interest and performance of an activity. Social cognitive theory predicts that rewards tied to level of performance enhance self-efficacy to the extent that a person is able to attain the performance standard (i.e., succeed). Greater self-efficacy leads to higher interest in a task and more time spent on the activity.

Social learning theory distinguishes between non–competency-contingent and competency-contingent rewards. Non–competency-contingent rewards include rewards given without regard to mastery of performance (e.g., rewards offered for doing an activity, doing it well, completing it, or repeating it). This type of reward contingency includes many of the studies that Deci's research team classified as using task-contingent, completion-contingent, and performance-contingent rewards.[15] From a social cognitive perspective, the bulk of experiments on rewards and intrinsic motivation has involved rewards offered for engaging in an activity without regard to a standard or criterion of performance. According to social cognitive theory, non–competency-contingent rewards impart little indication of competency, in that the rewards are only loosely tied to behavior.

Rewards given for mastery (i.e., achieving relatively challenging behavioral standards) are termed competency-contingent rewards, and it is this type of reward contingency that is said to develop perceptions of self-efficacy and task interest. In our analyses, rewards given for surpassing a score or for exceeding others could be considered a subset of competency-contingent rewards, and positive effects may be a result of increased feelings of competence and self-efficacy. Thus, the predictions of social cognitive theory are compatible with our meta-analytic results. At present, however, there are no studies that have examined the mediating role of self-efficacy.

Behavioral Accounts

As discussed in Chapter 5, behavioral researchers have not provided a theory of reward and intrinsic motivation. Rather, they have suggested a number of hypotheses that could account for the findings, based on a consideration of reinforcement principles. In terms of the difference between high- and low-interest tasks, behavioral researchers have taken the same position as Bandura and question why anyone would use extrinsic rewards for behavior that is already at high strength (high interest). The fact that rewards increase free-choice behavior on low-interest tasks is most important from a behavior-analytic perspective. That is, our finding that rewarding performance on tasks of low initial interest increases measures of intrinsic motivation suggests that rewards may be used without detrimental effects in conditions under which they are most important (i.e., when people have little initial interest in the task). Under these conditions, the extrinsic rewards do not conflict with the natural consequences of the activity.

In terms of high-interest tasks, a useful distinction is made by Carton in his analysis of tangible and verbal rewards.[16] Carton noted that in studies of verbal reward, the rewards were given immediately, frequently, and without any indication of withdrawal. These procedures are typical of a contingency of reinforcement and would be expected to increase performance and interest. Our findings that verbal rewards increase free choice and task interest are in accord with this hypothesis.

In contrast, Carton suggested that in studies of rewards and intrinsic motivation, tangible rewards are usually delivered only once, with some delay between the performance and the reward. In addition, in such studies, participants
are presented with signals that indicate that the rewards are not available for the
free-choice session. Generally, then, tangible rewards are expected to have a
negative effect because the rewards are unlikely to be functioning as reinforcement. Our meta-analytic results do indicate a general negative effect for tangible
reward that could support Carton's hypothesis. This account is given more support by the single-subject studies on the topic, in which tangible rewards were
delivered repeatedly and immediately. No detrimental effect of reward was detected in these studies. Instead, when rewards were withdrawn and repeated
assessments of performance were taken, there was no indication of a change in
intrinsic motivation.

Results from our meta-analysis indicate that tangible rewards produce negative effects when they are offered for doing a task or for doing it well. One way
to understand this negative effect from a behavioral viewpoint is to note that
the rewards used in most of these studies were not shown to function as reinforcement. When non-reinforcing rewards are offered for simply doing a task
(with no regard to quality or level of performance), one possibility is that they
act like demands. Participants may view these nonreinforcing rewards as an
attempt to force them to behave in a given way and may react against the
experimenter's control by showing deliberate non-compliance. Deliberate noncompliance may also be a reaction to the coercive offer of reward by the experimenter. The coercive aspect of the situation will be more prominent when
rewards are given without regard to level of performance. Under these conditions, participants may react by reducing their time and performance on the task
in the free-choice phase.

In our meta-analysis, when tangible rewards were offered for each problem
or unit solved, a negative effect occurred when participants received less than
maximum reward. In this context, less than maximum reward indicates failure.
Failure is a conditioned punisher that temporarily decreases task performance
during the free-choice period. Also, because failure is paired with the natural
rewards of performing the activity, the value of the natural consequences could
decrease. Repeated encounters with failure could, in this way, undermine motivation.

When rewards are offered for success (for meeting or surpassing a performance standard or group norm), the reward procedure can be called *success
contingent*. Rewards programmed for success would not be expected to have a
detrimental effect on free choice intrinsic motivation. This is because the rewards function as reinforcement. Our meta-analytic findings support this interpretation in three ways: (1) when participants were successful at solving
problems and received maximal reward, there was no decrease in intrinsic motivation, (2) rewards offered for surpassing a specified score did not decrease

intrinsic motivation, and (3) rewards offered for exceeding others led to increases in measures of intrinsic motivation.

SUMMARY OF THEORETICAL IMPLICATIONS

In terms of theoretical considerations, the results from our meta-analysis do not support cognitive evaluation theory or the overjustification hypothesis. These two theories focus primarily on negative effects of reward and give little attention to reward contingencies that are shown to enhance performance, interest, or motivation. Our findings are well explained by theories that predict that the effects of reward on intrinsic motivation depend on a clear specification of the reward contingency. Social cognitive theory predicts that rewards tied to level of performance enhance self-efficacy to the extent that the person is able to attain the performance standard (i.e., succeed). Greater self-efficacy leads to higher interest in a task and to more time spent on the activity. In our analyses, the positive effects of rewards given for surpassing a score or exceeding others are in accord with this account. The results also support behavioral explanations in that rewards that are non-reinforcing, or coercive, decrease intrinsic motivation, while rewards that are reinforcing, or based on success, maintain or enhance interest and performance.

PRACTICAL IMPLICATIONS

Our meta-analytic findings indicate that extrinsic rewards do not have pervasive negative effects on people's intrinsic motivation. On tasks of low initial interest, extrinsic rewards can be used to increase motivation and performance. On high-interest tasks, verbal praise and tangible rewards linked to success or to obtaining or exceeding a specific performance standard can enhance people's interest without disrupting performance of the activity in a free-choice setting. These reward contingencies can be viewed as a subset of the many possible arrangements of the use of reward in everyday life. Rewards can be arranged to progressively shape performance,[17] cultivate initial interest in an activity,[18] and maintain or enhance effort and persistence at a task.[19]

A negative effect occurs when a task is of high initial interest and the rewards are tangible, offered beforehand, and delivered without regard to success on the task or any specified level of performance. Under this combination of conditions, experimental findings indicate that some rewarded participants spend less time on the task (in a free-choice period without reward) and report less task enjoyment than a nonrewarded group. This effect is statistically significant in all the meta-analyses to date on this topic, but the effect is small. In addition, the negative effect appears to be a temporary phenomenon; no long-term decremental effects of reward are detected when rewards are presented repeatedly and intrinsic motivation measures are assessed over time.

How relevant to everyday life is the decremental effect of reward found in the experimental studies? One would be hard pressed to find any real-life circumstances that directly parallel the laboratory conditions necessary to produce a negative effect. It is difficult to imagine an employer or manager who would shower incentives on employees for a temporary period regardless of how they behave, withdraw the system, and then expect them to work hard after hours. In educational environments, students are rarely rewarded simply for doing activities that they already enjoy. Rewards are most often used to shape successful performance and recognize student accomplishment. In addition, the rewards are usually presented over a period of time, and as proficiency in a task increases, they are gradually faded out. In contrast, in the typical between-groups reward and intrinsic motivation experiment, the procedure involves a single reward delivery followed by a single assessment of intrinsic motivation without reward. The point is that the procedures used in the experimental studies that obtained negative effects of reward on intrinsic motivation are not characteristic of the use of rewards in applied settings.

The comparability of the reward contingencies used in the laboratory experiments to those used in everyday settings is frequently ignored in discussions that emphasize the detrimental effects of reward on intrinsic task interest. Instead, those who argue that negative effects are pervasive tend to condemn the use of rewards in practical settings. Thus, it is important to consider any circumstances that could remotely resemble the laboratory conditions shown to produce a negative effect of reward.

In work settings, there are some circumstances in which individuals are rewarded irrespective of success or performance level. For example, because of compensation and promotion systems that are insensitive to performance (e.g., wages set by job classification), some employees can vary their performance substantially yet with little effect on tangible reward. In such a situation, employees may have considerable latitude in how well or poorly they perform their jobs, without any change in pay or fringe benefits. If an employee has high intrinsic interest in the job and receives a reward independent of performance, interest in the job may decrease, thereby producing poorer performance than if the reward were contingent on performance.

In educational settings, if a student has high interest in a particular subject matter, say a history course, and receives the same grade regardless of performance, interest in history could deteriorate. The student may be less likely to spend time reading history both during the course and following its conclusion.

In order to avoid poor performance and reduced task interest in business and educational settings, employers, teachers, and administrators need to consider the basis on which they allocate rewards, recognition, and advancement. Our meta-analysis suggests that when people are praised or given positive feedback for their work, task interest and performance increase. When tangible rewards (e.g., money) are made contingent on success or on meeting a performance standard, motivation is enhanced.

The findings from our meta-analysis and the results of single-subject, repeated-measures experiments are in accord with a retrospective survey on the effects of extrinsic reward offered to children for reading. Flora and Flora examined the effects of parental pay for reading as well as participation in the "Book It" reading program sponsored by the Pizza Hut chain.[20] The "Book It" program involved over 22 million children in Australia, Canada, and the United States. The children set reading goals and were rewarded with coupons redeemable for pizzas if they met their objectives. Flora and Flora's findings indicate that neither offers of money nor pizzas negatively affected reading or intrinsic motivation for reading in everyday life. These results indicate that the findings from our meta-analysis have external validity. That is, in both laboratory situations and everyday settings, rewards offered contingent on meeting a specific level of performance do not negatively affect people's intrinsic motivation.

In some of the studies of rewards linked to performance standards, individuals were told in advance that reward depended on surpassing the performance of some percentage of others who had previously performed the task. In business and education, this type of reward contingency is quite common. Rewards are frequently given for surpassing the past or current performance of others. For example, the criteria that many teachers use to grade students typically depends on how well other students have done in the past.

In business, bonuses or promotions are often paid to individuals or groups for outperforming others. In many cases, the comparison of performance with others is implicit; organizations typically attempt to set commissions on sales high enough to motivate increased performance but not so high as to allow income to exceed that paid to higher level employees. Because the experimental studies found that reward offered for exceeding others increased participants' expressed interest and time spent on an activity, such a reward contingency might be used by employers without the detrimental effects that accompany rewards offered simply for doing a task. Unfortunately, at this point in time, we lack information concerning the durability of the effect of this type of reward on intrinsic task interest.

In many practical settings, the reward contingencies are not clearly related to those examined in the intrinsic interest studies conducted in the laboratory. An employee may have to meet a rather low performance standard, in order to avoid being fired. Systematic research is needed concerning the effect of stringency of the standard on intrinsic task interest. In other job or school settings, the magnitude of reward is often a continuous function or step-function of performance; the greater the performance, the greater is the reward. This differs from the typical laboratory use of an all-or-none performance standard to study reward. Sliding scales of reward, which are frequently used in everyday life, may have strong beneficial effects on intrinsic interest because they allow individuals to experience increasing levels of reward while feeling increasingly competent.

CONCLUSION

In this chapter, we have shown that rewards are not inherently either bad or good for people. Rewards can have negative effects, but such effects are circumscribed, limited, and easily prevented. A careful arrangement of rewards in educational settings and the work environment can enhance employees' interest and performance. This occurs when rewards are closely tied to the attainment of performance standards.

Our meta-analytic findings can be placed in the broader context of rewards given for mastery or competency.[21] Under these conditions, rewards foster performance accomplishments. When tasks are challenging and graded in steps toward the mastery of skills, rewards given at each step of accomplishment can instill interest and high personal standards for performance.[22] In addition, when rewards are made contingent on effort, people work harder at the task to which they are assigned and show increased performance on other activities. Rewarding high effort builds a generalized "learned industriousness."[23] The implications are that rewards based on challenge, mastery, and high effort build skills, interest, performance standards, and persistence.

Educators, business mangers, and administrators are interested, not only in high levels of interest, performance, and motivation, but also in promoting creative and novel achievements by their students and employees. Creative performance involves the generation of novel behavior that meets a standard of quality or utility. Reward for working hard at being creative may increase creativity. Eisenberger has shown that when rewards are given for creative thinking and performance, people show generalized creativity on other tasks. When rewards are given for menial activities involving little effort, however, creativity will be low on the task and generalize to low creativity in other situations.[24] The point is that "you get what you reinforce." Creativity can be instilled by reward procedures that specify creative performance. On the other hand, people can learn to behave in a generally uncreative manner if low creativity and effort are reinforced.

Taken together, the findings from our meta-analysis and other experimental literature suggest that rewards increase performance and interest when rewards are:

- made contingent on success or are given for meeting clear standards of performance
- made contingent on challenging activities
- given for mastering each component of a complex skill
- delivered for high effort and creativity

In each of these situations, it is important to arrange the reward so that it closely follows the designated behavior. Rewards that are delayed allow for other performances to occur during the interval, and consequently, those involved may not learn the actual basis of reward. In addition, research indicates that reward plans are most effective in organizations in which the employees are involved in the design and implementation of the plan.[25] In sum, when students and employees participate in performance/reward plans and rewards are immediate and based on personal competence, effort, and accomplishment, individuals will enjoy their work and do it well.

Given these findings, it is surprising that some educators, psychologists, and business spokespersons continue to argue that rewards have generalized negative effects on human behavior. These advocates would have us remove all forms of incentive systems in business, education, and other major institutions of our society. If this could not be accomplished, they would advocate that rewards should be loosely tied to behavior, since this would have the least negative effect on the supposed innate human drive for competence and self-determination. In answer to this position, we note the unmitigated failure of collective farms in the former Soviet Union, a situation in which rewards for productivity were only loosely tied to actual performance. Our research suggests that when rewards are linked to specific standards of performance, people will be more contented and productive employees. Why, then, would managers implement loose incentive systems that fail to reward success, effort, accomplishment, and quality of performance? The answer from our research is that this would be a backward step. Instead, an evaluation of the experimental findings indicates that interest and performance will increase when businesses and schools succeed in tying rewards to high-level personal accomplishments.

NOTES

1. Deci, Koestner, and Ryan (2001) made this claim and suggested that the use of rewards should be of particular concern to those who work in educational settings.

2. Cameron and Pierce, 1994; Eisenberger and Cameron, 1996.

3. Ibid.

4. As indicated, this analysis is based on Cameron, Banko, and Pierce (2001).

5. Deci, Koestner, and Ryan, 1999.

6. Pretty and Seligman, 1984.

7. Deci (1971) also used the Soma™ puzzle, assessed the free time measure over an eight-minute period, and the pooled standard deviation was 2.4 minutes.

8. Based on Deci, Koestner, and Ryan's (1999) analysis of engagement-contingent reward, rewarded children would spend about 25 minutes reading in a 40-minute period.

9. The most recent statements of the tenets of cognitive evaluation theory can be found in Deci, Koestner, and Ryan (1999) and in Ryan and Deci (2000).

10. Deci, Koestner, and Ryan, 1999.

11. Eisenberger, Pierce, and Cameron, 1999.

12. Lepper, Greene, and Nisbett, 1973.

13. Lepper and Gilovich, 1981; Lepper and Henderlong, 2000.
14. Bandura, 1986, 1997.
15. Deci, Koestner, and Ryan, 1999.
16. Carton, 1996.
17. Schunk, 1983, 1984.
18. Bandura, 1986.
19. Eisenberger, 1992.
20. Flora and Flora, 1999.
21. Also see Bandura, 1986.
22. See Schunk, 1983.
23. Eisenberger, 1992.
24. Eisenberger and Armeli, 1997; Eisenberger and Cameron, 1996.
25. McAdams and Hawk, 1992.

PART V

REWARDS AND INTRINSIC MOTIVATION: A SOCIOHISTORICAL PERSPECTIVE

Chapter 10

A Sociohistorical Analysis of the Literature on Rewards and Intrinsic Motivation

Throughout human history, many wrong-headed ideas have been popularized as cherished beliefs. Once prevalent, these ideas are propagated and maintained for a long time, even in the face of disconfirming evidence. There was a time when everyone believed that the earth was flat, that the sun revolved around the earth, and that human flight was impossible. Today these beliefs seem silly. But an enormous amount of effort and evidence was required and a great deal of resistance was encountered before such ideas were replaced. The view that rewards (or any external control) disrupt or destroy intrinsic motivation is also a misguided notion.

As shown in Chapters 2 and 3, the early studies did not produce evidence of a generalized negative effect of rewards. In Part IV of this book, we showed that when all studies are considered, the negative effect remains highly circumscribed and minimal. Nonetheless, the view that rewards reduce people's intrinsic motivation continues to be held in high regard. Why have millions of dollars and thousands of human hours been spent on this topic? Why do researchers continue to advocate against the use of rewards, even when the evidence does not support this position? And why does the view that rewards are harmful remain popular? One way to understand why this view became popular is to examine the literature in the context in which it was instigated.

If rewards are not harmful, what sociohistorical trends contributed to the negative effect view and made it acceptable? Can we trace certain patterns of thought that culminated in the early research on rewards and intrinsic motivation? These are important questions; the answers help us to see that the bad reputation of rewards arose in a historical context. In this chapter, we analyze the rewards and intrinsic motivation controversy from a sociohistorical perspective. Our analysis indicates that the literature on rewards and intrinsic motivation is best understood as part of a historical debate between behaviorism and other views in psychology.

The chapter begins with a description of the rise of behavioral views in psychology, the dispute over mentalism and introspection, arguments about freedom and control, and the reemergence of mentalism as cognitive psychology. Each of these elements contributed to an opposition toward behaviorism and the view that the use of reinforcement and rewards is harmful.

THE RISE OF BEHAVIORISM AND THE DECLINE OF MENTALISM

The most commonly accepted date of the origin of psychology as a science is 1879, when Wilhelm Wundt founded the first psychological laboratory. In the beginning, psychology was the study of the mind, or psyche (i.e., mental events, structures, and processes). The aim of a psychology of mind was to describe and explain consciousness. In order to understand consciousness, psychologists used introspection (looking inside oneself) and self-observation as basic methods. These methods involved analyzing the content of consciousness into component parts such as sensations, images, feelings, and thoughts. An important aspect of a psychology of mind is that the human psyche is viewed as the center of action and creative thought. As conscious beings, people are said to create representations of the world and to act in accord with their perceptions, memories, and plans. This early view is reflected today in psychologies that view people as willful, intentional, and self-determined. From this perspective, external influences (e.g., reward) interfere with people's basic capacity for self-direction and, in doing so, disrupt an individual's intrinsic motivation.

During the 1890s in North America, psychology gradually moved away from a psychology of the mind and individual agency toward a behaviorist view. In 1892, the American Psychological Association (APA) was founded and professionalism required that psychologists define their role in society. Based on a pragmatic viewpoint, "reform, efficiency, and progress" were the major values of American society. The period has been called "the age of the news—the new education, the new ethics, the new woman, and the new psychology."[1] Psychologists began talking about a science of behavior that could be practical, objective and verifiable through natural science methods (direct observation and experimentation).

The new behavioral psychology stood in contrast to a psychology of the individual and the mind. Behaviorists argued that stimulation and feedback from the environment (both physical and social) are important determinants of human behavior. In the behaviorist view, creative thinking (often attributed to the mind) arises from the interaction between human behavior and the social and physical environments, rather than from an autonomous creative mind. From a behavioral perspective, external rewards can be arranged to enhance creativity, feelings of self-determination, and personal competence.

Some psychologists saw the new psychology of behavior as quantitative and experimental and claimed "wide reaching practical applications in education, medicine, the fine arts, political economy, and indeed, in the whole conduct of life."[2] John Dewey, a philosopher of education and president of the APA in 1899, saw educational reform as a central concern for the new psychology. One implication of Dewey's pragmatic philosophy was that psychology would have to understand the control of human behavior by stimulation and feedback from the environment (e.g., praise by teachers).[3] This movement toward an objective and practical science of behavior eventually predominated over the study of the mind and introspection. Several prominent researchers contributed to the rise of behaviorism and to the rejection of mentalistic psychology.

Ivan Petrovich Pavlov (1849–1936)

One person whose ideas were highly influential in behavioral psychology was Ivan Pavlov, a Russian physiologist who was well known at the time for his work on digestion. At the time, many people thought that all animals, with the exception of humans, were complex biological machines. The idea was that a specific stimulus would evoke a particular response in much the same way that turning a key starts an engine. In other words, animals would react to the environment in a simple cause-and-effect manner. Humans, on the other hand, were seen as different from other animals in that their actions were purposive. Humans were said to anticipate future events.

In the course of his experiments on digestive secretions in dogs, Pavlov noticed that when the experimenter appeared, the dogs would salivate, seemingly in anticipation of food. The appearance of the experimenter had not originally elicited salivation. The effect was observed only after the experimenter's presence had been paired with the presentation of food. Pavlov recognized that such a result challenged the conventional wisdom that only humans displayed forethought.

Pavlov had made an important observation in terms of the study of behavior. He reasoned that anticipatory reflexes were learned or conditioned. Further, Pavlov concluded that these conditioned reflexes were an essential part of the behavior of organisms. Although some behaviors were described as innate reflexes, other actions were based on conditioning that occurred during the animal's life.

Taking advantage of this observation, Pavlov set out to investigate the phenomenon experimentally. The question was how to study conditioned reflexes systematically. Pavlov's answer to this question represents a major advance in the experimental science of behavior. If dogs reliably salivated at the sight of a lab coat, Pavlov reasoned, any arbitrary stimulus that preceded food might also be conditioned to evoke salivation. Pavlov replaced the experimenter's lab coat with a stimulus that he could systematically manipulate and reliably control. In some experiments, a metronome (a device used to keep the beat while playing the piano) was presented to the dog just before it was fed. This procedure resulted in the dog eventually salivating to the sound of the metronome.

Overall, Pavlov's research shows that part of human and animal behavior is caused by external events. In terms of behaviorism, Pavlov showed that external stimuli can control specific responses. More important, he showed that the control by these stimuli can be transferred to other (arbitrary) parts of the environment (e.g., a white lab coat or a metronome). One implication of this research is that much human behavior that appears to be purposive, intentional, and conscious is, in fact, due to conditioning. Pavlov's work represented a major break from the view that human behavior arose from mental processes and events in the mind.

John Broadus Watson (1878–1958)

Pavlov's research became prominent in North America, and the conditioned reflex was incorporated into a more general theory of behavior by the famous behaviorist John B. Watson. Building on the work of Pavlov, Watson argued that there was no need to make up unobservable mental associations to account for human and animal behavior. He proposed that instead, psychology should be a science based on observable behavior.

In Watson's behaviorism, thoughts and feelings had no place in a scientific account and researchers were encouraged to direct their attention to observable movements and measured neural activity. Although this was an extreme position, Watson succeeded in directing the attention of psychologists to the study of behavior and its environmental determinants.

In 1913, Watson published his most influential work in *Psychological Review*, in an article titled, "Psychology as the Behaviorist Views It."[4] The article outlined Watson's views on behaviorism and argued that objectivity was the only way to build a science of psychology. In particular, Watson rejected people's reports of their thoughts and feelings as scientific data. Self-reports were seen as subjective and unreliable. Inferring mental states from self-reports was not, according to Watson, a scientific enterprise. Finally, Watson noted that the psychology of mind had little practical value for behavior control or public affairs.

Watson's behaviorism did not sit well with those psychologists who claimed the existence of a mental world within the skin. For his opponents, behaviorism seemed to dehumanize people, making them into puppets reacting to pulls on their strings. Based on this characterization of Watson's position, many psychologists and educators rejected the evidence of conditioning and claimed that humans were not subject to conditioning principles. The control of human behavior, even by positive external means, became viewed as an encroachment on human nature. From a humanistic (and a psychology of mind) perspective, people were conscious beings striving for freedom (from control), competence, and dignity. Control by external means was necessarily bad. These views were a forerunner to current claims that external rewards damage people's intrinsic motivation.

Edward Lee Thorndike (1874–1949)

Watson's behaviorism emphasized observable behavior and the conditioned reflex. His analysis focused on the events that precede action and is usually called a stimulus-response (S-R) approach. Another American psychologist, Edward Thorndike, was more concerned with how success and failure affect the behavior of organisms. His research emphasized the events or consequences that follow behavior. Thorndike was the first scientist to systematically study what B.F. Skinner later called "operant" behavior. Thorndike called these behavioral changes "trial-and-error learning."[5]

Thorndike was always intrigued with animal behavior. At Columbia University, Thorndike began his famous experiments on trial-and-error learning in cats. Cats were placed in what Thorndike called a "puzzle box," and food was placed outside the box. A cat that struggled to get out of the box would accidentally step on a treadle, pull a string, and so on. These responses resulted in the cat opening the puzzle-box door and obtaining food. Thorndike found that most cats took less and less time to solve the problem after they were repeatedly returned to the box (i.e., repeated trials). From these observations, Thorndike made the first formulation of the law of effect:

The cat that is clawing all over the box in her impulsive struggle will probably claw the string or loop or button so as to open the door. And gradually all the other non-successful impulses will be stamped out and the particular impulse leading to the successful act will be stamped in by the resulting pleasure, until after many trials, the cat will, when put in the box, immediately claw the button or loop in a definite way.[6]

Today, Thorndike's law of effect is restated as the principle of reinforcement, which states that behavior may be followed by consequences that increase or decrease that behavior in the same situation.

In terms of behaviorism, the research by Thorndike demonstrates that behavior is regulated by its feedback, or consequences. The cat pulls a string and gets out of the box; a person looks in a drawer and finds a lost object. In both cases, the behavior is likely to be repeated under similar conditions. The law of effect is not something a person chooses to obey. Just as the law of gravity determines that we will fall to the ground if we jump, the law of effect requires that human behavior will increase (or decrease) due to its past consequences.

Those who contend that rewards decrease intrinsic motivation often argue against the generality of the law of effect. From this position, the law of effect is not a basic principle of human nature. Humans are viewed as self-determining. Applying external consequences to activities is said to undermine this basic aspect of human nature and subvert interest in the activities.[7] The larger debate concerns the uniqueness of humans compared to other animals. Behaviorists view both animal and human behavior as determined by the laws of conditioning, whereas those who argue against the law of effect do not believe that the same principles operate for both animals and humans.

Burrhus Fredrick Skinner (1904–1990)

Although the ideas of many scientists and philosophers have had an impact on behaviorism, B.F. Skinner is largely responsible for the development of behavior analysis and the philosophy of modern behaviorism. Skinner emphasized operant behavior, which is behavior that "operates upon the environment to produce effects or consequences."[8] Some of these effects increase behavior and are called reinforcement. The claim by critics that reward and reinforcement have negative effects on intrinsic motivation is, in a large part, a challenge to the views of Skinner and his science of behavior.

In accord with Watson, Skinner talked about a science of behavior rather than of physiology or mental life. In contrast to Watson, however, Skinner did not reject mental events from scientific analysis. Skinner argued that remembering, thinking, feeling, and so on are private behaviors of the organism that require explanation. He proposed that contingencies of reinforcement control both public and private behavior (e.g., thinking) of animals and humans. A contingency of reinforcement involves events (S^D, or discriminative stimulus) that set the occasion for behavior, the operant (R), and the requirements for reinforcement (S^r).

Skinner's model of operant conditioning breaks with all other modes of psychology. Behavior is selected by the contingencies of reinforcement, and not directed by mental, cognitive, or physiological processes. Behavior has a range of variation, and the process of reinforcement selects the form of response that is appropriate to the situation

---

SKINNER'S BEHAVIORAL MODEL

- Study the behavior of organisms, including humans
- Behavior is selected by its consequences; it is not directed by mental processes
- Behavior (including thinking and feeling) is due to the biology of the species and selection by reinforcement during the lifetime of the individual

---

Reinforcement is a process at the behavioral level that is analogous to Charles Darwin's concept of natural selection at the biological level.[9] Darwin and Skinner were both vehemently attacked by critics. Darwin showed that humans were part of a process of evolution and natural selection and not unique in terms of a soul or spirit; instead, he stated that humans were simply one of many types of organisms on the planet. Skinner showed that behavior was not due to a creative mind or cognitive representations but to the biology of the species (Homo sapiens) and selection of behavior by reinforcement during the lifetime of the individual. Both Darwin and Skinner challenged the Western cultural ideal that humans are unique beings pursuing their creative and purposive goals and objectives.

Skinner advocated the use of positive reinforcement but noted that the most prevalent form of behavior control in our society is punishment.[10] That is, people often use punishment to get what they want or make people behave as they want. A literature of freedom has identified obvious sources of punitive control and advocated methods of escape from coercive environments. Because punishment and control are often associated, most people take the control of behavior (even by positive rewards) to be coercive. For this reason, the general idea of behavioral control is a concern to many people.

Skinner questioned whether it is possible to eliminate behavior control and whether control is the same as coercion. Experimental evidence convinced him that the control of behavior is a fact of nature that may be investigated and described. That is, the control of human conduct by the social and physical environment is a built-in aspect of the world. People cannot choose to accept or reject behavior control, because it is a fact of life. We all accept the control of physical objects, chemical reactions, and physiological processes. Skinner argued that the control of behavior was just as natural; humans adjust their behavior on the basis of stimulation and feedback from the physical and social environment. If such stimulation and feedback are socially arranged (either inadvertently or by plan) for particular forms of conduct, then it follows that human behavior is controlled by the actions of others.

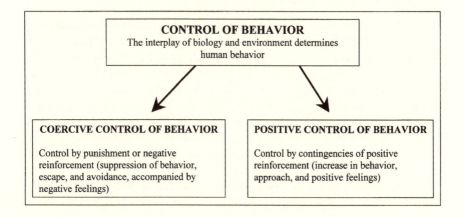

Is control the same as coercion? Skinner's answer is that the process of positive reinforcement is a form of control but the control is not punitive. Positive reinforcement is a type of control that is seldom identified and less frequently used in our society. A positive reinforcement system takes time to increase particular forms of conduct, but once it has been established, people often describe themselves as happy, contented, and self-fulfilled in such a system. According to Skinner, people do not show the negative by-products of punitive control (generalized escape and avoidance) when positive reinforcement is arranged for their behavior. A culture based on positive reinforcement not only teaches desired actions, it also instills a commitment to the survival of the culture, its values and practices.[11]

CHALLENGES TO BEHAVIORISM

The post–World War II years have been described as a period of "comfortable eclecticism" in psychology.[12] Many varieties of behaviorism were offered in the colleges and universities of North America.[13] At the same time, other schools of thought began to emerge (i.e., humanism, developmental psychology, and cognitive psychology). Three important developments occurred that set the stage for the research on rewards and intrinsic motivation. First, there were debates between humanists and behaviorists concerning the role of the environment and the control of human behavior. At the same time, the computer revolution led to the resurgence of mental representations and the rise of cognitive psychology. Finally, social psychologists challenged learning theory's claims about the relationship between rewards and attitude. This challenge paved the way for the subsequent attack on behaviorism by social psychologists, who claimed that rewards decreased intrinsic motivation.

Humanism and Behaviorism

The humanistic movement in psychology arose during the 1950s and 1960s as a reaction to both psychoanalysis and behaviorism. Humanists typically have strong negative reactions to behaviorism, and especially to Skinner's ideas. They believe that Skinner opposed the concepts of free will, purposeful action, self-actualization, and inner meanings of self. In fact, however, Skinner provided an account of freedom, purpose, and the self in behavioral terms.[14] The major point of disagreement was that humanists believed in the "autonomous human" as the guiding force in human behavior. Skinner rejected the individual as a causal agent. He argued that human behavior changed the environment and that these changes in turn caused subsequent human conduct. Only by acknowledging the role of the environment, Skinner stated, are humans able to shape behavior that is called creative, meaningful, and self-fulfilling.

The dispute between humanists and behaviorists is highlighted by the ideological debates between B.F. Skinner and Carl Rogers.[15] Carl Rogers founded a form of humanistic clinical psychology called client-centered therapy. He advocated for the use of encounter groups (a therapy group that focuses on self awareness and encourages open expression of feelings) and developed a theory of person-centered action.[16] Rogers believed that humans were basically good by nature, seeking growth, fulfillment, and meaningful relationships with others.

Humanists state that in order to achieve self-actualization and positive social relationships, people must become aware of, and express, their inner experiences (perceptions, thoughts, feelings, sensations, etc.). According to Rogers, many people fail in this quest because of their need for positive regard (acceptance and love) from others. Usually, significant others give love and acceptance only when the person lives up to their expectations. That is, positive regard is given on a conditional basis, and, according to Rogers, this interferes with a person's awareness of true feelings and beliefs. If people are to achieve self-actualization, argues Rogers, positive regard must be given unconditionally. That is, people must be completely accepted for what they are if they are to develop in positive ways.

Rogers founded client-centered therapy to enhance self-awareness and reduce the presumed detrimental influence of conditional positive regard by others. The therapy rested on three major tenets: (1) empathic understanding, (2) unconditional positive regard, and (3) genuineness. A client-centered therapist must sense, through empathy, the subjective meanings of a client's experiences and reflect this understanding. In this way, people gain more awareness about their experiences. At the same time, the therapist shows unconditional caring and accepting of the client's feelings and beliefs, allowing the person to become more self-accepting of the full range of sensations, thoughts, and emotions. Finally, the therapist strives to maintain genuineness, or honesty of interaction, with the client. Honesty of interaction leads to greater trust and more ease and comfort in expressing ones' true feelings.

Skinner rejected the idea that people could look within themselves and make free choices to change their self-concept. His analysis of the therapeutic situation suggested that the therapist and client were interacting in a way that shaped the client's behavior. If a therapist succeeded in being completely nonjudgmental and accepting, Skinner suggested that this only allowed the client's behavior to reflect its past history of reinforcement and current interaction with others outside the therapy session. For example, a therapist may use subtle ways to encourage the client to be more assertive in talking about his or her true feelings. Assertive talking may have an effect on significant others, who then reinforce this behavior by being more compliant with the client's requests. These changes in the social environment, stated Skinner, and not the need for self-actualization, account for any modification of behavior.

In terms of education and motivation, Rogers and Skinner also differed in opinions. Rogers's view of learning was in accord with the romanticism of Jean-Jacques Rousseau; the view was that learning is best accomplished in unstructured settings, with little interference by teachers and other adults.[17] A person is free to pursue personal interests and to choose his or her own, self-guided path to knowledge. Thus, Rogers emphasized freedom, independence, and self-actualization as the basis of education. Social influence by teachers, parents and other educators was viewed as detrimental to motivation and learning according Roger's humanist point of view.[18]

Skinner agreed that the goals of education were to develop positive feelings about learning and promote greater feelings of independence. For Skinner, however, a person feels free and enjoys learning when the educational environment is arranged (structured) to produce positive reinforcement for academic and social behavior. The task for educators is to reduce punitive control that leads students to "tune out or drop out" and to implement effective systems of positive reinforcement.[19] Skinner disagreed with Rogers's claim that unstructured settings and low involvement by teachers improves learning. If students learn under these conditions, claimed Skinner, it is because other sources of control, outside the classroom, have shaped their behavior. If educators do not teach by positive reinforcement, students may learn ways of acting from other sources that are not desirable from the point of view of parents, teachers, and other segments of society.[20]

Generally, behaviorists and humanists agree on the goals of education but disagree on the means to these ends. Humanists, on the basis of their philosophy of human nature, advocate for unstructured classrooms and less instruction by teachers. Behaviorists, on the basis of experimental evidence, propose to reduce punitive control and increase the regulation of academic and social behavior by positive reinforcement.

| A COMPARISON OF HUMANISM AND BEHAVIORISM ||
Humanism	*Behaviorism*
• free will and person as casual agent • purposeful action directed at goals • inner meanings • self-actualization	• control of human behavior • operant behavior due to past consequences • contingencies of reinforcement • interplay of biology and environment

The claim that rewards lessen a person's intrinsic motivation is a logical extension of the humanist thesis for education. From the humanist perspective, unstructured classrooms and minimal teacher involvement lessen external control. Rewards are sources of control, and humanists argue that any form of control has negative implications for self-actualization.[21] Behaviorists oppose this claim about rewards, just as they have opposed the general view that self-actualization is the center of learning and education. The behavioral view is that structured classrooms and planned intervention by teachers are necessary for successful learning because, from the behavioral perspective, control is inevitable. Rather than allow student behavior to be controlled by unplanned contingencies, educators can motivate students by designing a positive reinforcement system.

Cognitive Psychology and Behaviorism

The rise of cognitive psychology is another historical force contributing to the debate about rewards and intrinsic motivation. This rise has been heralded as a revolution, but it is more likely that cognitive psychology represents a return to purposive models of human behavior.[22] Edwin Tolman's book, *Purposive Behavior in Animals and Men*, written in 1932, focused on anticipatory thinking (cognitive maps and expectations) in humans and animals.[23] Forward thinking about goals, actions, and outcomes was said to direct behavior. Modern cognitive psychologists have adopted Tolman's views but have substituted "cognitive representations" for "forward thinking."

The reemergence of cognitive psychology is also associated with the computer revolution and work on artificial intelligence.[24] Cognitive theories postulate thought and memory processes as determinants of human behavior, much as software programs of the computer determine output. Thus, the computer metaphor gave a major impetus to the rise of cognitive psychology.

Cognitive researchers claim that human behavior is due to underlying cognitive processes that are much like information processing by computers. The causes of behavior lie within a person and that person's cognitive representations of the world. Cognitive psychologists emphasize the person as a source of causation and self-determination.[25] External rewards are harmful in this view because these events change people's cognitive representations. More specifically, rewards shift attributions of control from the person to the environment, thus undermining perceptions of self-determination. This change in attribution results in less interest in the activities for which the person was rewarded.

The notion of cognitive representations of actions and outcomes is in contrast to the modern behavioral view that began with B.F. Skinner.[26] In a behavioral account, remembering, thinking, and feeling are not cognitive processes that direct behavior; rather, they are private behaviors of an individual. These private events do not explain behavior but rather constitute more behavior to be explained. The explanation of both private behaviors and overt actions rests on an analysis of the biology of the species and the contingencies of reinforcement encountered by people over their lifetimes.[27]

Social Psychology, Rewards, and Attitudes

Another development in the debate about rewards and intrinsic motivation came from studies in social psychology conducted during the 1950s and 1960s. Social psychologists had developed cognitive accounts of human behavior prior to the emergence of the information-processing view. Specifically, social psychologists were interested in personal and interpersonal attitudes and how attitudes influenced human behavior. One important question concerned the factors that produced attitude change. Leon Festinger proposed the theory of cognitive dissonance as an account of how people change their attitudes based on information.[28] When information about attitudes and behavior is inconsistent, people experience a state of tension called "cognitive dissonance." In order to reduce dissonance, people change their attitudes to bring them in line with their behavior. That is, people make their attitudes consistent with their behavior.

An important aspect of attitude change and dissonance is the effect of rewards or incentives. Festinger argued that the larger the external reward a person receives for doing something in which he or she does not believe, the less will be the attitude change. Rewards and incentives are good justifications for actions that are inconsistent with attitudes. The greater the justification for the action, the less will be the dissonance and the smaller will be the attitude change.

In terms of dissonance theory, consider the following situation.Two people are engaged in a dull, boring task, toward which both have a negative attitude. One person is paid $20 to say that the task is fun and enjoyable; the other person is paid $1 to say the same thing. The prediction from dissonance theory is that the person who is paid the smaller amount of money will end up liking the task more (have a more positive attitude) than the higher paid individual. The person who was paid $20 has good justification for saying that he or she likes the task. The large reward justifies the statement and reduces the dissonance caused by the inconsistency between the attitude (the task is boring) and the behavior (saying that the task is enjoyable). Because dissonance is low, attitude change is minimal. That is, the person continues to believe that the task is dull and boring. On the other hand, the person who was paid $1 has less justification for the counterattitudinal statement and thus encounters high dissonance. In order to reduce the dissonance, the person changes his or her attitude toward the task (begins to like it). Festinger and Carlsmith carried out an experiment that confirmed that there was more attitude change (liking of a boring task) with less monetary reward.[29]

Generally, dissonance research appeared to show that external incentives were detrimental to attitude change. From this perspective, in order to get children to like reading, writing, and arithmetic, one would use the least amount of inducement to get them to do these activities.[30] Because children cannot justify reading (or other academic activities) in terms of external rewards, they will have high dissonance, which in turn will lead to an attitude change. In this case, the children will change their attitudes toward the school subject (come to like it). That is, the smaller the reward, the more positive will be the attitude toward an activity.

In the 1960s, dissonance theory's predictions about reward and attitude change were viewed as a direct contradiction to theories of learning and behaviorism. The claim was that learning theories would predict that the person who was paid $20 should be more enthusiastic about the task than the person paid only one dollar. Because theories about rewards and reinforcement did not account for the creation of more attitude change with less reward, behavioral principles of reinforcement were brought into question.

Daryl Bem carried out research based on a behavioral analysis of reward, attitude, and dissonance in the late 1960s.[31] Using standard behavior principles and Skinner's analysis of verbal behavior, Bem showed that people judged their attitudes based on their behavior. Just as an outside observer would use the amount of reward to judge the "true beliefs" of an individual, so the person him- or herself uses the amount of reward to infer his or her own attitudes. For example, a promotional message by an advertiser or politician is less credible and persuasive if the viewer or listener finds out that the speaker is being paid to say it. From Bem's perspective, the same process occurs in self-persuasion. Thus, the person who is paid $20 to say that a boring task is fun and enjoyable uses the large amount of money to infer low credibility of the statement and is not persuaded by the message (the task continues to be seen as boring). There is no dissonance reduction in Bem's self-persuasion analysis. Notice also that rewards do not serve as reinforcement for behavior in this scenario but rather serve as stimuli exerting control over verbal behavior (i.e., attitude statements). Thus, the principle of reinforcement is not inconsistent with Bem's reanalysis of dissonance effects.

Although Bem's reanalysis of dissonance, reward, and attitude change serves as a strong defense of behaviorism and behavior principles, social psychologists were not convinced. As cognitive psychology became more prominent, social psychologists began to talk about causal reasoning in humans and attributions to internal or external causes.[32] External influences, like money, shifted the attribution for causation from the person to the environment. When people see themselves as doing things for external reasons, social psychologists claimed that they will conclude that internal causes are weak. Thus, a person who is paid to do an activity will reason that the cause of the activity was the money and not his or her interest (internal cause) in it. Attribution theory upheld the position that rewards are harmful, shifting causal attributions to external sources and undermining internal motives for action. At this point, behaviorism and social psychology became locked into a battle over rewards and intrinsic motivation.

THE INTRINSIC MOTIVATION LITERATURE IN CONTEXT

As we have seen, three developments that began in the 1950s set the stage for research on how rewards destroy intrinsic motivation. These developments involved (a) humanism's general distaste for Skinner's view of freedom, control, and technology, (b) the reemergence of cognitive psychology and the view that people were an agent of causation, and (c) social psychology's concern with cognitive dissonance, reward, and attitude change.

By the 1960s and 1970s, both cognitive psychology and behaviorism had become established schools within psychology. Behaviorists emphasized the importance of behavior-environment relationships; cognitivists attended to internal processes and mental events within the individual. This difference in focus led advocates from the two camps to debate and criticize each other's positions. In addition, Skinner's strict determinism and emphasis on control roused a great deal of controversy. It ran contrary to the basic belief in free will that is held by most North Americans and led several psychologists to put forth a position of humans as willful and self-determining. It was during this period of rivalry and unrest that the research on the effects of reward and reinforcement on intrinsic motivation was instigated.

Cognitive science gained numerous supporters in the 1960s and 1970s. Because Skinner's behaviorism represented the major behavioral influence in psychology, he and his followers came under increasing attack.[33] Many of the criticisms were based on misconceptions about behaviorism. One would often hear behaviorism described as a mechanistic, stimulus-response account of humans that did not consider genetic determinants of behavior. Behaviorists were accused of representing people as nonthinking, nonfeeling automatons (as an aside, it is interesting to point out that it is cognitive psychologists who view humans as computers, not behaviorists). One author stated:

Of all the contemporary psychologists, B.F. Skinner is perhaps the most honored and the most maligned, the most widely recognized and the most misrepresented, the most cited and the most misunderstood. Some still say that he is a stimulus-response psychologist (he is not); some still say that stimulus-response chains play a central role in his treatment of verbal behavior (they do not); some still say that he disavows evolutionary determinants of behavior (he does not). These and other misconceptions are common.[34]

Howard Rachlin suggested that Skinner's views have been largely misunderstood because people think that mentalistic vocabulary is forbidden to the behaviorist.[35] He pointed out that the critical difference between a behaviorist and a mentalist is the point at which explanation stops. The behaviorist explains behavior (and mental states) as the result of past external behavior-environment interactions, whereas the cognitivist infers mental processes (perceptions, beliefs, expectancies) as the causal focus of current behavior.

As well as the numerous misunderstandings that are sprinkled throughout the psychological literature, serious arguments were also directed at behaviorism. Several writers could not accept Skinner's rejection of mentalistic theories, statistical analyses, hypothesis testing, and inferred processes and argued that inferred processes and similar phenomena have played a major role in other sciences.[36] B. Schwartz, R. Schuldenfrei, and H. Lacey maintained that behaviorism has restricted explanatory power.[37] They saw no evidence that behavior principles operate outside laboratory settings and instead argued for a teleological explanation of human behavior based on purposes and intentions. The attacks and criticisms of behaviorism have, of course, not gone undefended, nor in many cases have they been unprovoked.[38]

Perhaps the issue that created the most furor concerned Skinner's position with regard to freedom, control, and technology. Many simply could not accept a view of humans as controlled nor accept the consequences of determinism.[39] "To accept a rigorous determinism and apply it to one's own behavior is extremely difficult, requiring the overthrow of a lifetime's habits of thought."[40] Instead, some psychologists stressed the notion of personal causation and argued that humans are goal-directed, self-determining, free agents.[41] With regard to Skinner's proposal for a technology of behavior, one author contended that following World War II, people became suspicious and skeptical "about the prospects for solving technologically generated problems with further technology of any sort."[42]

Amid the debates and the battles against behaviorism, Thomas Kuhn published his important book, *The Structure of Scientific Revolutions*.[43] Put simply, Kuhn's thesis was that anomalies or problems periodically arise in a science that cannot be resolved under the prevailing paradigm. A revolution occurs when one paradigm is discarded in favor of another. Inevitably, such times are marked by debate and resistance to paradigm change. Kuhn's work received wide recognition. In particular, in the 1960s and 1970s, psychologists began to claim that a scientific revolution was taking place in psychology right under their noses.[44] The view was that behaviorism would be replaced by cognitive science. Over the years, several writers have argued that a cognitive revolution did, in fact, take place in the 1960s.[45] For example, in 1977, MacKenzie declared behaviorism dead.[46]

Leahey suggested that there never has been a cognitive revolution and instead, that the idea was ignited in the 1960s and 1970s by Kuhn's publication itself.[47] Kuhn's work served as a "rallying flag" for cognitivists.[48] From this perspective, many of the criticisms aimed at behaviorism can be construed as resulting from a zeal for revolution spurred by a reading of Kuhn.

Psychology in the 1960s and 1970s can be characterized as undergoing a period of turmoil. Many psychologists became convinced that cognitive processes and mental events should be the focus of their discipline. Given this view, they attempted to discredit behavioral views. Kuhn's work was often cited to support the cognitive position and point a finger at behaviorists. Interestingly, at the same time that psychologists were attacking behavioral views and voicing their suspicions about behavioral technology, the use of behavioral techniques was expanding in applied settings (e.g., classroom token economies and incentive systems).

Given the pervasive influence of cognitive psychology and the growing application of behavior modification techniques, the research examining the effects of reinforcement on intrinsic motivation was a timely and relevant consideration. In addition, because most of the criticisms aimed at behaviorism were based on logical argument rather than experimental findings, the time was ripe to produce research evidence demonstrating negative effects of reinforcement. Research findings that showed the detrimental effects of rewards attacked the very heart of behaviorism—reinforcement—and had widespread implications for behavioral technology. It is within this context that the early studies by Edward Deci and by M.R. Lepper,[49] D. Greene, and R.E. Nisbett were conducted and interpreted.[50]

As indicated, the research on intrinsic motivation came out of social psychology. Cognitive dissonance theory, which was prominent in social psychology in the 1960s, seemed to show that rewards and incentives were detrimental to attitude change. By the late 1960s, attribution theory and self-perception accounts of attitudes were gaining popularity.[51] Although Bem's (1972) self-perception account upheld behavior principles, Kelly's (1967) attribution theory implied that rewards would shift attributions of causation from internal to external sources and thereby undermine internal reasons or motives for action. Thus, social psychologists arrived at the topic of rewards and intrinsic motivation via an interest in attitudes and attitude change; subsequently, rewards were seen as harmful based on people's causal reasoning and a view that people were causal agents of action.

SUMMARY AND CONCLUSIONS

The argument put forth in this chapter is that the literature concerned with the negative effects of reward and reinforcement on intrinsic motivation is historically grounded in the debate between behaviorism and other psychologies. As part of the confrontation, social psychologists of the 1970s began an empirical attack on reinforcement theory and practice. This was a time when behaviorism came under fire, especially in terms of its applications and technology. Cognitive psychology was becoming well established, and many psychologists argued that internal cognitive processes and not reinforcement contingencies, were direct causes of behavior. Fueled by Kuhn's (1962) publication on scientific revolutions and a fear and suspicion of behavioral technology, many critics set out to demonstrate the inadequacies of behavioral views. Coming out of concepts in social psychology and a general climate of dissatisfaction about behaviorism, numerous studies on the effects of reward and reinforcement were generated.

Deci's initial studies established the research paradigm under which the negative effects of reward and reinforcement on intrinsic motivation were, and continue to be, investigated.[52] Although Deci's findings were weak, he argued that reinforcement did indeed produce decrements in intrinsic motivation. Given the prevailing cognitive orientation toward psychology, it is not surprising that Deci's claims were quickly seized on and further investigations were conducted to confirm his conclusions. In addition, a number of psychologists began to issue warnings that Deci's demonstrations of the negative effects of reward directly

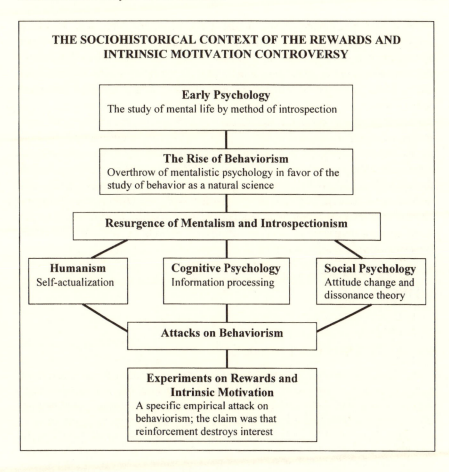

THE SOCIOHISTORICAL CONTEXT OF THE REWARDS AND INTRINSIC MOTIVATION CONTROVERSY

Early Psychology
The study of mental life by method of introspection

The Rise of Behaviorism
Overthrow of mentalistic psychology in favor of the study of behavior as a natural science

Resurgence of Mentalism and Introspectionism

Humanism
Self-actualization

Cognitive Psychology
Information processing

Social Psychology
Attitude change and dissonance theory

Attacks on Behaviorism

Experiments on Rewards and Intrinsic Motivation
A specific empirical attack on behaviorism; the claim was that reinforcement destroys interest

contradicted reinforcement theory and had relevance to the use of incentive programs in schools and other institutional settings.

The experiment by Lepper, Greene, and Nisbett[53] is perhaps the most widely cited example of the detrimental effects of reinforcement. What is striking about this study is that only children who were promised a reward showed a decrease in intrinsic motivation relative to a control group (see Chapters 2 and 3 for details). Children who received, but were not promised, a reward demonstrated an increase in intrinsic interest. Given these findings, a logical conclusion is that the promise, rather than the reward per se, may have produced the differences. Unfortunately, however, the results have seldom, if ever, been interpreted in this way.

Instead, many psychologists have asserted that the study by Lepper, Greene, and Nisbett (1973) is yet another demonstration of the undermining effects of reinforcement. In their enthusiasm to attack the general tenets of the behavioral position, many have mistakenly equated promised rewards with rewards and rewards with reinforcers.

As shown in Chapters 2 and 3, the early research on negative effects of rewards and reinforcement was weak and inconclusive. Nonetheless, the findings have frequently been used to discredit behavioral views and reinforcement theory. Our sociohistoric analysis of this literature suggests that overgeneralizations and misinterpretations of the studies were a result of the fervor of the times (which sought to overthrow behaviorism) rather than a careful analysis of the data. Our examination of the studies, however, shows that the literature on rewards and intrinsic motivation has not resulted in a discrediting of behavioral theory or, specifically, the principle of reinforcement. Instead, what resulted was a literature that points to conditions under which a negative effect of promised reward will occur, and, inadvertently, it has revealed several conditions that result in positive effects of rewards. Thus, it is our contention that if the studies on rewards and intrinsic motivation had been conducted in another time or place, with different dominant psychological views, the findings might have been interpreted in a very different light.

NOTES

1. Leahey, 1987, p. 262.

2. Ibid.

3. Dewey, 1900/1978.

4. Watson, 1913.

5. Thorndike, 1898. Although Thorndike talked about "trial and error" learning, this is not the way in which modern behaviorists understand the puzzle box experiments. Instead of trial and error learning, the experiments are better described as "trial and success" learning. The cats' behavior of pulling on a string (or pressing a treadle) resulted in opening the door to the puzzle box (success). These repeated successes account for the increasing efficiency of the cats in this situation.

6. Thorndike, 1911/1965, p. 40.

7. Deci and Ryan, 1985.

8. Skinner, 1938. Operant conditioning principles are criticized as dehumanizing. Critics argue that Skinner characterized people as passive responders to events from the environment. In fact, however, operant conditioning requires an active person, who emits behavior in various situations. When people act on the world, they change it. These changes, in turn, feed back on the actions that produce them, either increasing or decreasing the likelihood of this behavior.

9. Skinner, 1987. In this essay on selection by consequences, Skinner aligns himself with Darwin in advocating three levels of selection: (1) natural selection and the evolution of the species, (2) behavioral selection at the level of the individual during his or her lifetime, and (3) cultural selection (the change in cultural practices over generations).

10. Skinner, 1971.

11. Skinner, 1953.

12. Leahey, 1997.

13. See Zuriff, 1979, 1985.

14. Skinner, 1953.

15. Rogers and Skinner, 1956. This article concerns the argument between Rogers

and Skinner at a symposium held by the American Psychological Association. Both Rogers and Skinner discussed various issues regarding the topic of how values emerge in our society.

16. Rogers, 1964.

17. Rousseau, 1762/1974.

18. Rogers, 1969.

19. Sidman, 1989.

20. Skinner, 1968.

21. In the decades of the 1950s, 1960s and 1970s, the humanist movement led to the establishment of a variety of alternative schools. The aim of many of these institutions was to reduce teacher intervention and to create an atmosphere where students would come to discover their own inner potential. Proponents of these goals held the view that students should not be rewarded or reinforced for engaging in activities; instead, they assumed that the children would come to engage in school-related tasks because of the self-satisfaction inherent in such activities. This view was reflected in the writings of A.S. Neil (1959), who stated:

The danger in rewarding a child is not as extreme as that of punishing him, but the undermining of the child's morale through the giving of rewards is more subtle. Rewards are superfluous and negative. To offer a prize for doing a deed is tantamount to declaring that the deed is not worth doing for its own sake. . . . A reward should, for the most part be subjective: self-satisfaction for the work accomplished. (pp. 162–163)

Neil and other humanists were highly influential in the 1960s and 1970s and many teachers adopted the view that children would flourish best in an unstructured environment. Unfortunately, in many cases, the consequences of such a system were not good. Many students did not find the academic tasks self-satisfying; the result was that such students did not learn the basic skills of reading, writing, and mathematics. Some parents and educators began a backlash, and several books appeared that were critiques of the humanist movement and its effects on education (e.g., see Engelmann, 1992; Flesch, 1965, 1981; Kline, 1973).

22. Leahey, 1992.

23. Tolman, 1932.

24. Simon, 1956; Newell, Shaw, and Simon, 1958.

25. See Neisser, 1967; Miller, 1962.

26. Skinner, 1978.

27. Skinner, 1969.

28. Festinger, 1957.

29. Festinger and Carlsmith, 1959.

30. Freedman, 1965.

31. Bem, 1965.

32. Heider, 1958; DeCharms, 1968.

33. Although most of the attacks on behaviorism were aimed at the views of Skinner, several researchers who investigated the effects of rewards on intrinsic motivation included Bandura as a behaviorist (e.g., see Ryan and Deci, 1996).

34. Catania, 1984, p. 473.

35. Rachlin, 1984.

36. For example, see Wessels, 1981.

37. Schwartz, Schuldenfrei, and Lacey, 1978.

38. Skinner, 1974, 1978.

39. For example, see Krutch, 1953.

40. Leahey, 1987, p. 461.

41. DeCharms, 1968; Deci, 1975.

42. Smith, 1992, p. 221.

43. Kuhn, 1962.

44. Palermo, 1971.

45. For example, see Baars, 1986.

46. See MacKenzie, 1977. However, also see Zuriff, 1979, who pointed out that MacKenzie's conception of behaviorism was Hullian, not radical behaviorist.

47. Leahey, 1992.

48. Peterson, 1981.

49. Deci, 1971, 1972a, 1972b; Lepper, Greene, and Nisbett, 1973.

50. Although the early findings were weak and circumscribed, they have been frequently interpreted as demonstrations of the negative impact of reinforcement. They have also been used to reject the science of behavior, its principles, and its programs.

By the 1970s, behavioral psychologists had developed a number of behavioral programs in educational settings, hospitals, and the workplace. Such programs used reinforcement principles and were designed to teach a range of life skills and to increase socially appropriate behavior. An extensive literature documented the beneficial outcomes of such programs (Ayllon and Azrin, 1968; Kazdin, 1975a, 1975b; Kazdin and Bootzin, 1972). A central issue of concern in the behavioral literature was whether gains made in treatment settings would be maintained in non-treatment environments (Carlson, Hersen, and Eisler, 1972; Kazdin, 1975b). In other words, once a person had acquired particular skills and behaviors in the program setting, the concern was whether these skills and behaviors would be maintained in everyday settings.

Many nonbehavioral psychologists and educators seized upon the research findings on reward and loss of intrinsic interest as directly relevant to this issue. The laboratory results indicating that expected rewards decreased intrinsic motivation were used to argue that behavioral programs would fail in the long run because they would undermine people's intrinsic motivation. In a 1974 article in *American Psychologist*, Levine and Fasnacht criticized behavioral programs as harmful to intrinsic motivation and used this criticism to attack behaviorism. The authors stated that "the time has come for us to avoid a narrow operant [behavioral] perspective. Operant procedures have their place and their dangers" (p. 819). One problem with this conclusion is that it was based on a circumscribed laboratory finding that has not been shown to hold in applied settings. That is, there is no evidence that behavioral programs undermine intrinsic motivation. The issue of behavioral maintenance is far more complex than a simple undermining of intrinsic motivation. Maintaining behavior involves an understanding of the reinforcement contingencies of the program and the reinforcement contingencies operating in everyday settings (see Martin and Pear, 1999; Stokes and Baer, 1977).

The original studies on rewards and intrinsic motivation generated further research. Some reviewers of the literature noted that the results were mixed and concluded that few generalizations could be made about the negative effects of reward, let alone those of reinforcement. Other writers, however, threw caution to the wind and interpreted the results as clear evidence that reinforcement theory (and behaviorism, in general) was flawed (DeCharms and Muir, 1978; Kohn, 1993a, 1993b; Lepper and Gilovich, 1981; Lepper and Greene, 1978; Schwartz, 1990). Over the years, the view that rewards and reinforcement are harmful has been extolled in psychology texts (e.g., Zimbardo, 1992), as well as in education (e.g., Tegano, Moran, and Sawyers, 1991), business (e.g., Kohn, 1993b), and even the natural sciences (e.g., Sutherland, 1993).

51. Kelley, 1967; Bem, 1965.
52. Deci, 1971, 1972a, 1972b.
53. Lepper, Greene, and Nisbett, 1973.

PART VI

PRACTICAL APPLICATIONS OF REWARDS

Chapter 11

The Effective Use of Rewards in Everyday Life

The use of rewards in everyday life is a tricky business. One problem is that rewards are often given to get people to do what we want. Under such conditions, rewards are not positive motivators of behavior; instead, they serve as negative incentives. For example, teachers may offer students gold stars for being "good" and employees may be promised recognition and advancement if they are "productive." In such instances, teachers and managers offer and give rewards based on their judgments and evaluations of student and employee performance. Because the standards of performance are often vague in these circumstances, rewards can be manipulated to the advantage of those in charge. Such a reward system, from the point of view of students and employees, can quickly become unfair and coercive. What is "good" today may not be good tomorrow. Thus, those in supervisory positions can withhold the rewards that are currently being given for acceptable performance and require better and better levels of accomplishment. Reward systems arranged in this way are programmed to backfire; people will eventually show willful noncompliance, escape, avoidance, and, in some cases, rebellion.

These negative side effects of rewards have not gone unnoticed. The literature on intrinsic motivation pointed to the so-called undermining effect of rewards and claimed that all extrinsic rewards had negative effects on people's interests. Our analysis of the research on rewards and intrinsic motivation makes it clear that certain reward procedures do reduce motivation; at the same time, the meta-analysis shows that there are also ways to use rewards to enhance performance and interest.

The effective use of rewards in everyday life requires that we make a distinction between rewards as incentives and rewards as behavioral consequences. When rewards are used as incentives, the offer of reward comes before the behavior. Much of the literature on rewards and intrinsic motivation concerns the use of incentives (expected rewards) and is instructive about how to arrange offers of reward to motivate performance. Rewards also can be used as behavioral consequences. In this case, rewards often function as reinforcement for behavior, strengthening the action. The studies of reward and intrinsic motivation that used repeated rewards show that reinforcement can be used without a loss of intrinsic motivation. In this chapter, we provide guidelines for using incentives and reinforcement in everyday life to motivate performance and interest.

EFFECTIVE USE OF INCENTIVES IN EVERYDAY LIFE

One way to use rewards in everyday life is to offer payment, prizes, or recognition for some action. The offer of reward describes what will happen if the person does some action, performs at a specified level, completes assigned tasks, and so on. Offers, then, are verbal descriptions of contingences rather than the actual contingencies themselves.[1] These verbal descriptions come before the target behavior and are usually stated to "motivate the person to behave in a given way." Because offers of reward precede action and are attempts by people to motivate and guide behavior, we refer to these offers as incentives.

When people use incentives rather than actual contingencies to motivate and guide behavior, the effects often depend on the person's history of behavioral consequences. The effect of such a personal history is usually called an expectancy and, when offered an incentive, people differ in their expectations. A person who has complied with incentives in the past will be motivated (behave as instructed) or not by current incentives depending on the previous consequences of following incentives.

For example, a student who is offered rewards (e.g., coupons for pizzas) for reading for one hour a day may benefit in many ways (e.g., he or she may enjoy reading books, reading a menu to order food, reading directions to find a location, and so on). Based on this behavioral history, the student expects positive outcomes and is motivated by current incentives offered by parents or teachers. Another student may be given an incentive to sit quietly in his or her seat (e.g., a "good student" certificate) and discover that incentive-following behavior removes or reduces other rewards (e.g., seeing interesting things through the window, discussing events with classmates, getting the teacher's attention). This student may expect negative outcomes for incentive following and be less inclined to behave in accord with subsequent incentives from those in authority. The general point is that for a specific person, the effects of an incentive will depend on features associated with prior consequences (whether positive or aversive). These features may have to do with the person who offers the incentive, the context or setting in which the offer occurs, and the verbal form of the incentive itself (how it is stated).

Although the effects of offers of reward depend on personal history, the research on rewards and intrinsic motivation, as well as studies of social learning, suggest guidelines for the effective use of incentives. One guideline is to use incentives (offers of reward) for the benefit of the learner (or employee) and not for the benefit of social agents or persons in authority. Rewards that are used "to get people to do what we want" are frequently offered and given for the benefit of those in authority (parents, teachers, managers, etc.). Offers of rewards for students to sit quietly in class are usually arranged for the benefit of the teacher, not the students. Similarly, incentives to increase production in a factory are often given for the benefit of managers rather than workers. Most of these motivational systems are ultimately based on coercion rather than positive reinforcement. In such cases, the offer of reward is often backed up by punishment or threats of punishment (loss of employment, being sent to the principal, and so on).

In contrast, incentives given to "help a person learn or master a task" operate for the benefit of the student or worker. That is, beyond the rewards offered to motivate behavior (the incentive itself), people benefit in other ways when rewards are tied to mastery and skillful performance (e.g., increased perceived competence or self-efficacy, contact with alternative sources of reward, etc.). Incentive programs designed for the benefit of learners (and workers) are likely to involve the positive motivation of behavior and generate high performance and enjoyment of the activities.

Incentives for Performing Uninteresting Activities

At the present time, the research on rewards and intrinsic motivation suggests that incentives can be used to enhance performance and interest of activities that people do not like to do. One way of knowing whether the activity is enjoyable is to assess its relative frequency of occurrence. That is, what proportion of time does a person spend on this activity in a given setting? In a school situation, students may spend relatively little time on academic activities and much more time on off-task behavior. Our meta-analysis indicates that the use of incentives for activities of low initial interest (relatively low-frequency behavior) may enhance the motivation to engage in these activities. An important point is that the effects on performance and interest (in the laboratory) are moderate and temporary. In applied settings, incentives could be used to "get the behavior going," but these stimuli will have to be supplemented by behavioral contingencies to keep the behavior at high strength (see the section on reinforcement later in this chapter).

Tangible Incentives for Performing Interesting Activities

The most robust finding in the rewards and intrinsic motivation research concerns the negative effects of tangible incentives for merely "doing" activities that people like to do. That is, offers of reward without clear performance standards were consistently found to reduce performance and interest. A student who enjoys artistic activities may do less of them if a teacher offers gold stars for doing art and sculpture to the class (on the other hand, students who are not interested in artistic activities may benefit from the incentive). The exact basis of this effect is not yet resolved; it could be due to a loss of intrinsic motivation, a shift in attribution to external sources, a weakening of control by natural consequences, or deliberate noncompliance to a directive given by those in authority (backed up by punishment or the threat of punishment). Whatever the explanation, people seem to "turn off" when confronted with this kind of incentive. The best advice is not to use offers of tangible rewards for "doing" activities that people already enjoy doing.

If offers of tangible rewards are to be used, it is important to tie material incentives to the attainment of performance standards. Our meta-analysis[2] indicated that tangible rewards that are offered for exceeding a criterion or performance standard can enhance performance and interest, even when people already enjoy the activity. In addition, research in social learning indicates that tangible rewards that are offered for mastery, effort, and meeting challenges have positive effects on performance, perceived competence and interest. As a general rule, material incentives should be linked to specific, reasonable, and attainable performance standards.[3] An employee who is offered rewards based on a gradually increasing mastery of computers and the relevant software programs is likely to gain in performance, competence, and interest. The most important guideline for the use of mastery-based incentives is to ensure that people have the requisite skills to meet the performance standards required for reward at each step (incentives tied to success).

The use of incentives for exceeding a performance standard has been a successful strategy in business and industry.[4] In one case (Honeywell Inc.), management implemented a program of recognition called "The Winning Edge" for superior performance "above and beyond one's job." Employees were recommended to a review committee by their workmates for the award ($100 and having their names listed in the company's newsletter). The program increased employee cooperation and the general morale of the work environment and was considered successful and cost-effective by the company and workers.

In another industry (Blanchard Training and Development, Inc.), the management established the "Eagle Award" to recognize the provision of "legendary service" to customers by staying late to ship materials, helping to locate a lost order, resolving a billing problem, and so on. Again, employees were nominated by their workmates, who provided a brief description of the exceptional performance. A review committee that ensured that the described performance exceeded the job description considered the nominations. Winners were surprised with a visit from the Eagle Committee, and the winner received an Eagle Award trophy. In addition, a picture of the winner holding the Eagle Award was displayed in the lobby bulletin board with a brief description of the exceptional performance. The winner got to keep the trophy on his or her desk for a week or so until it was needed for another recipient. The program was viewed as successful, and "legendary service" became part of the company's culture.

A division of American Express of New York (Travel Related Services) implemented an exceptional performance program. The program, called "Great Performers," recognized and rewarded exceptional performances of employees by placing life-sized posters of winners and their accomplishments throughout the company. Winners took home their posters and were also eligible to become Grand Award winners (no limit on number of winners) of an expense-paid trip, $4,000 in traveler's checks, and a platinum "GP" logo pin and framed certificate. The Great Performers program increased Travel Related Services' income 500 percent over 11 years, and the company's return on equity has increased by 28 percent since the program began.

The research on rewards and intrinsic motivation has examined a limited set of tangible reward contingencies focused mainly on activities that people like to do. Even so, there is a clear message about the superfluous use of material rewards. The basic principle is that tangible rewards can undermine performance and interest when offered, without regard to performance standards, for activities that people enjoy doing. The negative effects of material incentives are lessened or reversed by tying rewards to specific performance standards.

USING INCENTIVES EFFECTIVELY

- Use incentives (offers of reward) for the benefit of the learner or worker, not for the benefit of the social agent (teacher, manager, etc.).
- Use incentives to enhance performance of activities that people do not like to do (relatively low frequency of occurrence).
- Reduce the use of material incentives for activities that people already like to do (relatively high frequency of occurrence).
- Reduce the use of tangible incentives offered to people for merely "doing" activities that they already like to do.
- Tie material incentives to specific, reasonable, and attainable standards of performance (rewards for success).

Encouragement: Use of Praise as an Incentive

As an alternative to tangible incentives, the research on rewards and intrinsic motivation indicates that incentives based on praise usually enhance measures of intrinsic motivation, even for activities that people already like to do. In applied research,[5] praise is defined as a response of teachers (or managers) that goes beyond the corrective feedback of "right," "yes," "OK," and so on. Praise involves an evaluative response such as "very good" and signs of positive affect such as excitement or warmth. A reaction to a student who succeeds at a mathematics assignment such as, "You got them all right, great work!" is an example of praise.

The distinction between praise and corrective feedback is useful because human learning requires corrective feedback but does not require praise. That is, people require feedback on their performance to gain proficiency and skill;[6] they do not need praise from others in order to learn and perform at high levels. Thus, the role of praise in work or school settings is open to question, even though the laboratory studies support its use. One issue is that laboratory research on rewards and intrinsic motivation has not made a clear distinction between praise and feedback. Without such a distinction, the effects of praise on intrinsic motivation partially may be due to corrective feedback, thus biasing the meta-analytic findings in a positive direction. An implication is that the laboratory results on praise and intrinsic motivation should be viewed with caution.

Although praise can function as reinforcement (see the next section) for specific behavior, applied educational research indicates that it is seldom used in this way in classroom settings.[7] Studies suggest that, in order for praise to serve as effective reinforcement in the classroom, teachers would have to move about, praising students' performance about once every 15 seconds, or 200 times in 50 minutes—a rate that is incompatible with traditional teaching practices (e.g., sitting at the front of the room).[8]

Teachers often use deliberate or planned praise as encouragement (incentives) to motivate higher levels of performance from students with limited ability. Deliberate praise by teachers is typically based on signs of effort rather than accomplishments. Because of the discrepancy between effort and accomplishment, deliberate praise can sometimes lack credibility with students, leading to embarrassment or discouragement. In contrast, spontaneous praise based on surprise or admiration of students' accomplishments usually has high credibility and enhances students' academic motivation.

Unfortunately, the applied educational findings suggest that planned praise is less effective for motivation than unplanned praise, making the deliberate use of praise for motivation less viable in classroom settings (and perhaps in business and industry). Also, even spontaneous praise can lead to negative side effects, as when the emphasis of praise is on surprise more than admiration ("Boy, I never thought you could do that!"). The general guideline is that praise can (at least momentarily) enhance performance and interest but that this form of encouragement can backfire, as in cases where praise lacks credibility or is overused.

EFFECTIVE USE OF REINFORCEMENT IN EVERYDAY LIFE

The use of rewards as incentives for behavior has its place. Incentives can be used to guide and motivate behavior in the short run, especially when activities lack initial interest. In the long run, however, incentives must be backed by behavioral consequences or else performance and interest in an activity will return to previous levels (before the offered reward). The effective use of rewards as behavioral consequences involves the principle of reinforcement. In this section, we outline the basic idea of reinforcement and suggest guidelines for its successful use in everyday life.

Reinforcement occurs when a person acts in a way that produces effects or consequences. Some of these behavioral consequences feed back on the person's behavior, strengthening or increasing the action that produced them. We may speak of reinforcement only if a specific behavior is strengthened by a particular behavioral consequence. In a work setting, an employee files records and observes a count of how many records have been filed at a given moment. One possibility is that "observing the count" serves as reinforcement for filing records by the employee. That is, the record-filing behavior is strengthened and maintained by its effects (observing the count).

Many of the behavioral consequences that affect behavior are called rewards; thus, rewards can be used as consequences of behavior to increase its frequency of occurrence. Notice that the use of rewards as reinforcement is different from the use of rewards as incentives for action. Rewards as incentives come before action, whereas rewards as reinforcement come after the behavior has occurred. Our review of the literature on rewards and intrinsic motivation identified a handful of studies that involved the use of repeated rewards following the occurrence of a target behavior. In these experiments, the target behavior increased during the reward phase so that the rewards functioned as reinforcement. Under these conditions, rewards either enhanced or did not affect measures of intrinsic motivation. As a general guideline, rewards that operate as reinforcement for an activity can be used to increase a target behavior without a loss of intrinsic motivation.

Although rewards can be used as effective behavioral consequences, most people not familiar with the manner in which to implement a successful reinforcement system in the home, classroom, or work setting. We are not able to outline all the ins and outs of reinforcement principles in this book;[9] we are, however, able to give some guidelines and refer interested readers to the literature on reinforcement in applied settings.[10]

Aspects of Reward and Reinforcement

Positive reinforcement involves presenting a reward or behavioral consequence when the person gives the target response.[11] Reinforcement is also a name for a process—the increase in an action that results from reinforcing consequences. Reinforcement describes a relationship between behavior and its consequences, which has three components: (1) the behavior must produce consequences, (2) the behavior must increase more with the consequences present than when they are absent, and (3) the increase in behavior must occur because of the consequences and not for some other reason.[12]

The effects of behavioral consequences can be classified as unconditioned and conditioned reinforcement. With unconditioned reinforcement, the reinforcing effects of behavioral consequences do not depend on other reinforcement relations. A large amount of human behavior is strengthened by food, water, sexual contact, and other biologically significant forms of reinforcement. Sensory stimulation such as flashing lights can also function as unconditioned reinforcement even though there is no obvious biological importance. Other behavioral consequences strengthen behavior because of a relationship to other sources of reinforcement. In a work setting, a "pat on the back" by the boss can function as conditioned reinforcement for "detecting a flawed component" by a worker; the reinforcement effectiveness of the boss's response presumably depends on its association with other kinds of reinforcement (including money, which is exchangeable for numerous goods and services). Rewards such as attention, approval, and recognition act as conditioned reinforcement when these social consequences have been associated with other sources of reinforcement.

Many behavioral consequences that increase human behavior are not called rewards in everyday language. For example, falling from high places or being tossed, twisted, and shaken hardly seem like rewards; yet these consequences of amusement park rides keep us coming back. This example shows that the reinforcing effects of behavioral consequences often depend on the situation or context. The effectiveness of a behavioral consequence also can depend on the behavior that produces it. Laughter can function as reinforcement for telling jokes but not for telling puns. Groaning can be used as reinforcement for puns but not for telling jokes. Generally, the reinforcing effects of behavioral consequences are relative rather than absolute.

The relative nature of reinforcement is observed when the opportunity for one activity is used as reinforcement for another activity. A parent who makes playing with friends contingent on practicing the piano is likely to see an increase in piano practice. The basic idea is that a higher frequency behavior (playing with friends) will reinforce a lower frequency behavior.[13] For most children, playing with friends has a higher probability of occurrence than playing the piano; playing with friends therefore will reinforce piano practice.

On the other hand, take the case of Mary, an accomplished pianist. For Mary, playing the piano has a higher probability than being with her friends. In this instance, being with friends will not reinforce playing the piano. In fact, for Mary, piano playing will reinforce being with her friends. In a classroom, painting and drawing (art) are usually higher probability activities than solving mathematical problems. Thus, teachers can use painting and drawing to reinforce mathematical problem solving. In contrast, for a particular child, Stephanie, who excels at mathematics, painting and drawing may be at a lower frequency than solving mathematical problems. In Stepanie's case, painting and drawing will not reinforce finding mathematical solutions. Practicing mathematics, however, will reinforce Stephanie's artistic behavior or another lower probability activity, perhaps playing sports. Notice that the relativity of reinforcement means that a reinforcement contingency has to be tailored to the person, situation, and behavior.

The use of reinforcement is not a straightforward extension of giving people things that we call rewards. Rewards are usually things that are "satisfying" and that people "like." Even so, these qualities do not guarantee that any reward or behavioral consequence will reinforce a particular behavior. Although the use of reinforcement involves many subtleties, there are several guidelines that can make reinforcement more effective in applied settings.

Rules for Effective Reinforcement

Rule 1: Specify the Target Behavior

Recall that reinforcement involves an increase in a specific target behavior. Behavior is what a person does. A target behavior should be observable, countable, and important (an action that, if increased in frequency, will make a practical difference in the everyday life of the student, worker, or client). Most parents, teachers, and managers use generalized and vague terms to describe the performance of children, students and employees. A student (or worker) should "develop an appreciation" of the written material, or should show "an understanding" of the assigned task.

Such generalized terms must be made concrete by giving examples of behaviors that are observed when we say that a student (or worker) appreciates or understands. In a classroom, a student's behavior is best expressed by action verbs that are directly observable. For example, a precise behavioral description could involve the following statements:

The students will:

- write sentences in their notebooks using the active voice
- count out loud the equivalent in quarters
- point to the picture that is the same as the word "dog"

A useful guide to selecting observable action verbs is available to teachers.[14] Table 11.1 shows the classification of action verbs as observable, ambiguous, or not observable based on agreement among independent classroom observers. The classification helps pinpoint behavior in school settings and is informative for anyone concerned with behavior change.

In business and industry, we usually talk about performance. Aubry Daniels

Table 11.1
Example of Action Verbs That Differ in Observability

CLASSIFICATION OF ACTION VERBS

Directly Observable	Ambiguous	Not Directly Observable
to mark	to use	to distinguish
to underline	to arrange	to recognize
to write	to demonstrate	to think critically
to fill in	to choose	to appreciate
to remove	to see	to discover
to point to	to utilize	to know
to put on	to construct	to understand
to cross out	to complete	to perceive
to circle	to identify	to be curious
to read orally	to perform	to learn

Source: Based on verbs from Deno and Jenkins (1967); reprinted in Alberto and Troutman (1999, p. 69).

suggested that we think of performance as a sequence of behaviors directed at some outcome or goal.[15] For example, the performance of a filing clerk could involve a sequence of behaviors such as opening the mail, sorting the correspondence, and filing it into appropriate folders. The goal or objective might be to have daily correspondence filed so that order desk clerks can easily find letters and memos to service customers. In another work setting, performance "may consist of the behaviors of picking up a sheet of plastic, placing it on a machine, pressing a button, removing the molded part, and stacking it neatly on a pile."[16] The objective could be to produce a given number of molds in a certain time and within certain specifications of tolerance (i.e., quality).

In order to create a change in performance, a manager needs to analyze the component behaviors. For example, all behavioral components for producing molds might be precisely carried out each time except for the final behavior of "stacking neatly." The lack of precision in this behavioral component may cause breakage, thus reducing the number and quality of molds made in a given time. In this example, behavior change would be targeted at "stacking neatly" behavior rather than some other component of the behavioral sequence. As an aside, one reason that an employee might not show the requisite behavior is that the term "neatly" is not clearly defined. Overall, the point is that a change in performance requires a change in one or more component behaviors.

In terms of targeting behavior, the rewards and intrinsic motivation literature is problematic. Most of the studies involve vague definitions of behavior or performance, and it is possible that any loss of interest or motivation is due to the imprecise specification of the target behavior. The studies using repeated reward found no loss of intrinsic motivation, but the target behavior was also more clearly described and counted. Further research is necessary to examine whether the definition of the target behavior plays a role in reducing measures of intrinsic motivation.

Rule 2: Arrange a Favorable Situation

An important aspect of training animals in the laboratory is the Skinner box, or operant chamber. The chamber is designed to accommodate animals (such as rats or pigeons). The space in the chamber is small so that the range of behaviors is restricted, and the chamber is designed to signal the target response (e.g., pressing a lever) to provide immediate reinforcement (food pellets) when the behavior occurs. In general terms, the operant chamber structures the situation so that the desired behavior will occur and incompatible behavior is reduced. Thus, lever pressing is likely and exploring of the chamber is minimized.[17]

The necessity of providing a favorable situation for teaching, training, and performance has not gone unnoticed. In a home, the kitchen is a favorable situation for food preparation and cooking. Schools have classrooms that are set up to support academic behavior and reduce incompatible behavior such as talking to classmates and wandering around the room. A work setting such as a factory is designed to enable an orderly sequence of actions that result in specific manufactured units or products. Although there is a naïve appreciation of the "favorable situation" for behavior, many of the problems of work, school, or home could relate to the training or performance situation.

For example, a classroom is not the same situation from one school to another or even within a particular school. There are traditional classrooms with desks arranged in rows and columns and a supervisory desk at the front of the room. Usually, there are blackboards to write on and bulletin boards for posting items. A small part of the classroom may contain bookshelves and books and perhaps a reading area. In contrast, there are less structured classrooms with movable chairs and tables, materials for projects and discovery throughout the room, and a teacher who interacts with the children in a low supervisory manor (e.g., seated on the floor with students gathered around). Rather than debate the merits of different types of classrooms in terms of ideology, a better strategy is to ask what behaviors are to be taught. The ideal setting for teaching scientific behaviors would likely be different from a situation that is best arranged to teach reading and writing skills. The point is that a flexible classroom that allows a teacher to arrange and rearrange the setting in terms of the target behavior will be one that promotes the desired academic or social behaviors while reducing actions that are incompatible with learning.

In business and industry, the arrangement of the factory, warehouse, or office may not structure the target performance. That is, aspects of the situation may interfere with the sequence of behaviors (or a particular behavior), thereby reducing performance and productivity. Employers and managers are used to talking about the design of materials and machinery, but the design of the work setting as a means to promote target behaviors and decrease incompatible activities is not well recognized.

Rule 3: Select Effective Rewards and Behavioral Consequences

Once you have identified the target behavior and established a favorable situation, the next step is to select effective rewards and behavioral consequences. Behavioral consequences can increase or decrease the target behavior, but in this book we will deal only with positive reinforcement. Positive reinforcement involves (1) the presentation of rewards and other behavioral consequences following the target behavior and (2) an increase in frequency of the target behavior. Therefore, before one can use positive reinforcement it is necessary to select one or more items, events, or activities (or any other thing) that serves to reinforce the target behavior.

Most consequences of behavior involve conditioned reinforcement (rather than primary reinforcement). That is, the things, activities, and behavior of others (social consequences) that affect our behavior are mostly based on an association with other sources of reinforcement. The rewards and other behavioral consequences that enter into positive reinforcement are unique to each individual. Fortunately, some reinforcing consequences are effective for many people; however, the larger the group or organization, the less is the probability that any particular reward or consequence will serve as reinforcement for everyone. How, then, can teachers and managers find the effective rewards and consequences for the individuals and groups with which they work?

In an attempt to identify effective rewards and behavioral consequences, Aubrey Daniels suggested that behavior managers[18] (1) think in terms of what the person or group wants, desires, or values; (2) ask people what they like; and (3) observe what people do and what they get out of it.[19] In terms of wants, desires, and values, it is likely that people who share a common social background will uphold similar values and enjoy similar rewards and behavioral consequences. Even so, the rule is that if something does not increase behavior, the reward or consequence is not reinforcing. Daniels explains it in this way:

Many plant managers have offered to take a top performer and spouse to dinner at a fancy restaurant when that was the last thing that particular couple wanted. They may well have preferred beer and pizza or dinner alone! Of course, the opposite mistake is also made when we assume that because of certain background factors they would prefer beer and pizza when in fact they want to go to a fancy restaurant.[20]

The point is that an analysis of cultural values can be helpful for spotting potential reinforcing consequences, but it is not a guarantee that the specified rewards will be reinforcing for a particular individual or group.

Another way to identify potential reinforcing rewards and behavioral consequences is simply to ask people what they like. Explain to the workers or employees that you are hoping to implement a positive reward system and need their help. Talk to them about the kinds of leisure-time activities they like to do, such as staying at a cottage, attending the movies or theater, playing sports, fishing, going to a concert, and so on. In addition, spend time talking to people about their family, friends, and other social relationships. The general point is to get to know people's interests through casual conversation.

A casual discussion of likes and interests can be supplemented by a reinforcement survey. The survey is another way of getting at potential reinforcing consequences. Again, explain to the person what you want to do and why you want to do it, before conducting a survey. The idea is to involve people in the design of their own positive reward system. As a first step, managers in business could simply have employees list the things they like and want. The problems are that people often do not know what they want or like, will not tell you, or ask for things that you cannot deliver. Thus, it is sometimes useful to use a structured questionnaire for a reinforcement survey.

As shown in Table 11.2, the reinforcement questionnaire lists activities and things that people often say they like. Each item is measured on a five-point scale of liking, from "not at all" to "very much." The survey can cover everyday social, tangible, and activity rewards, as well as rewards that are particular to the work setting. There are many intricacies about collecting and using reinforcement surveys that are beyond the scope of this book but are addressed in the performance management literature.[21] Overall, if used with sensitivity and care, a reinforcement survey can be helpful in identifying rewards that can serve as reinforcing consequences.

Potential reinforcing consequences can sometimes be spotted by direct observation rather than talks and surveys. Pay attention to what people do and talk about. For example, workers in a plant may talk a lot about upcoming breaks or rest periods. They also may take longer breaks than is acceptable to management. One assumption is that "having a break" will function as reinforcement for completing a production quota on time (e.g., 100 units per hour). A plant supervisor might test this contingency and find an increase in productivity, indicating that work breaks are reinforcing consequences.

Although a reinforcement contingency between units per hour and opportunities for breaks could increase production, bosses may complain about employees sitting around during work time (employees "sitting around" is not usually reinforcing for bosses). The point is that identifying reinforcing consequences (by talk, survey, and observation) does not resolve all problems of implementing a reinforcement system. Other sectors of a company or organization initially may oppose the reinforcement system,[22] even if it is effective in changing employees' (or students') performance.

One way to ensure that you have identified reinforcing consequences is to hedge your bets by using a reinforcement menu. After specifying potential reinforcing consequences by talk, survey, and observation, make up a menu of rewards and behavioral consequences that are likely to be reinforcing. As with the survey, the reinforcement menu lists social, tangible, and activity rewards.

Table 11.2
Reinforcement Survey Example

Please indicate your degree of liking (amount of pleasure you obtain) for each of the following things, events, or activities. Circle a number between 0 and 4.

Item	None	A Bit	Some	Much	Very Much
1. Listening to Music (specify)					
Rock	0	1	2	3	4
R & B	0	1	2	3	4
Jazz	0	1	2	3	4
Reggae	0	1	2	3	4
Classical	0	1	2	3	4
Country	0	1	2	3	4
Opera	0	1	2	3	4
2. Reading About (specify)					
Romance	0	1	2	3	4
History	0	1	2	3	4
Mystery	0	1	2	3	4
Science Fiction	0	1	2	3	4
Self-Help	0	1	2	3	4
Sports	0	1	2	3	4
Adventure	0	1	2	3	4

Each of these activities could be further specified (what kind of concert, sports, etc.)

Item	None	A Bit	Some	Much	Very Much
3. Attending concerts	0	1	2	3	4
4. Watching sports	0	1	2	3	4
5. Playing sports	0	1	2	3	4
6. Watching movies	0	1	2	3	4
7. Going to parties	0	1	2	3	4
8. Singing	0	1	2	3	4
9. Dancing	0	1	2	3	4
10. Painting	0	1	2	3	4
11. Cooking	0	1	2	3	4
12. Writing	0	1	2	3	4
13. Playing Cards	0	1	2	3	4
14. Playing musical instrument	0	1	2	3	4
15. Shopping	0	1	2	3	4
16. Talking about (topic)	0	1	2	3	4

17. Being recognized at a meeting for

Item	None	A Bit	Some	Much	Very Much
Solving a problem	0	1	2	3	4
Exceeding job requirements	0	1	2	3	4
Helping customers	0	1	2	3	4

Table 11.2 (*continued*)

18. Receiving from your supervisor or boss

Remarks on report	0	1	2	3	4
Phone call on work done well	0	1	2	3	4
A favorite book	0	1	2	3	4
Private talk about your project	0	1	2	3	4
Tickets to events (specify)	0	1	2	3	4
A favorite musical CD	0	1	2	3	4
Opportunity to give your opinion on a project	0	1	2	3	4
Dinner at a gourmet restaurant	0	1	2	3	4
A coupon for a book	0	1	2	3	4
Name on bulletin board	0	1	2	3	4
A touch on the shoulder for work well done	0	1	2	3	4
A coupon for a musical CD	0	1	2	3	4

19. Other activities, things, or events . . .

The idea is that the person gets to choose items from the menu whenever the performance exceeds a predetermined standard. The reinforcement menu ensures that a variety of behavioral consequences will be reinforcing at any moment; a reinforcement menu also works against satiation by not using the same rewards over time.

Rule 4: Set the Reinforcement Contingency

Once potential reinforcing consequences have been identified, it is useful to conduct a test. Does the reward or behavioral consequence actually increase the target behavior? In order to conduct a test, the behavior manager (teacher, supervisor, boss, etc.) must state the contingency between behavior and its consequences. For example, "If John completes the assigned homework problems, then he gets to choose a reward from a preestablished menu." Each day for a week, the homework is given, and if it is completed, the rewards follow. If John's homework is completed more often with the reinforcement contingency in effect than without it (baseline period), the evidence suggests positive reinforcement. At this point, the reinforcement system can be implemented on a full-time basis.

The performance criterion between the target behavior and its consequences can be increased slowly over time. In the case of John and his homework assignments, the number of homework problems each day could be increased in small steps so that John is always successful. Thus, the teacher may assign one take-home problem each day in the first week, two in the second, three in the third, and so on. This progressive contingency could be used to move John's performance from a low level to a final performance that is acceptable to John, his parents, and the teacher (e.g., John will do five homework problems each day for at least four out of five weekdays).

Rule 5: Wait for the Target Behavior to Occur and Then Reinforce It

Those involved in teaching or management are used to telling people what to do rather than waiting for them to do it. The problem is that reinforcement works best when the target behavior occurs without prompting, cajoling, or telling. For example, in a laboratory situation, a rat is trained to press a lever by waiting for a close approximation and following the response with food reinforcement. There is no way to "tell" the animal what to do, either verbally or by demonstration. Following the animal example, the best thing to do in applied settings is to discuss the reinforcement contingency before it is implemented, ensure that the person can meet the requirements for reinforcement, wait for the target behavior to occur, and then reinforce it.

In the case of John and his homework, the teacher should give the homework assignment for the day and, if John completes it, let him pick a reward from the menu. Notice that with this procedure, John is not told to do his homework by the teacher or reminded by his parents of the rewards he can earn. Rather, the reinforcement contingency is set, and if the target behavior occurs, the consequences follow. If the target behavior does not occur or has a low probability of occurrence, then the strategy is to use shaping (not telling), reinforcing closer and closer approximations to the final performance (the behavioral goal or objective).

The use of shaping, rather than telling, in the regulation of human behavior was discussed by Karen Pryor in her book *Don't Shoot the Dog!*[23] Pryor indicated:

In informal situations in real life, however, you are probably better off shaping with out instructions or verbal discussion. Suppose you have a messy roommate who leaves dirty clothes all over the place. . . . You would of course draw up a shaping plan, the initial and intermediate steps by which you would reach the desired goal. To get dirty clothes into the hamper every time, for example, you might start with one sock, and "target" the behavior by holding out the open hamper just as the sock is about to go on the floor. The reinforcer can be verbal, tactile, or whatever you think the roommate would be likely to respond to or accept. . . . There are, however, two traps in this use of shaping. The first is that it is easier to notice mistakes than to notice improvement, so, verbal creatures that we are, it is much easier for us to remonstrate when the criteria are not met than to reinforce when they are. And that can undo the progress. The second trap is that if you are calculating to shape someone's behavior, it is very tempting to talk about it. And talking about it can ruin it. If you say, "I am going to reinforce you"—for putting your laundry in the hamper, for not smoking marijuana, for spending less, or whatever—you are bribing or promising, not actually reinforcing; on learning of your plans, the person may rebel, instantly, and escalate the misbehavior. To get results you have to *do* shaping, not talk about it.[24]

Pryor's distinction between talking about rewards and delivering effective consequences is what this book is all about. The rewards and intrinsic motivation literature makes it clear that talking about rewards can backfire by reducing the target behavior and subverting interest in an activity. In contrast, reinforcement builds and maintains performance while at the same time generating motivation and interest.

Rule 6: Move from Continuous to Intermittent Reinforcement

To get behavior going, it is necessary that reinforcement be almost continuous. Continuous reinforcement has two properties that are critical to establishing performance: (1) reinforcement is immediate and (2) reinforcement is certain. The certainty of reinforcement concerns how likely it is that reinforcement follows the target behavior; the immediacy of reinforcement involves how quickly the reinforcing consequences are delivered.

The more closely the target behavior is followed by the reinforcing consequence, the more likely it is to be effective. Delays between the target behavior and reinforcement allow time for other behavior to occur, resulting in accidental reinforcement of the unwanted behavior. In his recent book on applied behavior analysis, Paul Chance discussed immediate reinforcement in the following example:

Suppose you would like to increase your 10-year-old daughter's tendency to read. You know from past experience that giving her the opportunity to read aloud to you is reinforcing. After dinner, while you are washing dishes, you notice that instead of watching TV, your daughter has picked up a book and begun reading. You decide that to reinforce this behavior, you will ask her to read to you as soon as you finish the dishes. Unfortunately, 5 minutes later when you are ready, she is no longer reading; she is now watching TV. Odd as it may seem, if you ask her to stop watching television and read to you, you might actually reinforce TV viewing.[25]

To avoid the delay problem, Chance recommends that behavior managers provide reinforcement while the behavior is in progress, thereby ensuring immediate reinforcement.

The other property of continuous reinforcement is certainty. The greater is the likelihood of reinforcement for the target behavior, the more rapidly the behavior will increase. With continuous reinforcement, every time the target behavior occurs, it is followed by the reinforcing consequence. Also, the reinforcing consequence almost never follows any other behavior. Thus, the probability of reinforcement for the target behavior is essentially one (certain), and it is zero for any other behavior. Chance noted that in human behavior, unfortunately, reinforcement is often no more certain to follow desired behavior than at other times:

Parents and teachers often ignore children when they behave well, for example—but let those children whine or cry or be destructive, and suddenly they have the adult's undivided attention. If attention is reinforcing, these parents and teachers are making reinforcement likely when undesirable behavior occurs and unlikely when desirable behavior occurs. Strange as it may seem, some [professionals] actually advocate making reinforcers more likely when children misbehave or act crazy than at other times.[26]

The overall point is that almost continuous reinforcement is necessary to establish a target behavior at high strength. This means that reinforcement must be immediate and certain for each instance of the target behavior and must almost never follow undesired behavior.

Once a performance has been well established, the rule is to change the schedule from continuous to intermittent reinforcement. A major advantage of intermittent reinforcement is that behavior is maintained in strength better with intermittent than with continuous reinforcement. For example, take the behavior of gambling on the "slots" in Los Vegas. Gambling behavior involves placing money in a slot machine and pressing a button or pulling a handle to activate a spin or draw. The reinforcing consequences are the payoffs following the gamble. A novice is only likely to repeatedly gamble if the early history of reinforcement is most often successful (almost continuous reinforcement). Once the performance has been well established, however, it is the intermittent payoffs that keep the gambler coming back. That is, slot machines are designed to occasionally reinforce gambling—usually the schedules can be quite extended so that many gambles occur before the person "hits a payoff." The changes in the schedules of reinforcement from an initial high rate of success to a lean rate of intermittent payoffs help to explain the maintenance of gambling behavior.

In classrooms or workplaces, intermittent reinforcement accounts for the continued performance of students or employees with limited supervision. Daniels elaborated on this point:

Salespeople working away from the office for extended periods of time, long-distance truck drivers, service technicians, security guards, night shift employees, auditors, entrepreneurs, and consultants are a few of the jobs that must be established on intermittent reinforcement for best performance. An additional advantage of intermittent schedules is that they allow a manager to be away from the office for a long time and not have decreases in performance due to lack of reinforcement.[27]

Notice that people who are called self-motivated, inner driven, or self-starters are those with a history of intermittent reinforcement for performance. Ultimately, "self-motivated" performance depends on at least occasional reinforcement; when all sources of reinforcement are withdrawn, even self-motivated people decline in performance. As a rule, teachers or managers should ensure that occasional reinforcement is arranged for performance—even for students or employees who seem to keep going without reinforcement.

Intermittent schedules are typically classified as either ratio or interval. Ratio schedules of reinforcement are based on the amount of work accomplished or the number of responses required for reinforcement. Interval schedules are based on how much time must pass before the designated behavior is reinforced. The reason why these schedules are important is that each kind produces a distinctive pattern of performance.

Behavior may be reinforced only after an interval of time has passed. A fixed-interval schedule stipulates that the first response following a specified interval is reinforced. Looking for a bus is behavior that is reinforced after a fixed time set by the bus schedule. If you just missed a bus, the probability of looking for the next one is quite low. As time passes, the rate of response increases with the highest rate occurring just before the bus arrives. Thus, the rate of response is initially zero but gradually rises to a peak at the moment of reinforcement. This response pattern is called scalloping and is characteristic of fixed-interval reinforcement.

A scalloping pattern of behavior would be expected if a teacher inspected the students' math homework at the end of each week. On Monday through Wednesday, students would do few problems, but as the end of the week approached and inspection became imminent, more and more of the homework would be accomplished—to be ready to submit for inspection (reinforcement) on Friday morning.

Stipulating a variable-interval schedule of reinforcement can eliminate scalloping. In this case, the first response after a variable amount of time is reinforced. A teacher could check homework after variable amounts of time have elapsed—the next day, after three days, at the end of the week, and so on. With variable interval reinforcement, behavior can be reinforced at any time, even if it was reinforced just a short while ago. Depending on the workload of the teacher, she could inspect homework two days in a row and then wait a week to do the next inspection. The variable-interval schedule produces steady and regular responding. Students will do homework at a stable, moderate rate throughout the week if the schedule of teacher inspection is variable interval.

In contrast to interval schedules that reinforce behavior after the passage of time, ratio schedules reinforce on the basis of the frequency or number of responses. With ratio schedules, the faster one accomplishes the performance requirement, the more reinforcement one obtains—the harder you work, the more you get! Thus, a worker who is paid for each finished O-ring will produce more units than a worker who is paid by the hour. With a fixed-ratio schedule, reinforcement occurs after a fixed number of responses. In a factory, piecerate of payment are examples of fixed-ratio schedules. Thus, a worker may receive $1 for sewing 100 of elastic wristband. When the ratio of responses to reinforcement is high, fixed-ratio schedules produce long postreinforcement pauses followed by a burst of activity—known as "break and run" performance. Without knowledge of this fixed-ratio effect, managers often complain about "slacking off" by the workers, especially if inspections occur during a "break" period. Daniels suggested that managers view the postreinforcement pause as a time to celebrate rather than a waste of time away from work. Organizations that take time to celebrate accomplishments or victories are typically highly productive because "people work harder to get the celebration and work harder following the celebration than they would have done without it."[28]

Ratio schedules of reinforcement can also be programmed on a variable basis. On a variable-ratio schedule, reinforcement is delivered after a variable amount of work or behavior. People never know when reinforcement will occur—it comes as a surprise. The best-known example of variable ratio reinforcement is the slot machine. The number of times you have to put your money in and pull the handle before a payoff is varied (as is the amount of winnings). On this kind of schedule, there is little waiting between bets because winning on a given pull does not mean that you cannot win on the next pull. The sooner you bet and pull the handle, the sooner you will discover if you are a winner.

Variable-ratio schedules eliminate the long pauses found on fixed-ratio reinforcement because the next response can always be reinforced. Variable-ratio reinforcement therefore produces very steady levels of performance. Also, research shows that variable-ratio schedules produce the highest response rates of any of the four basic schedules. The average ratio (responses to reinforcement) can be slowly increased so that high levels of performance are maintained by very infrequent reinforcement. In the laboratory, a pigeon pecking a key for food may emit many thousands of responses before receiving reinforcement. Overall, the pattern of behavior produced by variable-ratio schedules is "high and steady"—referring to a high and steady response rate.

In everyday life, variable-ratio schedules may explain behavior often attributed to individual persistence. A scientist may test thousands of chemical compounds before finding one that works and a door-to-door salesman may knock on hundreds of doors before making a sale. Also, variable-ratio schedules probably are involved in behavior that is said to be obsessive. We call people zealots, workaholics, or neurotic when they pursue one thing without letting up. These people work incessantly because experience has taught them that just around the corner it will pay off.[29]

As far as the practical use of variable-ratio reinforcement is concerned, one of the common mistakes is to raise the ratio of responses to reinforcement too rapidly. Many people who give up in school or work may be those who were placed in settings in which reinforcement was too infrequent before they achieved a high and steady level of performance. In business, sales trainees are often sent into the field before they become proficient, with the result that the amount of calls to sales is extremely low—leading to high dropout rates. Giving more reinforcement during training and supplementary reinforcement when trainees move into the field can solve the problem.

Generally, behavior is due to the schedule of reinforcement. When people are learning new behavior, continuous reinforcement will quickly establish a high level of performance. Once behavior is occurring at some level of proficiency, it is best to change to intermittent reinforcement in order to maintain the performance. Of the four basic intermittent schedules, variable-ratio schedules produce very high and steady rates of behavior; one problem is that people will give up if the ratio of responses to reinforcement is too large. Providing supplementary reinforcement during training and in the field can alleviate the problem of ratio strain on variable-ratio schedules of reinforcement.

Rule 7: Monitor the Results of Your Reward Program

A teacher or manager cannot assume that the reward procedure will have the intended effects. Just because you intend to increase the frequency of a target behavior, this does not mean that you will get this result. The only way in which behavior managers can be sure that they are using positive reinforcement is to look at the effects of the rewards on behavior. What is needed is a systematic way of monitoring the target behavior. That is, the behavior manager should be able to measure behavior and depict changes in performance on a graph. If the desired behavior increases following the presentation of a reward, you have succeeded in reinforcing it; if there is no increase, you are not providing reinforcement, no matter what your intention.

One of the most useful and least time consuming ways of monitoring performance is simply to count each instance of the target behavior. A teacher can use a golf counter worn on the wrist to record each occurrence.[30] Performance levels are found by tallying the count over a specified period of time. For example, in the classroom, a teacher could count each time a child completes a problem, answers a question, or writes in a notebook. The count can then be tallied over a day.

In business, managers are often interested in the rate at which something is done. The rate is simply the number of occurrences in a specified amount of time. Managers usually are concerned with the number of parts assembled per hour, the listings per week, or the calls completed each day. Converting counts to rates allows us to compare data when we are unable to standardize the period of observation or opportunities to respond. For example, suppose Tom is away from his desk six times in a 30-minute period of observation and eight times in another observational interval of 40 minutes. In this situation, the rate in both cases is 0.2 per minute.

Other measures of behavior are useful to ensure that reinforcement is effective. When behavior is not easily separated into discrete responses, duration may be a useful measure. The duration of behavior is a measure of how long a person does it. Thus, Sally spent 30 minutes talking to customers and John spent an average of 10 minutes each night on homework. In another context, the latency of behavior may be a useful measure. The latency is the length of time between an instruction and the occurrence of behavior. For example, the teacher told Sylvia to sit in her seat and it took her 20 seconds to sit down. The latency is useful when a behavior manager is concerned about how long it takes the student or worker to begin something or get started.[31]

It is not always possible to obtain count, duration, or latency measures of behavior. In such cases, measurement by judgment is sometimes useful. However, judgments by supervisors are often arbitrary and biased. That is, the evaluation of performance varies from one day to the next. One way to overcome this problem is to establish specific performance criteria that can be consistently observed by several people. Systems of judging in sports like gymnastics, figure skating, and diving illustrate the use of judging performance to determine winners.

In business, subjectivity in judgment can be overcome by constructing a behaviorally anchored rating scale.[32] The scale is usually constructed by employees and their boss and stipulates the degree of completion (or not) of specified behaviors or tasks. For example, an employee's performance could be judged in terms of carrying out required tests, identifying problems, and scheduling repairs. A score of 1 could be assigned to a performance in which none of these tasks are accomplished and a score of 10 could be assigned when all of these tasks are completed. Scores between 1 and 10 are assigned on the basis of the percentage of tests completed, problems identified, or repairs scheduled.[33] Once a behavioral rating scale has been constructed, contingent reinforcement can be arranged for the desired behavior as well as for an assessment of behavior change.

A final issue in monitoring the effectiveness of a reinforcement program concerns social validation.[34] In addition to the direct assessment of behavior change, it is important to obtain an assessment of feelings and sentiments of those involved in (or associated with) the program. If the procedures (objectives and results) are not acceptable to the parents or students, a teacher's reinforcement program may backfire—the students may avoid or escape it and the parents may complain about it.

In a business context, employees and bosses should be consulted before and after implementing a reinforcement system. For example, a supervisor may have identified "taking a break" as reinforcement for an employee's job-related behavior but upper level management might complain about the reward procedure ("You can't use breaks as a reward.") and sabotage the program. In another example, a reinforcement program may increase the target behavior but the behavior changes do not correlate with desired results of the corporation. That is, in a sales organization, the number of listings and calls may increase due to reinforcement but weekly sales may stay stable or decline. Again, the intervention may not be acceptable to corporate bosses even though the target behavior has increased. The general point is that consumer satisfaction is an important element in a reinforcement program; behavior managers should ensure that goals, procedures, and outcomes are favorable to those involved in, or affected by, the reward system.

Rule 8: Experiment—Be Ready to Change and Change Again

We indicated at the beginning of this chapter that using rewards in everyday life is a tricky business. The dictum to "be ready to change and change again," acknowledges that even the best-laid plans may not work—or at least, not as you expected. When faced with evidence that a reinforcement procedure does not have the desired effect, it is tempting to say that the principles of reinforcement are wrong and a behavioral view is incorrect.

An alternative to the dismissal of reinforcement principles is to take a pragmatic view of the problem. Perhaps the intended reinforcing consequences do not actually reinforce the target behavior. In this case, one answer may be to further identify items, events, or activities that function as reinforcement for the particular student or employee. Or perhaps the reinforcing consequences are delayed and other behavior is strengthened rather than the desired performance. Switching to reinforcing consequences that can be delivered more immediately or presenting the reinforcement when the target behavior is in progress might overcome this problem.

A reinforcement procedure may also have negative side effects. For example, an increase in the frequency of the target behavior may inadvertently lead to a decrease in some other desired behavior. The decline in another behavior might occur because the relative rate of behavior (or relative time spent on an activity) is a function of the relative rate of reinforcement.[35] That is, when considering two behaviors (e.g., playing music and reading) as reinforcement is added to one (reading), the relative rate of reinforcement for the other (playing music) will decline. With a drop in the relative rate of reinforcement, the other desired behavior (playing music) will inadvertently decrease—an unintended side effect of the reinforcement program.

The general point is that it is not possible to foresee every problem that can arise from a reinforcement program. But when faced with problems, there is no reason to give up. Careful monitoring of the target behavior, possible side effects, and social acceptance can help to pinpoint problems and suggest new intervention strategies. Based on a reanalysis of the reinforcement plan, new procedures can be implemented and tested for effectiveness in terms of behavior change. Overall, it is best to maintain an experimental attitude regarding the use of rewards in everyday life. B.F. Skinner encouraged us to "regard no practice as immutable. Change and be ready to change again. Accept no eternal verity. Experiment."[36]

USING REWARDS AS REINFORCEMENT

- Define the target behavior so that it can be observed and counted.
- Establish a favorable situation where target behavior is likely to occur.
- Select appropriate rewards of behavioral consequences (develop a reinforcement menu).
- Set the reward contingency (e.g., if ... then ...).
- Wait for the target behavior to occur and then reward it.
- Ensure that the reward is initially immediate and reliable following the target behavior; then program for maintenance.
- Monitor the results of your reward program.
- Be ready to change and change again—*experiment*.

NOTES

1. Pierce and Epling (1999, pp. 225–231) discussed the distinction between rule-governed behavior and contingency-shaped behavior. An offer of reward or an incentive, in this view, is an instance of rule-governed behavior. Analysis of rules such as instructions and advice shows that compliance with the rule is due to a history of reinforcement for following rules. People without such a history are not compliant with rules and people who have received aversive consequences for rule following may avoid behaving as the rule specifies (noncompliance).

2. Our meta-analysis supports the use of tangible rewards tied to performance standards (even with high-interest tasks). In contrast, the meta-analysis by Deci, Koestner, and Ryan (1999) indicated that these performance-based contingencies have negative effects on measures of intrinsic motivation. We have suggested, in this book and elsewhere (Cameron, Banko, and Pierce, 2001), that the meta-analysis by Deci and colleagues collapsed the data for reward procedures with distinct effects, leading them to the erroneous conclusion that all reward contingencies negatively affect intrinsic motivation.

3. See Bandura (1986). These rules for the effective use of mastery-based incentives are extracted from the theoretical writings of Bandura and the research literature on social learning concerned with reward and performance standards. The reader is referred to Chapter 5 in this book for an overview of social learning theory, rewards, and intrinsic motivation.

4. The examples of strategies used by Honeywell Inc., Blanchard Training and Development Inc., and American Express are taken from Nelson (1996).

5. See Brophy (1981), which makes a useful distinction between praise and corrective feedback that is not usually made in the intrinsic motivation and rewards literature.

6. Feedback is very important for behavior change but feedback alone will not sustain a target behavior (see Daniels, 1994, pp. 100–105). Behavior analysis of feedback in industry shows that feedback acts as an antecedent stimulus, telling people what behavior to change. The effect of feedback on people's performance "depends on the consequences they experience, have experienced, or expect to experience" (Daniels, 1994, p. 100). A combination of feedback and positive reinforcement is the best way to sustain behavior change.

7. Brophy (1981) indicates that few teachers use praise as reward for conduct or accomplishments. The applied research indicates that teacher praise is cued by a variety of personal characteristics and behaviors of students and not a systematic attempt to shape behavior through reinforcement.

8. See Chance (1992), in which the author argues that "to teach without using extrinsic rewards is analogous to asking our students to learn to draw with their eyes closed" (p. 200). The article points to problems with the use of rewards in classrooms but suggests these problems can and must be overcome.

9. The interested reader is referred to Catania (1998), Mazur (1998), or Pierce and Epling (1999) for a general overview of the principles of behavior, which involve reinforcement, discrimination and generalization, conditioned reinforcement, schedules of reinforcement, and several other areas of behavior analysis. An easier introduction to teaching and training by reinforcement principles is presented in Pryor (1999). Research on reinforcement principles often appears in the *Journal of the Experimental Analysis of Behavior*.

10. Readers interested in the use of rewards as reinforcement in applied settings can benefit from the discussion in Chance (1998). The use of reinforcement in classroom settings can be found in Alberto and Troutman (1999) and Schloss and Smith (1994). In business and industry, the use of rewards as reinforcement is found in the performance management literature (e.g., Daniels, 1994). Research on reinforcement in applied settings often appears in the *Journal of Applied Behavior Analysis*.

11. Another kind of reinforcement process is called negative reinforcement. The term *negative* refers to the operation of removing or taking away something when a response occurs. For example, on a rainy day, a person inflates an umbrella and thus removes the rain. If the use of an umbrella on a rainy day increases, the process is called reinforcement. Thus, negative reinforcement involves an increase in a response by the removal of an ongoing aversive stimulation.

12. See Catania (1998) concerning the difficulty of attributing an increase in behavior to its consequences. Catania states that "the infant coos and the parent comes, and now the cooing increases. How do we decide whether the infant is now cooing because cooing has been reinforced or because the parent is now present making cooing more likely?" (p. 70). If we use rewards as behavioral consequences in applied settings, we must be sure that the increases in performance are due to the rewards and not to other, extraneous events.

13. The Premack principle (Premack, 1959, 1971) states that if response A is more probable than response B, an opportunity to engage in A can be used to reinforce B. In the laboratory (with rats), if eating has a higher probability of occurrence than wheel running, an opportunity to eat will reinforce wheel running.

14. The classification of verbs is from Deno and Jenkins (1967) and was republished in Alberto and Troutman (1999, p. 69). Another helpful source for descriptions of target behavior is Morris (1976), who provides the following test questions: (1) can you count

the number of times the behavior occurs (e.g., four times a day)? (2) Would a stranger know exactly what to look for when you tell him or her the target behavior you are going to change (can you actually see the behavior when it occurs)? (3) Are you still able to break down the target behavior into smaller components that are more specific and observable than the original target behavior (the answer should be no)?

15. The behavior analysis of performance in business and industry is found in Daniels (1989), which presents approach an called performance management, or the ABC model of behavior change. The basic idea is to specify the antecedents (A), the target behavior (B), and the consequences (C). In this section of the book, we have emphasized behavior and its consequences rather than the events or stimuli that precede behavior. The full ABC system is necessary for effective behavior management.

16. Daniels, 1989, p. 13.

17. A discussion of the operant chamber as a favorable situation for conditioning by reinforcement appears in Pierce and Epling (1999, pp. 102–103).

18. *Behavior manager* is used here to refer to anyone who is involved in behavior change. The rules for selecting reinforcing consequences not only relate to business and industry but also can be adapted to home, schools and a variety of organizations (e.g., hospitals, legal systems, and so on).

19. Daniels, 1989, pp. 56–63.

20. Daniels, 1989, p. 56.

21. See Daniels (1989, pp. 57–59) for a more complete discussion of the reinforcement survey.

22. The answer to this kind of opposition is to discuss the behavioral intervention with the upper level management before the reinforcement contingency is implemented. For most bosses, productivity and profit are reinforcing consequences and rests or breaks usually reduce these outcomes. If a contingency between units per hour and taking breaks increases productivity and profit, the bosses should eventually adopt and support the reinforcement system.

23. Pryor, 1999.

24. Pryor, 1999, pp. 65–66. In the section on shaping without words, Pryor also points out that once you have achieved success in shaping, you had "better not brag about it." Such bragging is patronizing and usually results in making a lifelong enemy of the person targeted for behavior change.

25. Chance, 1998, p. 115. Chance provides a well-written and succinct overview of the rules of reinforcement.

26. Ibid.

27. Daniels, 1989, p. 98. Daniels notes that intermittent reinforcement avoids the problem of satiation with tangible reinforcing consequences. Satiation occurs when reinforcement has been repeatedly presented—as when food is presented following each lever press and the rat eventually stops pressing the lever (the rat is satiated). Intermittent reinforcement is also useful for managers (and teachers) because a single manager can maintain the behavior of several employees (or students) by using occasional reinforcement.

28. Daniels, 1989, p. 105. Daniels noted that writers, directors, and others who take on long-term projects may show post-reinforcement pauses that last weeks, months, or even years.

29. One by-product of variable ratio reinforcement is excitement. One reason why athletics and sports are exciting is the variable ratio payoff, in terms of goals, runs, or

baskets, for watching the game. The lack of excitement in school and work may reflect the lack of variable ratio schedules in these situations.

30. See Lindsley (1968) on the use of wrist counters for recording rates of behavior.

31. Other measures of behavior may include its form or topography, force, and locus. A discussion of these measures is found in Alberto and Troutman (1999, pp. 97–100).

32. See Daniels (1994, pp. 94–95) for a discussion and example of this kind of scale.

33. Daniels (1994, p. 94) indicated that although ranking is one of the most frequently used measures,

I strongly advise against it. Ranking should not be used because it sets one employee against another. . . . By using ratings we compare performance against established criteria. In this way, it is possible for everyone who meets the required criteria to be rated as a top performer.

34. Wolf (1978) introduced the importance of social validation of applied behavioral interventions. The use of questionnaires, interviews and surveys are important ways of assessing the acceptability of reinforcement programs to various sectors and consumers.

35. See Herrnstein (1961) on the matching law, which states that for two behaviors, B1 and B2, maintained on two schedules of reinforcement, R1 and R2, respectively, the proportional rate of behavior [B1/ (B1 + B2)] equals or matches the proportional rate of reinforcement [R1/ (R1 + R2)]. Based on this equation, if reinforcement is added to R2, then the relative time spent on B1 must decline. This requirement of the matching law would be detected as a side effect of reinforcement in applied settings.

36. Skinner (1979, p. 346). Although this quote refers more to basic research, maintaining an experimental attitude in terms of application of reinforcement principles is also important. In fact, given the complexities of applied settings, the willingness to change repeatedly may be essential to solving practical problems involving human behavior. In other areas of technology, "fine-tuning" a system is an acceptable strategy. For example, although the basic principles of physics allows for the propulsion of a rocket into space, the guidance system must obtain data that allows for corrections in trajectory. Similarly, the basic principles of reinforcement can be used for behavioral technology, but there also must be fine-tuning of the reinforcement system.

PART VII

CONCLUSION

Chapter 12

Resolving the Controversy over Rewards and Intrinsic Motivation

The rewards and intrinsic motivation controversy concerns the dispute over the use of rewards and reinforcement to motivate people's performance and interest. Many teachers use gold stars, recognition, bonuses, access to preferred activities, or other types of rewards to encourage high levels of performance by their students. In business, managers frequently offer incentives to employees for exceptional performance. Over the past 30 years, a number of psychologists have questioned the wisdom of these practices. The concern is that rewards undermine people's intrinsic motivation and performance. If students and employees are rewarded for doing an interesting task, the claim is that they will come to like the task less and engage in it less once the rewards are no longer forthcoming.

The contention that rewards undermine intrinsic motivation rests on a body of experimental research from social psychology. A few years ago, our research team conducted a meta-analysis of this literature to determine when, and under what conditions, rewards produce either increases or decreases in measures of intrinsic motivation.[1] We concluded that negative effects of reward occur under a circumscribed set of conditions and that, when appropriately arranged, rewards can be used to enhance motivation and performance.

Our findings and recommendations were highly contentious to those who argue that rewards are inherently harmful. Spurred by our research, certain investigators who view rewards as negative conducted a reanalysis of the literature.[2] These investigators suggested that our previous meta-analysis was seriously flawed and that rewards do, in fact, have a substantial undermining effect. In this book, we have shown that there is no inherent negative property of reward. On the basis of an updated meta-analysis on this topic (see Chapter 8),[3] a careful examination of previous research, and a historical overview of the literature (see Chapter 10), we found no reason to accept the claim that rewards have pervasive negative effects on people's intrinsic motivation.

In terms of the meta-analysis presented in this book, the research findings on the topic indicate that rewards can be used to increase motivation and performance on tasks that are of low initial interest. On high-interest tasks, positive effects are obtained when participants are verbally praised for their work and tangible rewards are offered and explicitly tied to performance standards and success. The only negative effect occurs when tangible rewards signify failure or are only loosely tied to behavior. Overall, our research suggests that negative effects of reward can be easily prevented and that teachers and managers can use rewards effectively to motivate performance and interest.

Although the negative effects of reward are highly circumscribed, over the past 30 years, many researchers and educators have argued against the use of rewards and reinforcement in everyday life. To understand this reluctance to use positive incentive systems, we point to the sociohistorical context of the rewards and intrinsic motivation controversy. Studies on negative effects of reward were instigated at a time when many people were suspicious of science and technology, especially as they applied to human behavior.

A prominent view in the 1960s and 1970s concerned human beings as willful and self-determined; a major goal was to seek self-actualization. Any external influences (including the use of rewards) were seen as harmful to an individual's psychological development. It is within this context that experiments on rewards and intrinsic motivation were conducted, and although the findings were weak, the research was interpreted as evidence for the harmful effects of rewards and reinforcement. This view led to inertia in management and teaching. Rather than design programs that used positive reinforcement to instill habits and values, individuals involved in performance management were being told that doing nothing was better than using an incentive system.

What we have shown in this book is that rewards and reinforcement can be used to promote desired behavior and, at the same time, maintain people's interest. In other words, there is no need to ban the use of rewards in classrooms and industry. Instead, more effort needs to be devoted to the effective management of rewards in applied settings.

Prominent values of contemporary Western culture include human happiness, the individual pursuit of self-discovery and creative potential, and persistence in the face of adversity. These values are related to the more general values of individualism concerning freedom, dignity, and individual responsibility. In the pursuit of these values, our society has often resorted to punishment when behaviors conflict with cherished beliefs. In this book, we have shown that there is no need to use punishment and coercion to attain our valued goals. Human freedom and happiness can be better attained through the effective use of rewards and positive reinforcement in everyday life.

NOTES

1. Cameron and Pierce, 1994; Eisenberger and Cameron, 1996.
2. Deci, Koestner, and Ryan, 1999.
3. Cameron, Banko, and Pierce, 2001.

References

Studies marked with an asterisk (*) were those included in the meta-analysis presented in this book.

*Adorney, K.M. (1983). *Facilitating and undermining intrinsic motivation: A test of attribution, cognitive evaluation and competence theories*. Unpublished doctoral dissertation, Columbia University.

Alberto, P.A., & Troutman, A.C. (1999). *Applied behavior analysis for teachers*. Upper Saddle River, NJ: Prentice Hall.

*Amabile, T.M., Hennesey, B.A., & Grossman, B.S. (1986). Social influences on creativity: The effects of contracted-for reward. *Journal of Personality and Social Psychology, 50,* 14–23.

*Anderson, R., Manoogian, S.T., & Reznick, J.S. (1976). The undermining and enhancing of intrinsic motivation in preschool children. *Journal of Personality and Social Psychology, 34,* 915–922.

*Anderson, S., & Rodin, J. (1989). Is bad news always bad? Cue and feedback effects on intrinsic motivation. *Journal of Applied Social Psychology, 19,* 449–467.

*Arkes, H.R. (1979). Competence and the overjustification effect. *Motivation and Emotion, 3,* 143–150.

*Arnold, H.J. (1976). Effects of performance feedback and extrinsic reward upon high intrinsic motivation. *Organizational Behavior and Human Performance, 17,* 275–288.

*Arnold, H.J. (1985). Task performance, perceived competence, and attributed causes of performance as determinants of intrinsic motivation. *Academy of Management Journal, 28,* 876–888.

Ayllon, T., & Azrin, N.H. (1968). *The token economy*. Upper Saddle River, NJ: Prentice-Hall.

Azrin, N.H., & Holz, W.C. (1966). Punishment. In W.K. Honig (Ed.), *Operant behavior: Areas of research and application* (pp. 380–447). New York: Appleton-Century-Crofts.

Baars, B.J. (1986). *The cognitive revolution in psychology*. New York: Guilford Press.

Balsam, P.D., & Bondy, A.S. (1983). The negative side effects of reward. *Journal of Applied Behavior Analysis, 16*, 283–296.

Bandura, A. (1986). *Social foundations of thought and action: A social cognitive theory*. Upper Saddle River, NJ: Prentice Hall.

Bandura, A. (1997). *Self-efficacy: The exercise of control*. New York: Freeman.

Bandura, A., & Schunk, D.H. (1981). Cultivating competence, self-efficacy and intrinsic interest through proximal self-motivation. *Journal of Personality and Social Psychology, 41*, 586–598.

*Bartelme, L.A. (1983). *The effects of choice and rewards on intrinsic motivation and performance*. Unpublished doctoral dissertation, University of Iowa.

Bates, J.A. (1979). Extrinsic reward and intrinsic motivation: A review with implications for the classroom. *Review of Educational Research, 49*, 557–576.

Bem, D.J. (1965). An experimental analysis of self-persuasion. *Journal of Experimental Social Psychology, 1*, 199–218.

Bem, D.J. (1972). Self-perception theory. In L. Berkowitz (Ed.), *Advances in experimental social psychology* (Vol. 6) (pp. 2–62). New York: Acadmic Press.

Bernstein, D.J. (1990). Of carrots and sticks: A review of Deci and Ryan's *Intrinsic motivation and self-determination in human behavior*. *Journal of the Experimental Analysis of Behavior, 54*, 323–332.

*Blanck, P.D., Reis, H.T., & Jackson, L. (1984). The effects of verbal reinforcement of intrinsic motivation for sex-linked tasks. *Sex Roles, 10*, 369–386.

Boal, K.B., & Cummings, L.L. (1981). Cognitive evaluation theory: An experimental test of processes and outcomes. *Organizational Behavior and Human Performance, 28*, 289–310.

*Boggiano, A.K., & Barrett, M. (1985). Performance and motivational deficits of helplessness: The role of motivational orientations. *Journal of Personality and Social Psychology, 19*, 1753–1761.

*Boggiano, A.K., Harackiewicz, J.M., Besette, J.M., & Main, D.S. (1985). Increasing children's interest through performance contingent reward. *Social Cognition, 3*, 400–411.

Boggiano, A.K. & Hertel, P.T. (1983). Bonuses and bribes: Mood effects in memory. *Social Cognition, 2*, 49–61.

*Boggiano, A.K., Main, D.S., & Katz, P.A. (1988). Children's preference for challenge: The role of perceived competence and control. *Journal of Personality and Social Psychology, 54*, 131–141.

*Boggiano, A.K., & Ruble, D.N. (1979). Competence and the overjustification effect: A developmental study. *Journal of Personality and Social Psychology, 37*, 1462–1468.

*Boggiano, A.K., Ruble, D.N., & Pittman, T.S. (1982). The mastery hypothesis and the overjustification effect. *Social Cognition, 1*, 38–49.

*Brennan, T.P., & Glover, J.A. (1980). An examination of the effect of extrinsic reinforcers on intrinsically motivated behavior: experimental and theoretical. *Social Behavior and Personality, 8*, 27–32.

*Brewer, J. (1980). *The undermining and enhancing effects of intrinsic motivation: A developmental study.* Unpublished doctoral dissertation, Ohio State University.

*Brockner, J., & Vasta, R. (1981). Do causal attributions mediate the effects of extrinsic rewards on intrinsic interest? *Journal of Research in Personality, 15,* 201–209.

Brophy, J. (1981). On praising effectively. *The Elementary School Journal, 81,* 270–278.

*Butler, R. (1987). Task-involving and ego-involving properties of evaluation: Effects of different feedback conditions on motivational perceptions, interest, and performance. *Journal of Educational Psychology, 79,* 474–482.

*Calder, B.J., & Staw, B.M. (1975). Self-perception of intrinsic and extrinsic motivation. *Journal of Personality and Social Psychology, 31,* 599–605.

Cameron, J., Banko, K.M., & Pierce, W.D. (2001). Pervasive negative effects of rewards on intrinsic motivation: The myth continues. *The Behavior Analyst, 24,* 1–44.

Cameron, J., & Pierce, W.D. (1994). Reinforcement, reward and intrinsic motivation: A meta-analysis. *Review of Educational Research, 64,* 363–423.

Cameron, J., & Pierce, W.D. (1996). The debate about rewards and intrinsic motivation: Protests and accusations do not alter the results. *Review of Educational Research, 66,* 39–51.

Cameron, J., & Pierce, W.D. (1997). Rewards, interest and performance: An evaluation of experimental findings. *American Compensation Association [ACA] Journal, 6,* 6–15.

Carlson, C.G., Hersen, M., & Eisler, R.M. (1972). Token economy programs in the treatment of hospitalized adult psychiatric patients: Current status and recent trends. *Journal of Nervous and Mental Disease, 155,* 192–204.

Carton, J.S. (1996). The differential effects of tangible rewards and praise on intrinsic motivation: A comparison of cognitive evaluation theory and operant theory. *The Behavior Analyst, 19,* 237–255.

*Carton, J.S., & Nowicki, S. (1998). Should behavior therapists stop using reinforcement? A reexamination of the undermining effect of reinforcement on intrinsic motivation. *Behavior Therapy, 29,* 65–86.

Catania, A.C. (1984). The operant behaviorism of B.F. Skinner. *Behavioral and Brain Sciences, 7,* 473.

Catania, A.C. (1998). *Learning.* Upper Saddle River, NJ: Prentice Hall.

Chance, P. (1992, November), The rewards of learning. *Phi Delta Kappa,* 200–207.

Chance, P. (1998). *First course in applied behavior analysis.* Pacific Grove, CA: Brooks/Cole Publishing.

*Chung, K.T. (1995). The effects of extrinsic reinforcement on intrinsic motivation amongst mildly mentally handicapped children. *Curriculum Forum, 4,* 98–114.

*Cohen, D.S. (1974). *The effects of task choice, monetary, and verbal reward on intrinsic motivation: A closer look at Deci's cognitive evaluation theory.* Unpublished doctoral dissertation, Ohio State University.

Cohen, J. (1988). *Statistical power analysis for the behavioral sciences* (2nd ed.). Mahwah, NJ: Erlbaum.

Cooper, H.M. (1989). *Integrating research: A guide for literature reviews.* Beverly Hills, CA: Sage.

*Crino, M.D., & White, M.C. (1982). Feedback effects in intrinsic/extrinsic reward paradigms. *Journal of Management, 8,* 95–108.

*Dafoe, J.L. (1985). *Use of rewards in teaching a skill: Effects on competence, self-efficacy and intrinsic motivation.* Unpublished doctoral dissertation, Stanford University.

Daly, H.B. (1969a). Is instrumental responding necessary for nonreward following reward to be frustrating? *Journal of Experimental Psychology, 80,* 186–187.

Daly, H.B. (1969b). Learning of a hurdle-jump response to escape cues paired with reduced reward or frustrative nonreward. *Journal of Experimental Psychology, 79,* 146–157.

*Daniel, T.L., & Esser, J.K. (1980). Intrinsic motivation as influenced by rewards, task interest and task structure. *Journal of Applied Psychology, 65,* 566–573.

Daniels, A.C. (1989). *Performance management: Improving quality productivity through positive reinforcement.* Tucker, GA: Performance Management Publications.

Daniels, A.C. (1994). *Bringing out the best in people: How to apply the astonishing power of positive reinforcement.* New York: McGraw-Hill.

*Danner, F.W., & Lonkey, E. (1981). A cognitive developmental approach to the effects of rewards on intrinsic motivation. *Child Development, 52,* 1043–1052.

Davidson, P., & Bucher, B. (1978). Intrinsic interest and extrinsic reward: The effects of a continuing token program on continuing nonconstrained preference. *Behavior Therapy, 9,* 222–234.

DeCharms, R. (1968). *Personal causation.* New York: Academic Press.

DeCharms, R., & Muir, M.S. (1978). Motivation: Social approaches. *Annual Review of Psychology, 29,* 91–113.

*Deci, E.L. (1971). Effects of externally mediated rewards on intrinsic motivation. *Journal of Personality and Social Psychology, 18,* 105–115.

*Deci, E.L. (1972a). The effects of contingent and noncontingent rewards and controls on intrinsic motivation. *Organizational Behavior and Human Performance, 8,* 217–229.

*Deci, E.L. (1972b). Intrinsic motivation, extrinsic reinforcement, and inequity. *Journal of Personality and Social Psychology, 22,* 113–120.

Deci, E.L. (1975). *Intrinsic motivation.* New York: Plenum Press.

*Deci, E.L., Cascio, W.F., & Krusell, J. (1975). Cognitive evaluation theory and some comments on the Calder and Staw critique. *Journal of Personality and Social Psychology, 31,* 81–85.

Deci, E.L., Koestner, R., & Ryan, R.M. (1999). A meta-analytic review of experiments examining the effects of extrinsic rewards on intrinsic motivation. *Psychological Bulletin, 125,* 627–668.

Deci, E.L., Koestner, R. & Ryan, R.M. (2001). Extrinsic rewards and intrinsic motivation in education: Reconsidered once again. *Review of Educational Research, 71,* 1–27.

Deci, E.L & Ryan, R.M. (1985). *Intrinsic motivation and self-determination in human behavior.* New York: Plenum Press.

*DeLoach, L.L., Griffith, K., & LaBarba, R.C. (1983). The relationship of group context and intelligence to the overjustification effect. *Bulletin of the Psychonomic Society, 21,* 291–293.

Deno, S., & Jenkins, J. (1967). *Evaluating preplanning curriculum objectives.* Philadelphia: Research for Better Schools.

Dewey, J. (1900). Psychology and social practice. *Psychological Review, 7,* 105–124. Reprinted in E.R. Hilgard (Ed.) (1978), *American psychology in historical perspective: Addresses of the presidents of the American Psychological Association 1892–1977* (pp. 65–79). Washington, DC: APA.

Dickinson, A.M. (1989). The detrimental effects of extrinsic reinforcement on "intrinsic motivation." *The Behavior Analyst, 12,* 1–15.

About the Authors

JUDY CAMERON is an Associate Professor of educational psychology at the University of Alberta.

W. DAVID PIERCE is a Professor in the Department of Sociology at the University of Alberta, Director of the Centre for Experimental Sociology, and retired Adjunct Professor in the Department of Neuroscience (Medicine).

*Dimitroff, G. (1984). *Depression of intrinsically motivated performance by rewards: The role of frustration-mediated contrast effects.* Unpublished doctoral dissertation, University of Toronto.

*Dollinger, S.J., & Thelen, M.H. (1978). Overjustification and children's intrinsic motivation: Comparative effects of four rewards. *Journal of Personality and Social Psychology, 36,* 1259–1269.

Dunham, P.J. (1968). Contrasted conditions of reinforcement. *Psychological Bulletin, 69,* 295–315.

*Earn, B.M. (1982). Intrinsic motivation as a function of extrinsic financial rewards and subjects' locus of control. *Journal of Personality, 50,* 360–373.

*Effron, B. (1976). *Effects of self-mediated competency feedback and external incentives on intrinsic motivation and quality of task performance.* Unpublished doctoral dissertation, University of Pittsburgh.

Egan, T. (1995, November 12). Take this bribe, please, for values to be received. *New York Times, "Week in Review,"* 5.

Eisenberger, R. (1992). Learned industriousness. *Psychological Review, 99,* 248–267.

*Eisenberger, R. (1999). *Effects of gender and cooperative-versus-individual performance-contingent reward on intrinsic motivation.* Unpublished manuscript.

Eisenberger, R., & Armeli, S. (1997). Can salient reward increase creative performance without reducing intrinsic creative interest? *Journal of Personality and Social Psychology, 72,* 652–653.

Eisenberger, R., & Cameron, J. (1996). The detrimental effects of reward: Myth or reality? *American Psychologist, 51,* 1153–1166.

Eisenberger, R., & Cameron, J. (1998). Rewards, intrinsic interest and creativity: New findings. *American Psychologist., 53,* 676–679.

Eisenberger, R., Kaplan, R.M., & Singer, R.D. (1974). Decremental and nondecremental effects of noncontingent social approval. *Journal of Personality and Social Psychology, 30,* 716–722.

Eisenberger, R., Leonard, J.M., Carlson, J., & Park, D.C. (1979). Transfer effects of contingent and noncontingent positive reinforcement: Mechanisms and generality. *American Journal of Psychology, 92,* 525–535.

Eisenberger, R., Pierce, W.D., & Cameron, J. (1999). Effects of reward on intrinsic motivation: Negative, neutral, and positive. *Psychological Bulletin, 125,* 677–691.

*Eisenberger, R., Rhoades, L., & Cameron, J. (1999). Does pay for performance increase or decrease self-determination and intrinsic motivation? *Journal of Personality and Social Psychology, 77,* 1026–1040.

*Eisenstein, N. (1985). Effects of contractual, endogenous, or unexpected rewards on high and low interest presechoolers. *The Psychological Record, 35,* 29–39.

Engelmann, S. (1992). *War against the schools' academic abuse.* Portland, OR: Halcyon House.

*Enzle, M.E., Roogeveen, J.P., & Look, S.C. (1991). Self- versus other-reward administration and intrinsic motivation. *Journal of Experimental Social Psychology, 27,* 468–479.

Enzle, M.E., & Ross, J.M. (1978). Increasing and decreasing intrinsic interest with contingent rewards: A test of cognitive evaluation theory. *Journal of Experimental Social Psychology, 14,* 588–597.

Epling, W.F. & Pierce, W.D. (1992). *Solving the anorexia puzzle: A scientific approach.* Toronto: Hogrefe & Huber. (Original work published 1991.)

*Fabes, R.A. (1987). Effects of reward contexts on young children's task interest. *Journal of Psychology, 121,* 5–19.

*Fabes, R.A., Eisenberg, N., Fultz, J., & Miller, P. (1988). Reward, affect and young children's motivational orientation. *Motivation and Emotion, 12,* 155–169.

*Fabes, R.A., Fultz, J., Eisenberg, N., May-Plumlee, T., & Christopher, F.S. (1989). Effects of rewards on children's prosocial motivation: A socialization study. *Developmental Psychology, 25,* 509–515.

*Fabes, R.A., McCullers, J.C., & Horn, H. (1986). Children's task interest and performance: Immediate vs. subsequent effects of rewards. *Personality and Social Psychology Bulletin, 12,* 17–30.

*Feehan, G.G., & Enzle, M.E. (1991). Subjective control over rewards: Effects of perceived choice of reward schedule on intrinsic motivation and behavior maintenance. *Perceptual and Motor Skills, 72,* 995–1006.

Feingold, B.D., & Mahoney, M.J. (1975). Reinforcement effects on intrinsic interest: Undermining the overjustification hypothesis. *Behavior Therapy, 6,* 357–377.

Festinger, L. (1957). *A theory of cognitive dissonance.* Evanston, Il: Row, Peterson.

Festinger, L., & Carlsmith, J.M. (1959). Cognitive consequences of forced-compliance. *Journal of Abnormal and Social Psychology, 58,* 203–210.

Flesch, R. (1965). *Why Johnny can't read.* New York: Harper & Row. (Original work published 1955)

Flesch, R. (1981). *Why Johnny still can't read: A new look at the scandal of our schools.* New York: Harper & Row.

Flora, S.R. (1990). Undermining intrinsic interest from the standpoint of a behaviorist. *The Psychological Record, 40,* 323–346.

Flora, S.R., & Flora, D.B. (1999). Effects of extrinsic reinforcement for reading during childhood on reported reading habits of college students. *The Psychological Record, 49,* 3–14.

Freedman, J.L. (1965). Long-term behavioral effects of cognitive dissonance. *Journal of Experimental Social Psychology, 1,* 145–155.

*Freedman, S.M., & Phillips, J.S. (1985). The effects of situational performance constraints on intrinsic motivation and satisfaction: The role of perceived competence and self-determination. *Organizational Behavior and Human Decision Processes, 35,* 397–416.

Geller, L. (1982). The failure of self-actualization therapy: A critique of Carl Rogers and Abraham Maslow. *Journal of Humanistic Psychology, 22,* 56–73.

Glass, G.V. (1976). Primary, secondary and meta-analysis of research. *Educational Researcher, 5,* 3–8.

Glass, G.V., McGaw, B., & Smith, M.L. (1981). *Meta-analysis in social research.* Beverly Hills, CA: Sage.

*Goldstein, G.S. (1980). *The effects of competition and external rewards on intrinsic motivation.* Unpublished doctoral dissertation, University of New Hampshire.

*Goldstein, L.W. (1977). *Intrinsic motivation: The role of reward and feedback on quality of performance and subsequent interest in photography.* Unpublished doctoral dissertation, Cornell University.

*Greene, D., & Lepper, M.R. (1974). Effects of extrinsic rewards on children's subsequent intrinsic interest. *Child Development, 45,* 1141–1145.

*Griffith, K.M. (1984). *The effects of group versus individual context, initial interest, and reward on intrinsic motivation*. Unpublished doctoral dissertation, University of South Florida.

*Griffith, K.M., DeLoach, L.L., & LaBarba, R.C. (1984). The effects of rewarder familiarity and differential reward preference in intrinsic motivation. *Bulletin of the Psychonomic Society, 22*, 313–316.

*Hamner, W.C., & Foster, L.W. (1975). Are intrinsic and extrinsic rewards additive? A test of Deci's cognitive evaluation theory of task motivation. *Organizational Behavior and Human Performance, 14*, 398–415.

*Harackiewicz, J.M. (1979). The effects of reward contingency and performance feedback on intrinsic motivation. *Journal of Personality and Social Psychology, 37*, 1352–1363.

*Harackiewicz, J.M., Abrahams, S., & Wageman, R. (1987). Performance evaluation and intrinsic motivation: The effects of evaluative focus, rewards, and achievement orientation. *Journal of Personality and Social Psychology, 53*, 1015–1023.

*Harackiewicz, J.M., & Manderlink, G. (1984). A process analysis of the effects of performance-contingent rewards on intrinsic motivation. *Journal of Experimental Social Psychology, 20*, 531–551.

*Harackiewicz, J.M., Manderlink, G., & Sansone, C. (1984). Rewarding pinball wizardry: Effects of evaluation and cue value on intrinsic interest. *Journal of Personality and Social Psychology, 47*, 287–300.

Harackiewicz, J.M., & Sansone, C. (2000). Rewarding competence: The importance of goals in the study of intrinsic motivation. In C. Sansone & J.M. Harackiewicz (Eds.), *Intrinsic and extrinsic motivation: The search for optimal motivation and performance* (pp. 79–103). San Diego, CA: Academic Press.

Harlow, H.F. (1950). Learning and satiation of response in intrinsically motivated complex puzzle performance by monkeys. *Journal of Comparative Physiological Psychology, 43*, 289–294.

Harlow, H.F., Harlow, M.K., & Meyer, D.R. (1950). Learning motivated by a manipulation drive. *Journal of Experimental Psychology, 40*, 228–234.

Hawkins, D. (1995, October 30). Johnny can read for cash and freebies: Is bribery the best way to get a kid to learn? *U.S. News and World Report*, 72–73.

Hedges, L.V. (1981). Distribution theory for Glass's estimator of effect size and related estimators. *Journal of Educational Statistics, 6*, 107–128.

Hedges, L.V. & Becker, B.J. (1986). Statistical methods in the meta-analysis of research on gender differences. In J. Hyde & M.C. Linn (Eds.), *The psychology of gender: Advances through meta-analysis* (pp. 14–50). Baltimore, MD: John Hopkins University Press.

Hedges, L.V. & Olkin, I. (1985). *Statistical methods for meta-analysis*. Orlando, FL: Academic Press.

Heider, F. (1958). *The psychology of interpersonal relations*. New York: John Wiley & Sons.

Hennessey, B.A., & Amabile, T.M. (1998). Reward, intrinsic motivation, and creativity. *American Psychologist, 53*, 674–675.

Herrnstein, R.J. (1961). Relative and absolute strength of responses as a function of the frequency of reinforcement. *Journal of the Experimental Analysis of Behavior, 4*, 267–272.

*Hitt, D.D., Marriott, R.G., & Esser, J.K. (1992). Effects of delayed rewards and task interest on intinsic motivation. *Basic and Applied Social Psychology, 13*, 405–414.

Hogan, R. (1975). Theoretical egocentrism and the problem of compliance. *American Psychologist, 30*, 533–540.

Horcones. (1983). Natural reinforcement in a Walden Two community. *Revista Mexicana de Analisis del la Conducta, 9*, 141–143.

Horcones. (1987). The concept of consequences in the analysis of behavior. *The Behavior Analyst, 10*, 291–294.

*Horn, H.L. (1987). A methodological note: Time of participation effects on intrinsic motivation. *Personality and Social Psychology Bulletin, 13*, 210–215.

Hunter, J.E., & Schmidt, F.L. (1990). Methods of meta-analysis: correcting error and bias in research findings. Newbury Park, CA: Sage Publications.

*Hyman, C. (1985). *Reward contingency, standards, and intrinsic motivation.* Unpublished doctoral dissertation, City University of New York.

*Karniol, R., & Ross, M. (1977). The effect of performance relevant and performance irrelevant rewards on children's intrinsic motivation. *Child Development, 48*, 482–487.

*Kast, A., & Connor, K. (1988). Sex and age differences in response to informational and controlling feedback. *Personality and Social Psychology Bulletin, 14*, 514–523.

Kazdin, A.E. (1975a). *Behavior modification in applied settings.* Homewood, IL: Dorsey Press.

Kazdin, A.E. (1975b). Recent advances in token economy research. In M. Hersen, R.M. Eisler, & P.M. Miller (eds.), *Progress in behavior modification* (Vol. 1) (pp. 233–274) New York: Academic Press.

Kazdin, A.E. (1994). *Behavior modification in applied settings.* Pacific Grove, CA: Brooks/Cole.

Kazdin, A.E., & Bootzin, R.R. (1972). The token economy: An evaluative review. *Journal of Applied Behavior Analysis, 5*, 343–372.

Kelley, H.H. (1967). Attribution theory in social psychology. In D. Levine (Ed.), *Nebraska symposium on motivation* (Vol. 15). Lincoln: University of Nebraska Press.

Kline, M. (1973). *Why Johnny can't add: The failure of the new math.* New York: Vantage Books.

*Koestner, R., Zuckerman, M., & Koestner, J. (1987). Praise, involvement, and intrinsic motivation. *Journal of Personality and Social Psychology, 53*, 383–390.

Kohn, A. (1993a). *Punished by rewards.* Boston: Houghton Mifflin.

Kohn, A. (1993b, September–October). Why incentive plans cannot work. *Harvard Business Review*, 54–63.

Kohn, A. (1996). By all available means: Cameron and Pierce's defense of extrinsic motivators. *Review of Educational Research, 66*, 1–4.

Kollins, S.H., Newland, M.C., & Critchfield, T.S. (1997). Human sensitivity to reinforcement in operant choice: How much do consequences matter? *Psychonomic Bulletin and Review, 4*, 208–220. Erratum. *Psychonomic Bulletin and Review, 4*, 431.

*Kruglanski, A.W., Alon, S., & Lewis, T. (1972). Retrospective misattribution and task enjoyment. *Journal of Experimental Social Psychology, 8*, 493–501.

*Kruglanski, A.W., Friedman, I., & Zeevi, G. (1971). The effects of extrinsic incentive on some qualitative aspects of task performance. *Journal of Personality, 39*, 606–617.

*Kruglanski, A.W., Riter, A., Amitai, A., Margolin, B.S., Shabatai, L., & Zaksh, D. (1975). Can money enhance intrinsic motivation? A test of the content-consequence hypothesis. *Journal of Personality and Social Psychology, 31*, 744–750.

Krutch, J.W. (1953). The idols of the laboratory. In F. Connolly (ed.), *Man and his measure* (pp. 1242–1251). New York: Harcourt, Brace & World.

Kuhlman, D.M., Camac, C.R., & Cunha, D.A. (1986). Individual differences in social orientation. In H. Wilke, D. Messick, & C. Rutte (Eds.), *Experimental social dilemmas* (pp. 151–176). Frankfurt: Verlag Peter Lang.

Kuhlman, D.M., & Marshello, A.F.J. (1975). Individual differences in game motivation as moderators of preprogrammed strategy effects in prisoner's dilemma. *Journal of Personality and Social Psychology, 32*, 922–931.

Kuhlman, D.M., & Wimberley, D. (1976). Expectations of choice behavior held by co-operators, competitors and individualists across four classes of experimental games. *Journal of Personality and Social Psychology, 34*, 69–81.

Kuhn, T.S. (1962). *The structure of scientific revolutions.* Chicago: University of Chicago Press.

Kuo, Z.Y. (1931). The genesis of the cat's responses to the rat. *Journal of Comparative Psychology, 11*, 1–35.

Leahey, T.H. (1992). The mythical revolutions of American psychology. *American Psychologist, 47*, 308–318.

Leahey, T.H. (1987). *A history of psychology: Main currents in psychological thought* Upper Saddle River, NJ: Prentice Hall.

*Lee, J. (1982). *Effects of absolute and normative feedback and reward on performance and affect.* Unpublished doctoral dissertation, University of Iowa.

Lepper, M.R. (1998). A whole much less than the sum of its parts. *American Psychologist, 53*, 675–676.

Lepper, M.R., & Gilovich, T. (1981). The multiple functions of reward: A social developmental perspective. In S.S. Brehm, S. Kassin, & F.X. Gibbions (Eds.), *Developmental social psychology* (pp. 5–31). New York: Oxford University Press.

Lepper, M.R., & Greene, D. (Eds.). (1978). *The hidden costs of rewards: New perspectives of the psychology of human motivation.* Hillsdale, NJ: Erlbaum.

*Lepper, M.R., Greene, D., & Nisbett, R.E. (1973). Undermining children's intrinsic interest with extrinsic reward: A test of the "overjustification" hypothesis. *Journal of Personality and Social Psychology, 28*, 129–137.

Lepper, M.R., & Henderlong, J. (2000). Turning "play" into "work" and "work" into "play": 25 years of research on intrinsic versus extrinsic motivation. In C. Sansone, & J.M. Harackiewicz (Eds.), *Intrinsic and extrinsic motivation: The search for optimal motivation and performance* (pp. 257–307). San Diego, CA: Academic Press.

Lepper, M.R., Keavney, M., & Drake, M. (1996). Intrinsic motivation and extrinsic rewards: A commentary on Cameron and Pierce's meta-analysis. *Review of Educational Research, 66*, 5–32.

*Lepper, M.R., Sagotsky, G., Dafoe, J.L., & Greene, D. (1982). Consequences of superfluous social constraints: Effects on young children's social inferences and subsequent intrinsic interest. *Journal of Personality and Social Psychology, 42*,

51–65.

Levine, F.M., & Fasnacht, G. (1974). Token rewards may lead to token learning. *American Psychologist, 29*, 817–820.

*Liberty, H.J. (1986). *Intrinsic motivation, extraversion, impulsivity, and reward in a computer game setting*. Unpublished doctoral dissertation, City University of New York.

Light, R.J., & Pillemer, D.B. (1984). *Summing up: The science of reviewing research*. Cambridge: Harvard University Press.

Lindsley, O.R. (1968). Technical note: A reliable wrist counter for recording behavior rates. *Journal of Applied Behavior Analysis, 1*, 77–78.

*Loveland, K.K., & Olley, J.G. (1979). The effect of external reward on interest and quality of task performance in children of high and low intrinsic motivation. *Child Development, 50*, 1207–1210.

*Luyten, H., & Lens, W. (1981). The effect of earlier experience and reward contingencies on intrinsic motivation. *Motivation and Emotion, 5*, 25–36.

MacKenzie, B.D. (1977). *Behaviorism and the limits of the scientific method*. Atlantic Highlands, NJ: Humanities Press.

Maier, S.F., & Seligman, M.E.P. (1976). Learned helplessness: Theory and evidence. *Journal of Experimental Psychology: General, 105*, 3–46.

Martin, G., & Pear, J. (1999). *Behavior modification: What is it and how to do it* (6th ed.). Upper Saddle River, NJ: Prentice-Hall.

Mawhinney, T.C. (1990). Decreasing intrinsic "motivation" with extrinsic rewards: Easier said than done. *Journal of Organizational Behavior Management, 11*, 175–191.

Mawhinney, T.C., Dickinson, A.M. & Taylor, L.A. (1989). The use of concurrent schedules to evaluate the effects of extrinsic rewards on "intrinsic motivation." *Journal of Organizational Behavior Management, 10*, 109–129.

Mazur, J.E. (1998). *Learning and behavior*. Upper Saddle River, NJ: Prentice-Hall.

McAdams, J.L., & Hawk, E.J. (1992). *Capitalizing on human assets: The benchmark study*. Scottsdale, AZ: American Compensation Association and Maritz Inc.

McDougall, W. (1908). *An introduction to social psychology*. London: Methuen.

*McGraw, K.O., & McCullers, J.C. (1979). Evidence of a detrimental effect of extrinsic incentives on breaking a mental set. *Journal of Experimental Social Psychology, 15*, 285–294.

*McLoyd, V.C. (1979). The effects of extrinsic rewards of differential value on high and low intrinsic interest. *Child Development, 50*, 1010–1019.

Miller, G.A. (1962). *Psychology: The science of mental life*. New York: Harper & Row.

*Morgan, M. (1981). The overjustification effect: A developmental test of self perception interpretations. *Journal of Personality and Social Psychology, 40*, 809–821.

*Morgan, M. (1983). Decrements in intrinsic interest among rewarded and observer subjects. *Child Development, 54*, 636–644.

Morgan, M. (1984). Reward-induced decrements and increments in intrinsic motivation. *Review of Educational Research, 54*, 5–30.

Morris, R. (1976). *Behavior modification with children*. Cambridge, MA: Winthrop Publications.

*Mynatt, C., Oakley, D., Piccione, A., Margolis, R., & Arkkelin, J. (1978). An examination of overjustification under conditions of extended observation and multiple reinforcement: Overjustification or boredom? *Cognitive Therapy and Research, 2*, 171–177.

Neil, A.S. (1959). *Summerhill: A radical approach to child rearing.* New York: Hart.

Neisser, U. (1967). *Cognitive psychology.* New York: Appleton-Century-Crofts.

Nelson, R. (1996). The use of informal rewards in recognizing performance. *Smart Business Supersite* (http://www.smarth.3.com). Available on http://www.p-management.com/reward/reward.htm

Newell, A., Shaw, J.C., & Simon, H.A. (1958). Elements of a theory of problem solving. *Psychological Review, 65,* 151–166.

*Newman, J., & Layton, B.D. (1984). Overjustification: A self-perception perspective. *Personality and Social Psychology Bulletin, 10,* 419–425.

Newman, L.S., & Ruble, D.N. (1992). Do young children use the discounting principle? *Journal of Experimental Social Psychology, 28,* 572–593.

Notz, W.W. (1975). Work motivation and the negative effects of extrinsic rewards. *American Psychologist, 30,* 884–891.

*Ogilvie, L., & Prior, M. (1982). The overjustification effect in retarded children: durability and generalizability. *Australia and New Zealand Journal of Developmental Disabilities, 8,* 213–218.

*Okano, K. (1981). The effects of extrinsic reward on intrinsic motivation. *Journal of Child Development, 17,* 11–23.

*Orlick, T.D., & Mosher, R. (1978). Extrinsic awards and participant motivation in a sport related task. *International Journal of Sport Psychology, 9,* 27–39.

Overmeier, J.B. (1985). Toward a reanalysis of the causal structure of the learned helplessness syndrome. In F.R. Brush & J.B. Overmeier (Eds.), *Affect, conditioning, and cognition: Essays on the determinants of behavior* (pp. 211–227). Mahwah, NJ: Erlbaum.

Overmier, J.B., & Seligman, M.E.P. (1967). Effects of inescapable shock upon subsequent escape and avoidance responding. *Journal of Comparative and Physiological Psychology, 63,* 28–33.

*Overskeid, G., & Svartdal, F. (1996). Effect of reward on subjective autonomy and interest when initial interest is low. *Psychological Record, 46,* 319–331.

Palermo, D.S. (1971). Is a scientific revolution taking place in psychology? *Science Studies, 1,* 135–155.

*Pallak, S.R., Costomotis, S., Sroka, S., & Pittman, T.S. (1982). School experience, reward characteristics and intrinsic motivation. *Child Development, 53,* 1382–1391.

*Patrick, C. (1985). *The effect of level of task difficulty on children's intrinsic motivation.* Unpublished doctoral dissertation, Purdue University.

*Perry, D.G., Bussey, K., & Redman, J. (1977). Reward-induced decreased play effects: Reattribution of motivation, competing responses, or avoiding frustration? *Child Development, 48,* 1369–1374.

Peterson, G.L. (1981). Historical self-understanding in the social sciences: The use of Thomas Kuhn in psychology. *Journal for the Theory of Social Behavior, 11,* 1–30.

*Phillips, J.S., & Freedman, S.M. (1985). Contingent pay and intrinsic task interest: Moderating effects of work values. *Journal of Applied Psychology, 70,* 306–313.

*Picek, J.S. (1976). *Effects of reward uncertainty and ability information on attributions of intrinsic motivation.* Unpublished doctoral dissertation, Indiana University.

Pierce, W.D., & Epling, W.F. (1999). *Behavior analysis and learning* (2nd ed.). Upper Saddle River, NJ: Prentice-Hall.

*Pittman, T.S., Cooper, E.E., & Smith, T.W. (1977). Attribution of causality and the overjustification effect. *Personality and Social Psychology Bulletin, 3,* 280–283.

*Pittman, T.S., Davey, M.E., Alafat, K.A., Wetherill, K.V., & Kramer, N.A. (1980). Informational versus controlling verbal rewards. *Personality and Social Psychology Bulletin, 6,* 228–233.

*Pittman, T.S., Emery, J., Boggiano, A.K. (1982). Intrinsic and extrinsic motivational orientations: reward-induced changes in preference for complexity. *Journal of Personality and Social Psychology, 42,* 789–797.

*Porac, J.F., & Meindl, J. (1982). Undermining overjustification: Inducing intrinsic and extrinsic task representations. *Organizational Behavior and Human Performance, 29,* 208–226.

Porter, L.W., & Lawler, E.E. (1968). *Managerial attitudes and performance.* Homewood, IL: Irwin-Dorsey.

Premack, D. (1959). Toward empirical behavior laws: 1. Positive reinforcement. *Psychological Review, 66,* 219–233.

Premack, D. (1971). Catching up with common sense or two sides of a generalization: Reinforcement and punishment. In R. Glaser (Ed.), *The nature of reinforcement* (pp. 121–150). New York: Academic Press.

*Pretty, G.H., & Seligman, C. (1984). Affect and the overjustification effect. *Journal of Personality and Social Psychology, 46,* 1241–1253.

Pryor, K. (1999). *Don't shoot the dog! The new art to teaching and training* (rev. ed.). New York: Bantam Books.

Rachlin, H. (1984). The explanatory power of Skinner's radical behaviorism. In S. Modgil & C. Modgil (Eds.), *B.F. Skinner: Consensus and controversy* (pp. 155–164). Philadelphia, PA: Falmer Press.

*Reiss, S., & Sushinsky, L.W. (1975). Overjustification, competing responses and the acquisition of intrinsic interest. *Journal of Personality and Social Psychology, 31,* 1116–1125.

Reiss, S., & Sushinsky, L.W. (1976). The competing response hypothesis of decreased play effects: A reply to Lepper and Greene. *Journal of Personality and Social Psychology, 33,* 233–245.

Rogers, C.R. (1964). Toward a science of the person. In T.W. Wann (Ed.), *Behaviorism and phenomenology* (pp. 109–140). Chicago: University of Chicago Press.

Rogers, C.R. (1969). *Freedom to learn.* Columbus, OH: Merrill.

Rogers, C.R., & Skinner, B.F. (1956). Some issues concerning the control of human behavior: A symposium. *Science, 124,* 1057–1066.

*Rosenfield, D., Folger, R., & Adelman, H.F. (1980). When rewards reflect competence: A qualification of the overjustification effect. *Journal of Personality and Social Psychology, 39,* 368–376.

*Ross, M. (1975). Salience of reward and intrinsic motivation. *Journal of Personality and Social Psychology, 32,* 245–254.

*Ross, M., Karniol, R., & Rothstein, M. (1976). Reward contingency and intrinsic motivation in children: A test of the delay of gratification hypothesis. *Journal of Personality and Social Psychology, 33,* 442–447.

Rousseau, J.J. (1974). *Emile* (B. Foxley, Trans.). London: Dent. (Original work published 1762)

Rummel, A., & Feinberg, R. (1988). Cognitive evaluation theory: A meta-analytic review of the literature. *Social Behavior and Personality, 16,* 147–164.

Ryan, R.M. (1982). Control and information in the intrapersonal sphere: An extension of cognitive evaluation theory. *Journal of Personality and Social Psychology, 43,* 450–461.

Ryan, R.M., & Deci, E.L. (1996). When paradigms clash: Comments on Cameron and Pierce's claim that rewards do not undermine intrinsic motivation. *Review of Educational Research, 66,* 33–38.

Ryan, R.M. & Deci, E.L. (2000) When rewards compete with nature: The undermining of intrinsic motivation and self-regulation. In C. Sansone & J.M. Harackiewicz (Eds.), *Intrinsic and extrinsic motivation: The search for optimal motivation and performance.* (pp. 13–54). San Diego, CA: Academic Press.

*Ryan, R.M., Mims, B., & Koestner, R. (1983). Relation of reward contingency and interpersonal context to intrinsic motivation: A review and test using cognitive evaluation theory. *Journal of Personality and Social Psychology, 45,* 736–750.

*Salincik, G.R. (1975). Interaction effects of performance and money on self-perception of intrinsic motivation. *Organizational Behavior and Human Performance, 13,* 339–351.

Sampson, E.E. (1988). The debate on individualism: Indigenous psychologies and their role in personal and societal functioning. *American Psychologist, 43,* 15–22.

*Sansone, C. (1986). A question of competence: The effects of competence and task feedback on intrinsic interest. *Journal of Personality and Social Psychology, 51,* 918–931.

*Sansone, C. (1989). Competence feedback, task feedback and intrinsic interest: An examination of process and context. *Journal of Experimental Social Psychology, 25,* 343–361.

Sansone, C., & Harackiewicz, J.M. (1998). "Reality" is complicated. *American Psychologist, 53,* 673–674.

Sansone, C., & Harackiewicz, J.M. (Eds.). (2000). *Intrinsic and extrinsic motivation: The search for optimal motivation and performance.* San Diego, CA: Academic Press.

*Sansone, C., Sachau, D.A., & Weir, C. (1989). Effects of instruction on intrinsic interest: The importance of context. *Journal of Personality and Social Psychology, 57,* 819–829.

*Sarafino, E.P. (1984). Intrinsic motivation and delay of gratification in preschoolers: The variables of reward salience and length of expected delay. *British Journal of Developmental Psychology, 2,* 149–156.

Schloss, P.J., & Smith, M.A. (1994). *Applied behavior analysis in the classroom.* Needham Heights, MA: Allyn & Bacon.

Schunk, D.H. (1983). Reward contingencies and the development of children's skills and self-efficacy. *Journal of Educational Psychology, 75,* 511–518.

Schunk, D.H. (1984). Enhancing self-efficacy and achievement through rewards and goals: Motivational and informational effects. *Journal of Educational Research, 78,* 29–34.

Schwartz, B. (1990). The creation and destruction of value. *American Psychologist, 45,* 7–15.

Schwartz, B., Schuldenfrei, R., & Lacey, H. (1978). Operant psychology as factory psychology. *Behaviorism, 2,* 229–254.

Schwarzer, R. (1991) *META: Programs for secondary data analysis.* MS-DOS Version 5.0 [Computer program]. Dubuque, IA: Wm. C. Brown.

Seligman, M.E.P. (1975). *Helplessness.* San Francisco: Freeman.

*Shanab, M.E., Peterson, D., Dargahi, S., & Deroian, P. (1981). The effects of positive and negative verbal feedback on the intrinsic motivation of male and female subjects. *The Journal of Social Psychology, 115*, 195–205.

*Shapira, Z. (1976). Expectancy determinants of intrinsically motivated behavior. *Journal of Personality and Social Psychology, 34*, 1235–1244.

*Shiffman-Kauffman, S.E. (1990). *The effects of reward contingency and type of learning experience on intrinsic motivation.* Unpublished doctoral dissertation, City University of New York.

Sidman, M. (1989). *Coercion and its fallout.* Boston, MA: Authors Cooperative.

Simon, H.A. (1956). Rational choice and the structure of the environment. *Psychological Review, 63*, 129–138.

Skaggs, K.J., Dickinson, A.M., & O'Connor, K.A. (1992). The use of concurrent schedules to evaluate the effects of extrinsic rewards on intrinsic motivation: A replication. *Journal of Organizational Behavior Management, 12*, 45–83.

Skinner, B.F. (1938). *The behavior of organisms: An experimental analysis.* Upper Saddle River, NJ: Prentice-Hall.

Skinner, B.F. (1953). *Science and human behavior.* New York: Macmillan.

Skinner, B.F. (1968). *The technology of teaching.* New York: Appleton-Century-Crofts.

Skinner, B.F. (1969). *Contingencies of reinforcement: A theoretical analysis.* Upper Saddle River NJ: Prentice-Hall.

Skinner, B.F. (1971). *Beyond freedom and dignity.* New York: Knopf.

Skinner, B.F. (1974). *About behaviorism.* New York: Knopf.

Skinner, B.F. (1978). Why I am not a cognitive psychologist. In *Reflections on behaviorism and society.* Upper Saddle River, NJ: Prentice-Hall.

Skinner, B.F. (1979). *The shaping of a behaviorist.* New York: Knopf.

Skinner, B.F. (1987). Selection by consequences. In *Upon further reflection.* Upper Saddle River, NJ: Prentice-Hall.

*Smith, A.T. (1980). *Effects of symbolic reward and positive feedback on high and low levels of intrinsic motivation in preschoolers.* Unpublished doctoral dissertation, University of Missouri–Columbia.

Smith, L.D. (1992). On prediction and control: B.F. Skinner and the technological ideal of science. *American Psychologist, 47*, 216–223.

*Smith, T.W., & Pittman, T.S. (1978). Reward, distraction, and the overjustification effect. Journal of Personality and Social Psychology, 36, 565–573.

*Smith, W.E. (1975). *The effect of anticipated vs. unanticipated social reward on subsequent intrinsic motivation.* Unpublished doctoral dissertation, Cornell University.

Smyth, J. (2001, June 20). Research vindicates bribery as school tool. Academic controversy: study says rewards whet an enduring appetite for learning. *National Post*, p. 1.

*Sorensen, R.L., & Maehr, M.L. (1976). Toward the experimental analysis of "continuing motivation." *The Journal of Educational Research, 69*, 319–322.

*Staw, B.M., Calder, B.J., Hess, R.K., & Sandelands, L.E. (1980). Intrinsic motivation and norms about payment. *Journal of Personality, 48*, 1–14.

Stokes, T.F., & Baer, D.M. (1977). An implicit technology of generalization. *Journal of Applied Behavior Analysis, 10*, 349–367.

Sutherland, S. (1993). Impoverished minds. *Nature, 364*, 767.

Svartdal, F. (1992). Sensitivity to nonverbal operant contingencies: Do limited processing resources affect operant conditioning in humans? *Learning and Motivation, 23,* 383–405.

*Swann, W.B., Jr., & Pittman, T.S. (1977). Moderating influence of verbal cues on intrinsic motivation. *Child Development, 48,* 1128–1132.

Tang, S.H., & Hall, V.C. (1995). The overjustification effect: A meta-analysis. *Applied Cognitive Psychology, 9,* 365–404.

*Taub, S.I., & Dollinger, S.J. (1975). Reward and purpose as incentives for children differing in locus of control expectancies. *Journal of Personality, 43,* 179–195.

Tegano, D.W., Moran, D.J., III & Sawyers, J.K. (1991). *Creativity in early childhood classrooms.* Washington, DC: National Education Association.

*Thompson, E.P., Chaiken, S., & Hazlewood, D. (1993). Need for cognition and desire for control as moderators of extrinsic reward effects: A person X situation approach to the study of intrinsic motivation. *Journal of Personality and Social Psychology, 64,* 987–999.

Thorndike, E.L. (1898). Animal intelligence. *Psychological Review Monograph Supplements* (Serial No. 8).

Thorndike, E.L. (1965). *Animal Intelligence: Experimental Studies.* New York: Macmillan. (Original work published 1911)

Tolman, E.C. (1932). *Purposive behavior in animals and men.* New York: Naiburg.

Triandis, H.C. (1995). *Individualism and collectivism.* Boulder, CO: Westview Press.

*Tripathi, K.N. (1991). Effect of contingency and timing of reward on intrinsic motivation. *The Journal of General Psychology, 118,* 97–105.

*Tripathi, K.N., & Agarwal, A. (1985). Effects of verbal and tangible rewards on intrinsic motivation in males and females. *Psychological Studies, 30,* 77–84.

*Tripathi, K.N., & Agarwal, A. (1988). Effect of reward contingency on intrinsic motivation. *The Journal of General Psychology, 115(3),* 241–246.

*Vallerand, R.J. (1983). The effect of differential amounts of postive verbal feedback on the intrinsic motivation of male hockey players. *Journal of Sport Psychology, 5,* 100–107.

*Vallerand, R.J., & Reid, G. (1984). On the causal effects of perceived competence on intrinsic motivation: A test of cognitive evaluation theory. *Journal of Sport Psychology, 6,* 94–102.

Vanderberg, G. (2001, June 21). Bribery: it may be the key to better grades. *The Edmonton Journal,* p. 1.

Vasta, R. (1981). On token rewards and real dangers. *Behavior Modification, 5,* 129–140.

Vasta, R., Andrews, D.E., McLaughlin, A.M., Stirpe, L.A., & Comfort, C. (1978). Reinforcement effects on intrinsic interest: A classroom analog. *Journal of School Psychology, 16,* 161–168.

*Vasta, R., & Stirpe, L.A. (1979). Reinforcement effects on three measures of children's interest in math. *Behavior Modification, 3,* 223–244.

Vaughan, M.E., & Michael, J. (1982). Automatic reinforcement: An important but ignored concept. *Behaviorism, 10,* 217–227.

Vroom, V. (1964). *Work and motivation.* New York: Wiley.

Watson, J.B. (1913). Psychology as the behaviorist views it. *Psychological Review, 20,* 158–177.

*Weinberg, R.S., & Jackson, A. (1979) Competition and extrinsic rewards: Effect on intrinsic motivation and attribution. *Research Quarterly, 50,* 494–502.

*Weiner, M.J. (1980). The effect of incentive and control over outcomes upon intrinsic motivation and performance. *The Journal of Social Psychology, 112*, 247–254.

*Weiner, M.J., & Mander, A.M. (1978). The effects of reward and perception of competency upon intrinsic motivation. *Motivation and Emotion, 2*, 67–73.

Wessels, M.G. (1981). A critique of Skinner's views on the explanatory inadequacy of cognitive theories. *Behaviorism, 9*, 153–170.

White, K.G., & Cameron, J. (2000). Resistance to change, contrast, and intrinsic motivation. *Behavioral and Brain Sciences, 23*, 115–116.

*Wicker, F.W., Brown, G., Wiehe, J.A., & Shim, W.Y. (1990). Moods, goals, and measures of intrinsic motivation. *The Journal of Psychology, 124*, 75–86.

Wiersma, U.J. (1992). The effects of extrinsic rewards in intrinsic motivation: A meta-analysis. *Journal of Occupational and Organizational Psychology, 65*, 101–114.

Williams, B.A. (1983). Another look at contrast in multiple schedules. *Journal of the Experimental Analysis of Behavior, 39*, 345–384.

*Williams, B.W. (1980). Reinforcement, behavior constraint and the overjustification effect. *Journal of Personality and Social Psychology, 39*, 599–614.

*Wilson, R.L. (1978). *The effect of reward on intrinsic motivation: An integration of dissonance and intrinsic motivation studies.* Unpublished doctoral dissertation, North Carolina State University.

*Wimperis, B.R., & Farr, J.L. (1979). The effects of task content and reward contingency upon task performance and satisfaction. *Journal of Applied Social Psychology, 9(3)*, 229–249.

Wolf, M.M. (1978). Social validity: The case for subjective measurement or how applied behavior analysis is finding its heart. *Journal of Applied Behavior Analysis, 11*, 203–214.

*Yuen, W.C. (1984). *Self-schema, task information, extrinsic reward and intrinsic motivation.* Unpublished doctoral dissertation, Simon Fraser University, Canada.

Zimbardo, P.G. (1992). *Psychology and life* (13th ed.). New York: HarperCollins Publishers Inc.

*Zinser, O., Young, J.G., & King, P.E. (1982). The influence of verbal reward on intrinsic motivation in children. *The Journal of General Psychology, 106*, 85–91.

Zuriff, G.E. (1979). The demise of behaviorism–Exaggerated rumor? A review of MacKenzie's "Behaviorism and the limits of the scientific method." *Journal of Experimental Analysis of Behavior, 32*, 129–136.

Zuriff, G.E. (1985). *Behaviorism: A conceptual reconstruction.* New York: Columbia University Press.

Index

DATE DUE